PENGUIN
COMPASS

VIVIANNE CROWLEY

The Magickal Life

A Wiccan Priestess Shares Her Secrets

PENGUIN COMPASS

PENGUIN COMPASS
Published by the Penguin Group
Penguin Group (USA) Inc., 375 Hudson Street,
New York, New York 10014, U.S.A.
Penguin Books Ltd, 80 Strand, London WC2R 0RL, England
Penguin Books Australia Ltd, 250 Camberwell Road, Camberwell,
Victoria 3124, Australia
Penguin Books Canada Ltd, 10 Alcorn Avenue,
Toronto, Ontario, Canada M4V 3B2
Penguin Books India (P) Ltd, 11 Community Centre, Panchsheel Park,
New Delhi – 110 017, India
Penguin Books (N.Z.) Ltd, Cnr Rosedale and Airborne Roads, Albany,
Auckland, New Zealand
Penguin Books (South Africa) (Pty) Ltd, 24 Sturdee Avenue,
Rosebank, Johannesburg 2196, South Africa

Penguin Books Ltd, Registered Offices:
80 Strand, London WC2R 0RL, England

First published in Great Britain as *The Natural Magician* by Michael Joseph,
an imprint of Penguin Books Ltd 2003
Published in the United States of Amnerica in Penguin Compass (U.S.A.) 2003

1   3   5   7   9   10   8   6   4   2

LIBRARY OF CONGRESS CATALOGING IN PUBLICATION DATA
Crowley, Vivianne.
The magickal life : a wiccan priestess shares her secrets / Vivianne Corwley.
p.   cm.
Includes bibliographical references.
ISBN 0 14 21.9624 X
1. Magic.   2. Witchcraft.   I. Title.
BF1611.C77 2003
133.4'3—dc21   2003043865

Printed in the United States of America
Set in Wilke and Weiss
Designed by Francesca Belanger

ACKNOWLEDGMENTS

I would like to thank especially Eileen Campbell, whose vision inspired this book; my husband Chris for his unfailing support; Janet Goldstein for sharing the vision; Fiona Brown and Lucia Watson for their insightful editing; and my agent Mandy Little, for her boundless enthusiasm. This book derives from teaching I have received from many different sources. Alex, Maxine, Madge, Arthur, and Gabriel taught me Wicca and Kabbalah. Marjorie Aarons, Janet Orman, and Ivy Northage taught me how to heal. Ian Gordon-Brown, Barbara Somers, and Joan and Reyn Swallow taught me transpersonal psychology and widened my vision. Paul Greenslade and Paul Kingsland gave me recipes for wonderful incense. Levanah, Shafeeq, and Mark created a labyrinth that has given many visions. Dawn, Tony, Paul, Marie, and Sue helped us make a stone circle that linked us to the land. Francesca, Peter, and Victoria introduced us to the wonders of Colorado and Arizona. An Ellie Baker workshop gave me the inspiration for the Cauldron Journey, and Jon's Kabbalah a new technique for talismans. And to all those with whom we have worked natural magic over the many years, thank you for your wisdom, inspiration, dedication, and fun.

CONTENTS

viii ❧ *Contents*

The
Magickal
Life

CHAPTER ONE

What is Magic?

"How many miles to Babylon?"
"Three score and ten."
"Can I get there by candlelight?"
"Aye, and back again."

NURSERY RHYME, ANONYMOUS

$\mathcal{M}$agic has always existed, practiced sometimes by many and sometimes by only the secret and initiated few. You can think of magic as a skill. It is a way of using energy. Energy is part of the fabric of matter. It existed before our cosmos came into being. It will exist when this cosmos dies and another is born. Some would call it the Tao; others the life force or sacred power. Human beings have always sensed it—just behind the veil of everyday reality. We love J. K. Rowling's Harry Potter books, *Lord of the Rings, Buffy the Vampire Slayer, Charmed,* and endless reruns of *Bewitched* because they take us into the magical universe that we believed in as children, lost faith with in late childhood, and sometimes dabbled with in adolescence. When we enter the "grown up" world, most of us put magic aside. This is a pity because if we give up magic we forget that the mind can influence the body; that though accidental events can seem to dictate our lives, it is possible to have the right kind of accidents and to avoid the wrong kind. We forget that we have the power to influence how others react to us. We forget to be open to the strange patterns of events that can help us achieve our destiny. We forget the creative power of the human imagination.

Magic is a strange, archaic, and exciting word. Deep down we know that while much of magic is medieval superstition, behind this is something real. Most of us have experienced synchronistic events that take our lives in new directions, dreams that come true, and telepathic experiences with close friends and relatives. Some of us have had the feeling that occasionally it is possible to break the laws of time and space; for our minds to do things that they cannot normally do.

Regardless of the intention and the means, there are five types of magic. There is magic to remove obstacles, magic to create opportunities, magic to achieve a particular goal, magic that heals or restores something or someone, and magic that changes the personality. The last is often called high magic. It is the magic of personal transformation, the magic of change. In addition to our everyday personalities, we have within us unrealized potential waiting to unfold. One of the processes of magic is to help us discover and unfold our potential selves. We are born with immense potential, but most of us never get to use all of ourselves. We have talents, qualities, and attributes that never get the opportunity to flourish. One of the purposes of magic is to help us flourish.

Magic can be a great force for good. It can heal. It can remove the doubts and fears that lurk within us, inhibiting us from fulfilling ourselves and becoming what we want to be. Magic helps us notice, process, and act upon the helpful hints that the universe tries to give us—but which we usually ignore. It is a way of reading the underlying currents, of sensing what will happen next in the story of life, of getting a preview before the movie is shown. It is also a way of rewriting the plot.

How does magic work? Magic is not about cats, cauldrons, and hocus-pocus. It is not about wizards' academies, dragons, or evil sorcerers, but about something much more down-to-earth—the powers of the human mind. If you read about magic in any tradition, Western or Eastern, in indigenous shamanic cultures, or in contemporary psychology, you will find a universal process. All these traditions teach practices that involve entering a meditative state, visualizing your goal, creating energy, and directing that energy toward the goal. Magical techniques are not far from those that sports stars now use. Football and tennis players train in visualization techniques once used only by shamans and magicians. The same process is used in cancer treatment, spiritual healing, and Reiki. Conventional medicine once laughed at these "alternatives." Now scientific journals publish learned articles on psychoneuroimmunology, and energy healing techniques are recognized as "complementary" medicine, an adjunct to standard medical practice.

Magic is ancient but is still practiced in the twenty-first century. Magic is about becoming aware of our natural bodily, emotional, and mental rhythms, and of when to do what. It is about listening to the subliminal signals that we often ignore—the instincts that tell us we can trust this person but not that; that this person can help us; that we must phone someone because we sense that he or she needs our help. When we become aware of magic, we notice that sometimes we know what is going to happen before the event occurs— and we have the confidence to act upon that information. Magic can help us be in the right place at the right time, to get the lucky break that changes the course of our lives. The scientific revolution rejected magic. In the twentieth and twenty-first centuries, we have rehabilitated it. We have found that mind and matter interact, that the mind can heal the body, and that time and space that once seemed "absolutes" and "givens" are but artificial constructs that in the higher reaches of science become one. Magicians know that there are modes of consciousness different from those we experience in everyday life. If you are steeped in quantum physics, you know that the time-space framework that we use to negotiate everyday reality—and which works perfectly well most of the time—is an illusion. Things are not at all how they appear. Other people come to this idea from a completely different starting point. They have vivid personal experiences that show them this is true. Maybe you had such experiences as a child. And maybe they were something like mine.

Once, when I was six years old, I was lying in bed and a voice was calling me. I couldn't understand the words, but I knew I had to follow. I got out of bed, following the voice, and floated out through the bedroom window. I was flying. I weaved and soared upon the air currents, flying like a bird. My body felt free, freer than if I were swimming in the sea. I was ecstatic. I flew across the fields and into the woods where I played during the day. Instead of being night, it was light—not normal daylight, more like a golden radiance. I flew around the magical golden woods until I was tired, then flew back through my bedroom window, lay down in my bed, and woke up. It was morning; my mother was calling me.

I ran downstairs, "Mommy, Mommy, I can fly."

Mommy was not impressed and told me to eat my cornflakes. I ate as quickly as I could and ran outside, eager to try out my new skill. I found a large fallen tree trunk, hauled myself on top, and leapt off, flapping my arms like a bird. I landed on the ground with a bump. Obviously, I didn't quite have the hang of it. I climbed on the tree trunk and tried again, but with the same result—bump. I tried again and again, each time without success. After ten minutes, I had bruised heels and decided to think things through. First, it seemed I could fly only at night. The night world must be different from the day world; different rules must apply. Second, most adults were not receptive to the idea of flying—or of different worlds. I would have to keep these ideas to myself, until I could find like-minded people. I was sure there were like-minded people out there somewhere because of a rhyme I had read in a children's book.

> "How many miles to Babylon?"
> "Three score and ten."
> "Can I get there by candlelight?"
> "Yes and back again."

I had no idea what this meant, but like all unsolved puzzles, it was grit in the oyster shell—it stuck in my mind. The words seemed like a magical incantation, but what did they mean? Now I felt I knew—or almost knew. There were at least two worlds—this world and the otherworld, the world of day and the world of dreaming night. These childhood experiences affected my worldview profoundly. They showed me that there were other states of consciousness from those of sleeping and waking. If we could enter these states of consciousness, we could see the world in another way. Things that normally seemed solid were composed of crystals, light, and moving energy. To see the world in a new way is a mystical experience common to people from all cultures. Usually, such experiences come spontaneously and unbidden. They are moments of grace, magical moments, and they can transform our lives. If our minds are trained in meditation and magic, we can learn to trigger these experiences at will. *Seeing* is an important part of magic in all sorts of ways. Magic is a way of seeing the world anew, as it really is. This gives us *in-sight*, to see where we want to go.

Living Magically

This book is about natural magic. It is "natural" in the sense that it is about learning to use the hidden powers of the human psyche, powers that are part of our natural selves. These powers were widely used by our ancestors, but in our urban, civilized, and somewhat "unnatural" lives, we have forgotten how to relate to our deeper instinctive and intuitive nature. Natural magic is "natural" in another sense—it follows the laws of nature. Nature creates a biosphere—an interlocking, mutually dependent complex of organisms that cannot exist alone. When one organism becomes too dominant, the balance is lost, and so too is the world. Natural magic adds energy to what we do, but it is not a way to impose our will on the universe in an egocentric effort to make everything go our way. There are plenty of people and other beings out there just as important as we are, and there are higher purposes than ours. Natural magic is about learning to ride the wave, or as Chinese Taoists would say, traveling the way of the water-courser. Natural magicians are people who can detach themselves from their egos. Their minds are objective and clear-seeing. Freed from the ego's emotional desires to pull us this way and that, they see what needs to be done and how to do it. Magic is about clarity.

Natural magic is latent in us all. It is a way of describing those powers of the body, mind, heart, and spirit that have been used by shamans, priesthoods, witches, healers, and magi for thousands of years. Magic involves looking at the world in a new way that sees life as full of endless possibilities. It is about responding to the ever-changing needs of contemporary society with spontaneous creativity. We live in a world where nothing is certain. Jobs change, corporations collapse, economies are volatile, and relationships are fragile. We have to be ready to respond to the moment. We cannot live in the past or assume that the future will look like the present. We have to have plans for how we want our lives to be, plus the flexibility to change them as outer circumstances force change. We are jugglers with the vagaries of the universe. The important thing is to keep the balls in the air. Magic happens when body, mind, emotions, spirit, and vision work in harmony and we direct our energies to clear and focused ends. Magic is working with the cosmic tides of the universe so we have an impetus of energy behind what we do. Magical living is skillful living. We learn to practice the art of living in the same way that dancers, artists, athletes, archers, musicians, martial arts experts, or entrepreneurs practice their arts. They turn energy into form and give birth to new creation. This is creative magic, and it can transform our lives. Magic depends on vision and imagination. It is important in the twenty-first century because it represents the leading edge of society—where we are going.

Natural magic has its own spirituality, a pre-Christian pagan spirituality that sees the Divine as Goddess and God, redressing the imbalanced images that male-dominated religions offer. Magic represents relinking with nature, but while we are part of the biological world, magic also teaches us that human beings are more than their biology. Each of us has a purpose and a function. A role of the spiritual growth processes of magic is to help us discover what that is. This is what some people call finding our True Will. It is what others call finding one's true vocation—what we are uniquely equipped to give. This is important for us and for the world, which needs our contribution. Ultimate happiness and satisfaction with life come from feeling that we are needed and valued, that we have a role, that there is purpose to our existence. Finding this purpose is part of our magical journey.

There are books on magic for specialists who want to be full-time magicians, witches, or shamans, and there are spell books that give you formulas that you can follow in the same way that you can follow cookery recipes. The first are for magical scientists and the second are fine for the occasional "quick-fix" spell. Real contemporary magic is a process. It is about living magically and integrating magic into everyday life, while understanding what we are doing and how it works. This book is for people who would like to know more about how magic works—maybe from natural curiosity, or maybe because you would like to try it for yourself. Maybe you are already a natural magician and would like to share the experiences of someone else who is exploring the magical path to see if they resonate with yours. This book is also for you.

Like me, you don't need to "believe" in magic to try it out. You have simply to work on the premise that it is a possibility and see what happens. Try it and see; experiment and enjoy. Believe what you have seen to be true, be interested in everything, deal in facts. This is the way of the natural magician. Magic is about doing. It is like learning to dance. It involves doing things with your body, emotions, and mind. Reading about magic will not turn you into a natural magician. If you are really interested in natural magic, read this book and try out the practices it describes. In this way, you internalize the processes of natural magic for yourself. Your life is a voyage of self-discovery, an uncharted voyage. No one's journey is the same as anyone else's. In our lives, we are all voyagers to unknown continents. We have no idea where we are going or what we will find when we get there. That's good. It's the not-knowing that makes the journey worthwhile.

★

POINTERS FOR PRACTICE

Natural magic is a skill, a way of using energy. To become natural magicians, we must develop our inner powers. Powerful people are people who empower others, not people who seek power over others. Natural magic is a method of empowerment. You don't have to believe in magic to make it work. Just try it and see.

CHAPTER TWO

Magic 101

"Where are you going?"

A voice floats out of the kitchen. My friend Jane and I stop dead in our tracks in the hallway. We're all dressed up in our teenwitch best—ankle-length black skirts, matching T-shirts, hennaed hair, Gothic street cred—you know the kind of thing. My handbag bulges with a copy of Idries Shah's *The Secret Lore of Magic.* A magic wand and a snooker triangle protrude from the top. I clutch the bag under my armpit to disguise the contents as Jane's mother wanders into the hall. Normally, she never asks us where we are going, especially on a Saturday afternoon.

I smile brightly. "We're going for a walk." It's true as far as it goes.

"Oh, good, you can take the dog."

We wait in fear and trembling while Jane's mother disappears into the kitchen and emerges with a brutish, snarling, under-exercised border collie that hates humans. Generations of breeding have destined it to be a working dog, earning its keep on wild Welsh hills, rounding up sheep. Suburban life does not suit it. It wants to get out and will only let you leave the house without it if you give it chocolate. We are out of chocolate.

Desperately, I try to think of a reason to refuse the vicious beast. My mind becomes the kind of blank that descends when you are caught out in teenage subterfuge. Jane somehow maneuvers so the dog is thrust at me. I clutch its lead as it leaps up to the top of the front door, clawing to get out. We leave with the dog and head for the woods at the bottom of the local golf course. We are planning to try a bit of demon evocation. A golf course on a Saturday afternoon is not the ideal venue for demon evocation, but it is less tricky than explaining to Jane's mother what a demon is doing in the bedroom. She's gotten used to the overnight boyfriends, but she's going to draw the line somewhere. It's not that we are budding Satanists. It's just that magical literature is scarce in the pre-Internet suburbs. Having ploughed my way through Eliphas Levi's *Transcendental Magic*, the only other magical book in the local bookstore is Sufi mystic Idries Shah's selected extracts from medieval and Renaissance grimoires. Unfortunately, either Idries Shah or the grimoire writers are obsessed with demons.

In Pursuit of Invisibility

All ancient grimoires have invisibility spells, often used for nefarious purposes. The Celtic magician Merlin cast an invisibility spell for King Uther Pendragon so he could commit adultery with Igraine, Duchess of Cornwall, and conceive King Arthur. Jane and I don't want invisibility for any particularly nefarious purposes—though it struck me as a useful alternative to a backstage pass—but invisibility sounds less dodgy than some of the other references in the index. Take "K," for instance, "Killing by magic." There are some teachers I'm not too keen on, but there are limits. "L" leads to "Lucifer, conjuration of," and sounds rather dodgy; so too does "I" for "Invisibility." Page 108, "To make oneself invisible," involves collecting seven black beans. Fine, I'm rampantly vegetarian and have every color of bean and lentil imaginable. "Take the head of a dead man." Er, no, I don't think so. My dedication to the magical arts doesn't stretch to grave-robbing. I turn to page 116. "Take the stone which is called Ophethalminus and wrap it in the leaf of the Laurel of Bay Tree." Sounds a lot safer; but what is Ophethalminus? I try page 191, a section on "Raising the spirits of the Lemegeton." Apparently, invisibility can be obtained by invoking Baal, "the most powerful of all Kings of demons." I'm not a total wimp, but I think we should practice on something smaller first. Page 200 involves invoking a "powerful President" with the appearance of a winged dog. Apparently, he can grant invisibility. He also causes murder. Doesn't sound like a good plan, either.

I give up on invisibility, but what to do? I'm dying to try out something. Who's the tiniest, least scary-sounding demon in the book? I scan the pages looking for innocuous demons—Dantalian— a strong Duke "with a multitude of male and female faces and carrying a book." Doesn't sound exactly photogenic, but it's a lot less scary than winged dogs. Apparently, he can "teach any art or science." Sounds okay. I'll invoke him to teach me the magical art. And maybe I'll do it in the afternoon. The golf course woods are a bit sinister after dark. Persuading Jane that she wanted to help me invoke a demon wasn't too difficult. She's a fire sign; they're very impulsive. The only drawback is that now we are accompanied by a vicious dog. Maybe it's a sign, a protection, I console myself optimistically, as I haul the dog off passersby to stop it turning them into snacks.

Further perusal of Idries Shah had produced a fine collection of demon conjurations, but lots of them seemed, well, rude. I mean, how would you like to be addressed, "I conjure thee, O evil and accursed Serpent" and asked to manifest without making any obnoxious smells? Making disparaging comments about personal hygiene doesn't sound like a great way to begin a relationship, does it? I find the most polite invocation in the book. It's long.

We cast the circle and set up the snooker triangle some way outside as a triangle of evocation. The idea is that the demon is supposed to stay in the triangle. I think the grimoires mention something fancier and the triangle looks rather small, but one has to start somewhere. And when it comes to demons, small sounds good. We tie the dog to a tree. It doesn't appreciate this at all, but, "Sit!" is not part of its vocabulary. I open *The Secret Lore of Magic*.

"O Dantalian, I conjure thee, empowered with the strength of the Greatest Power, and I order thee by Baralamensis, by Baldachiensis . . ."

Tricky one, that—magicians need to be great linguists. More complicated names. The dog barks furiously.

". . . by Paumachie, Apoloresedes . . ."

Who are these guys, anyway?

". . . and by the most powerful Princes Genio, Liachide: the Ministers of the Tartar Seat," pause for quick giggle, "commanding Princes of the Throne of Aplogia, in the ninth place."

I look at the triangle. Nothing is happening, but the dog barks insanely, as though we're trying to murder it. I wish it would shut up.

"I conjure thee, O Spirit Dantalian, by He whose Word created, by the Strong and Highest Names of Adonai, El, Elohim, Sabaoth, Elion, Escherce, Jah, Tetragrammaton, Shaddai."

It sounds very garbled. I'm not sure these guys knew their Hebrew, but I'm in the swing of it now.

"Appear immediately here so that I may see thee, in front of this Circle, in a pleasant and human body, without any unpleasantness."

A quick check—no demon in the triangle, and I'm worried that the barking will attract the attention of passing golfers. Oh well, plow on.

Some time later, "Come at once, from any part of the world; come pleasantly, come now, come and answer my questions, for thou art called in the Name of the Everlasting, Living and Real God, Heliorem."

"Likewise I conjure thee . . ."

This is getting very, very boring, but I plod on. Maybe persistence is a virtue of magicians. Many conjurations later, Jane and I stand in the circle, wondering what to do next. Even the dog is bored and has stopped barking. Nothing has happened.

"Let's go home."

We are halfway across the golf course when the abnormally quiet dog stops dead, rolls on its back, and lies staring into the sky. It's foaming at the mouth and making faint whimpering noises. It occurs to me that I've broken the first rule of magic—always banish what you evoke.

"Has this happened before?" I inquire nervously. "I mean, is it epileptic?"

"No." Jane's calm. She's taking it pretty well considering it's her mother's dog, not mine.

Shit! How do you exorcise a possessed dog? I leaf frantically through the index of *The Secret Lore of Magic*. Nothing under "dogs, possessed." A party of golfers is three holes away and this is getting seriously embarrassing. The dog's too heavy to carry and I don't fancy explaining to Jane's mother why her dog is in some kind of cataleptic fit.

"Try 'banishing,'" Jane suggests helpfully.

Nothing. Second Law of Magic—do not panic. Calm down, think slowly. I look through the book more carefully. How do people banish demons? Index—"D"—"demoniac possession to cause." No, we've got that, where's "uncause?" Further down "Dismissal of spirits," page 98—yes!

"Dismissal of spirits" is very short. I'm not convinced one sentence will work after such a lengthy conjuration. Third Law of Magic—if in doubt, try more Latin. All that convent education, curtseying to the Mother Superior and wearing silly hats had to come in useful one day. We pray over the dog.

"Pater noster, qui es in caelis, sanctificetur nomen tuum: adveniat regnum tuum: fiat voluntas tua sicut in caelo et in terra. Panem nostrum quotidianum da nobis hodie: et dimitte nobis debita nostra, sicut et nos dimittimus debitoribus nostris. Et ne nos inducas in tentationem: sed libera nos a malo. Amen."

The dog stops staring at the sky and looks at us. Seems promising. I carry on.

"Ite in pace ad local vestra et pax sit inter vos redituri ad mecum vos invocavero, in nomine Patris, et Filii, et Spiritus Sancti. Amen."

The dog stops foaming, stands up, and wags its tail. I'm astonished. This is better than horror movies. We walk home, thoughtfully, checking every few minutes that the dog's okay. It's as quiet as a lamb, the nicest it's ever been. I draw three conclusions—1: this stuff works; 2: never evoke anything without banishing it; 3: I'd better find someone to teach me how to do magic properly before I do some damage. I go in search of a teaching group and find an advertisement for a reputable Wiccan training group.

Some nervous phone calls to a contact number later, I descend a basement staircase just near London's Hyde Park. A glamorous young man opens the door. He looks like a rock star. I explain that Jane and I have come for the open evening. An intelligent-looking white cat joins him and gives me a superior glance. We go in.

Magical Synchronicity

The magic I learned in Wicca was natural magic—the magic of herbs, crystals, the stars, and the human heart and mind. And I discovered that witches do not believe in demons: a possessed dog does not a demon make. The *Buffy* version of magic is fun, but it is not the reality. When we evoke—or call forth—a demon, we are asking our psyches to manifest our own inner negativity. In my case, it was the fears and anxieties of two teen witches. Manifesting our inner negativity in this way is not a good idea, so demon evoking is best avoided. Natural magic is far removed from the masculine power trips of the medieval grimoire witches and their efforts to persuade angels and demons to do their bidding.

Magic is about creating synchronicity. Synchronicity is a term first used by psychologist Carl Jung to describe those moments when two seemingly unrelated events coincide and have important meaning. The universe opens itself to us and spirit, God, Goddess, the Divine, the Tao, whatever you wish to name it, gives us a sign. Psychiatrist Viktor Frankl had such a moment when near to despair during the Second World War. He was in a work party from a concentration camp, marching out to work on a freezing cold winter morning. Suddenly, when his thoughts were at their darkest, a light came on in a distant farmhouse and the Biblical phrase "out of the darkness comes light" came into his mind. We could dismiss this as a coincidence, but when we have such experiences, we know they have meaning. We resonate and respond to them as though our deepest being and the innermost Divine center of the universe are suddenly in harmony. The external world and our inner world reflect one another and the knowledge that comes into our minds at those times impresses itself upon us so deeply that we just "know." When he saw the light, Dr. Frankl "knew" he would survive the concentration camp—after darkness would come light. He did, living until his nineties, a man in love with the gift of conscious existence, the precious gift of life.

Often synchronicity comes to us unbidden, but magic is about taking an active role in the process and creating synchronicity. Let me give an example. The Wiccan group I joined as a teen witch taught me the basics of natural magic, but in my early twenties I found that I needed something else—a framework, a philosophy to piece together the fragments of teaching that I have acquired. The Western magical tradition draws on the philosophy of ancient Greece, which was influenced by the spirituality of Buddhist and Hindu India, and on the Renaissance Christian and Jewish reinterpretations of that Pagan Greek philosophy. These traditions meet in kabbalistic magic.

I wanted to find a teacher of kabbalah. One autumn evening, a Wednesday, the day of Mercury, patron of intellect and learning, I kneeled in front of the altar in my bedroom. It was a coffee table covered with a gold cloth with two lighted golden yellow candles in brass candlesticks—gold for success, to draw positive energy. I took an orange candle—orange for mind, intellect, teaching. I poured a small amount of frankincense oil on my fingers. Oil is a substance used in magic to carry energy. I smoothed the oil from the center of the candle toward each end, focusing on the intention—to find a teacher. I was careful to avoid putting oil on the wick. It would make it sputter. I tried to visualize a teacher, but the images I got were confused. Male and female images alternated. I stopped trying to visualize a person. I was imposing my idea and vision of who the teacher should be. Instead, I visualized a symbol—a book. I don't know why, but it seemed right. When I could no longer hold the visual image, I lit the orange candle and placed it on the altar, sending a thought out into the universe—help me to find that which I seek.

I was living in Stamford Hill, one of London's Jewish heartlands and home to the Hasidim Kabbalists. The next day, on my way to work, I clambered up to the top deck of a number 73 bus, as usual. The top deck of a red London bus—a world of rooftops, elaborate carvings at the top of Victorian buildings, passing glimpses into other people's houses and lives. The bus opens up the city. We see it differently, from another perspective. The nineteenth-century chemist Kekulé fell into a daydream on a London bus and dreamed his great discovery—his Structural Theory, which led to his discovery of the structure of the benzene molecule. And if you are not a great scientist developing your latest theory, the top of a double-decker bus is a great place to read. I sat down that morning and took out Dion Fortune's *The Mystical Qabalah.* Dion Fortune was one of the outstanding female magicians of the twentieth century. A middle-aged woman sat down beside me. After a while, I sensed that she was looking at what I was reading. She started a conversation. This was unusual; the English rarely speak to strangers in public. By the time I got off the bus some miles later in central London, I had discovered that she was the co-head of a kabbalistic ritual magic lodge and I had agreed to a meeting with her male counterpart. I was to wait at the foot of the Duke of York's steps on the Mall, just down from Buckingham Palace. A large black car would stop, driven by a man called Gabriel. I was to get in the car and go to a house in North London where I would meet members of the ritual magic lodge. Rationality and intuition competed. Rationality told me that in a big city like London this was a crazy thing to do, and possibly dangerous. Intuition told me it was the answer to my candle magic. Intuition won and I found myself that evening standing at the foot of the Duke of York's steps in the golden pool of light cast by one of the Mall's ornate lampposts. The car arrived; I got in. Some months later, I was initiated into the lodge.

What happened here? I consecrated an orange candle with a particular intention. Someone who could help me realize that intention sat next to me on a bus. If I hadn't been reading the right book, this person would never have spoken to me. If I hadn't been prepared to act on what had happened, my life would not have taken the course I wanted to make the cycle from wish to fulfillment complete. When we do magic, we enter a state of consciousness that is open to synchronistic events that may change our lives. In magic, we have original state and end state. Magic is something to change one to the other. If we want magic to work, we need to go through life in a state of open expectancy that the unexpected will happen and to notice when it does. We travel the world with an open mind, open eyes, and an open heart. We are willing to say "yes" to the universe. When we create a magical intention, we send out a particular type of energy and the universe reacts to us in a particular way; but the universe can only help to create the right conditions for us. When the conditions occur, we have the choice to take the opportunities the universe presents, or not. Magic does not negate free will.

There's Magic and There's Magic

Some magic is more psychological than magical. It is "feel good" magic that we do for others as an expression of empathic concern. A girlfriend knows that you practice a little magic. She asks you to do a spell for her to help her get over the traumatic breakup of her marriage. You do some candle magic and she feels better. Maybe no unusual energies are involved, but the realization that someone cares about her enough to do something for her gives her the psychological boost she needs. The message is that I care about you and am prepared to devote time and energy to your problem. Love is the driving force of "feel good" magic—love for others sufficient to sacrifice a bit of time and energy for them. Then there is true magic, magic where something happens that is quite unexpected, quite out of the ordinary, and not like anything we would have imagined. We create a current of energy in the universe, rather like the "butterfly flapping its wings" example of chaos theory. This tiny movement in the cosmic whole creates a ripple of chain reactions. Thought begets magic.

When I did candle magic to find a magical teacher, I started to visualize what I wanted, but I could not impose my vision on the universe. The perfect guru-teacher that my younger self was looking for was neither realistic nor appropriate, but by following my deeper intuition when I allowed my visualization to evolve into a book, I was led via a book to some wonderful teachers. In magic, we seek to achieve certain goals, but we have to be aware of the cosmic flow. We tailor our needs according to what is available and what arrives is usually more appropriate for us than what we originally wanted. The universe really does know more than we do. We need to listen as well as to seek.

While what we visualize may change, even during the course of a piece of magic, the importance of visual imagery as a way of mediating magic does not. Magic uses materials and techniques to focus our visualization and to channel our energies. We burn candles, we create talismans, we charge up crystals with energy. Crystals apart, often the materials we use in magic have no power in themselves, but we use them to help us concentrate. They provide a magical focus that allows us to harness our inner powers to bring about change. Other processes are important, and we will explore them in this book, but visualization is the foundation of magic. Our everyday thinking uses the left hemisphere of the brain, the hemisphere that controls the right hand. Magical thinking is right-brain thinking, creative thinking that sees the bigger picture and works with images, not words.

Visualization is a way of using our minds to create images that work both on our own unconscious and on the outer world to create magic—synchronistic happenings that cannot otherwise be explained. Magic is a way of creating images that become reality. Images are a key to using the mind fully, to making it work. When we have a precognitive dream, we are passive receivers of images that then unfold to become the future. When we do magic, we create images, empower them and turn them into reality. Magic is an active process in which we are transmitters. Clairvoyance is a passive procedure in which we are receptors. If you hear famous people describe how they achieved their goal or dream, you will find that it involved a lot of hard work but also that frequently the achievement was inspired by a vision. Michael Flatley, who transformed Irish dance through his performances in *Riverdance* and *Lord of the Dance*, often talks of how as a child he sat in school staring out of the window. This got him into trouble. His teachers criticized him for being a daydreamer, but he was not idly dreaming. He was visualizing himself as the extraordinary dancer that he wanted to be.

☉

Visualizing Your Goals

Is there a positive goal that you would like to achieve in your everyday life? No, I do not mean winning the lottery, but something you would like to work for and attain. The principle of magic is that you must put in effort on the material plane in order to get something out of the material plane, and besides there are too many competing psyches trying to win the lottery. Think about something useful that you want that would help you develop as a person—a new job, house, or course of study, something practical that helps you in your everyday life. Now practice your visualization skills. Imagine what you want to achieve. Now imagine yourself achieving it. Perhaps you are opening your new front door with a set of keys. Perhaps you are receiving a telephone call and someone is telling you, "You've got the job!" Perhaps a letter has been delivered and you are opening it. It says, "We are pleased to inform you that . . ." The important thing is to visualize achieving the desired outcome. Imagine the emotions that might surround this. Visualize this for five minutes morning and evening for two weeks. At the same time, do everything that you can on the material plane to make the desired aim come about. It is no use visualizing yourself in a wonderful job if you have not applied for one. See what results.

Here you are using creative visualization in the realm of the imagination to help you achieve outcomes in the outer world. To make visualization work, you must create the necessary channels for energy to manifest itself on the material plane. Your visualization acts as a "mold" in which to pour the energy and give it form. Energy, channels, forms, desire—these are the processes that help us create magic.

POINTERS FOR PRACTICE

Magic is about creating synchronicity. Magic helps create the right conditions for you to achieve your goals, but to make it work, you must create the necessary channels for energy to manifest itself on the material plane. Visualization is a foundation of magic. Practice visualization to improve your magical skills.

CHAPTER THREE

Mediumship 101

My teenage magical reading taught me that to do magic, we need visualization skills. We need vision that goes beyond the ordinary. We need to learn to "see" in a new way, to become sensitive to subtle energies that most people ignore. People who undergo training to finely tune these skills are the shamans and mediums of their societies. I first experimented with mediumship in my teens. I had seen movies set in the Victorian era with overdressed ladies and gentlemen sitting around tables with a ouija board in the center or a glass surrounded by letter cards. With the aid of a round table and the necessary props, my friends and I had some successful sessions with a spirit claiming to be the nineteenth-century Indian saint and Goddess worshipper Ramakrishna. We didn't know who he was. We had to look him up in a book. He came across in the séances as an admirable individual with advanced ideas about religious tolerance—the kind that get you murdered by religious fanatics, though fortunately this was not his fate. In any event, he became a benign presence in our lives and an astral gossip. He regaled us with interesting information about our friends' sex and love lives, as well as inspirational comments about our future spiritual direction and what we should be doing with our lives. Some of the gossip was known by at least one of us and we were probably unconsciously influencing the glass to produce it. Other details were a complete surprise. "Ramakrishna" produced predictions about the future that were unexpected and turned out to be true. Do I think we were communicating with the disembodied spirit of Ramakrishna? No. Whatever plane of material or nonmaterial existence Ramakrishna now inhabits, I think the revered devotee of the Goddess would have something better to do with his time than to drop in on our teenwitch psychic experiments. I think my conclusion is more interesting than being talked to by a dead mystic. Our séance group was tightly knit. We were close friends with strong emotional bonds. Some of us had already had telepathic experiences with one another. I think we were tapping our collective group mind and that when we were in the right state of consciousness we were clairvoyant, much more clairvoyant than any of us was individually. This is why magicians sometimes work with others in lodges, covens, or temples. They can create a magical group mind.

My Wicca training in my late teens and early twenties renewed my interest in mediumship. Much of magic seemed to involve using the same powers mediums used—clairvoyance and the ability to tap into subtle energies. I decided to explore mediumship further. Here is what happened during my first experience.

☾

MY FIRST MEDIUMSHIP ENCOUNTER

I go to a decaying mansion on the south side of Belgrave Square in London's embassy district. An open black door leads me into the reception hall of the Spiritual Association of Great Britain. Inside, smiling ladies in cardigans staff the reception desk. I ask for the events program. Life membership is amazingly cheap, a bargain offer. I sign up. I want to ask if I can enroll for more than one lifetime but I haven't got the nerve. There are healing sessions, demonstrations of clairvoyance, one-to-one sessions with mediums, small group sessions with mediums. What to choose? "Psychic portraiture"— what's that? I read that psychic artist and medium Coral Polge can draw your dead relatives, spirit guides, even your spirit pets. Pets sound fun. Maybe she will produce Whiskers, my black-and-white childhood cat, long gone to the happy hunting ground? I book an appointment for my first-ever private session with a medium.

In a downstairs room is a middle-aged lady with what I'm discovering is the universal mild-mannered calm of Spiritualists. She sits in an armchair with a drawing board propped on her knee, a large piece of drawing paper, and some colored chalks. Disappointingly, she doesn't go catatonic, produce any ectoplasm, or talk to any disincarnate entities. She chats. She tells me about mediumship, she describes the colors of my aura. I'm getting a bit bored with mediumship when I realize that something interesting is going on. She's talking with one part of her brain while going into a semitrance with the other. I sense that she's tuning in to my mind. I relax and open my psyche to her. She starts to draw. She tells me about her spirit guide, French pastel portrait artist Maurice Quentin de la Tour, who died in 1788 at the grand old age of eighty-four. She asks me if can see him. I look round the room for a floating entity. She indicates that he stands behind her. I get no vision of the esteemed eighteenth-century artist myself, but she tells me that other mediums see him leaning over her shoulder dressed in a wig and lace ruffles. When he was alive, de la Tour specialized in portraits that evoked the psychology of his sitters through their facial expressions. It seems that he's kept to the same line of work. His drawings were attempts to capture a short, instantaneous emotion characteristic of the sitter. He sounds like an appropriate mentor for what Coral Polge is attempting. She stops sketching and shows me her drawing. An Indian woman in a white sari—a widow then, I think. She tells me it is my spirit guide.

I was intrigued by Coral Polge and glad she did not produce a Tibetan monk or a Red Indian Chief. There are more mediums with these than chiefs and monks to go round. However, she didn't tell me anything that is verifiable, so I decided to try another medium.

☽

A SECOND MEDIUMSHIP ENCOUNTER

I go through the ads in the local newspaper and discover Mystic Mac. How can anyone resist going to see a medium named Mystic Mac?

Twelve of us turn up at the open night. Many are regulars, and everyone else has been before. Mystic Mac gives people messages from loved ones and some clairvoyant statements about future events. I'm not sure how this will work for me. I have a dearth of dead relatives. My astral connections are nonexistent, not a single Granny or deceased Uncle John.

It's my turn. He begins. "As I approach you, I feel a tremendous stillness and silence within. You are a very old soul and have had many, many incarnations. You were in Egypt and in Babylon. You were a Jewess in Babylon. 'By the waters of Babylon, I sat down and wept.' You were in India. One time you had many sons who were great in their time and you will meet them again through your incarnations. In India, you served a guru and eventually became a guru yourself. You sat by the waters of the Ganges where it reaches the plain. You were incarnated in Italy and Spain, and in Germany in the time of Maria-Theresa. You were a librarian then. You saw there was truth in all religions and took what was best from them. You could see there was some spiritual truth in Roman Catholicism. In five or six years, you will teach and will give lectures on spiritual matters in central London and will be well received. You will go to Germany and will meet people there who will be of great help to you. You will be a perpetual scholar and have a great love of books."

Not bad for a spiritualist medium at a large group session who didn't know me from Adam. Somehow, Mystic Mac had hit upon my childhood fantasies, or were they dreams or memories, or the result of reading too many books? Since early childhood, I had experienced what I called "time dreams," of living in different eras in all the places he had listed. I've been a book-a-holic since the age of four when I discovered the Aladdin's cave of musty country second-hand bookstores. Second-hand bookstores were more exciting for me than sweet shops. And yes, I did go to Germany. The lectures began six years after Mystic Mac's session and because of a misunderstanding of my Hindi, in 1988 I ended up on the wrong bus out of Delhi and went to where the waters of the Ganges meet the plain. The ticket seller mistook my "Agra" for "Hardwar." Mystic Mac gave me a description of the Indian incarnation. She sounded remarkably like the portrait drawn by Coral Polge.

Phantoms and Fantasy

When we visit mediums like Mystic Mac and they talk about previous incarnations, what are they sensing? Three spiritual traditions that have influenced my life are Wicca, Kabbalah, and Buddhism. One is a Goddess-oriented nature religion, one a Jewish mystical tradition, and the other an atheistic spiritual philosophy. One is Western, one Near Eastern, and the other Eastern. All three have reincarnation as an inherent part of the teaching. Do I believe in reincarnation? I feel no need to believe or disbelieve. Reincarnation is one of an interesting set of after-death possibilities. I am much more interested in the present and future. If we visit a medium, we can tell if he or she is sensing something that relates to us, but what is the status of the information? Past memories, auras, random experiences from the collective unconscious? Or how we see ourselves? Are the "memories" really thoughts, fantasies, and symbols that represent different parts of ourselves, parts that we would like to make manifest? We don't know, but their status matters less than what use we make of them. Their importance lies in insights they can give about our lives now. Fantasy in itself can be harmful or helpful, a substitute for reality or a way of visualizing the future. Past incarnations can seem fascinating but if they preoccupy you, it is likely that you are dissatisfied with your life in the present. And if you are dissatisfied with the present, you need to focus on changing it. Magically harnessed, fantasies turn into empowered visions to help you transform your life. Natural magic teaches us to live in the here and now. Even if reincarnation exists, incarnations are very short. It is important to live them well. Incarnation memories are of use if they tell us something about ourselves now; something that will help us to unveil our potential selves, to become all that we can be.

Despite my reservations about the explanations given by some mediums for their insights, my experiments with séances and visits to mediums inspired me to develop my psychic skills further. I decided to enroll for a new evening class—Beginners' Mediumship—and take my husband, Chris, with me. He had little interest in mediumship, but we were newly married and into togetherness. This is how it happened:

☽

BEGINNERS' MEDIUMSHIP

The College of Psychic Studies in London is a venerable nineteenth-century institution started by elderly ladies and gentlemen of the table rapping, ectoplasm, and inner planes adept persuasion. We go in nervously looking for stray ectoplasm. Oil paintings of distinguished bewhiskered gentlemen like avid spiritualist Sir Arthur Conan Doyle, creator of Sherlock Holmes, preside over the corridors, which are ideal for filming ghost movies. Former servants' bedrooms have become rooms for mediums' sittings but there's no ectoplasm and the library of dusty volumes that houses the reception desk seems normal enough. We are ushered into a small room to have our psychic potential assessed by a medium. We sit down nervously and project our best auras, not wanting to be turned away as psychic rejects. After a few minutes, I realize that the interview is to weed out the overexcitable and the mad. The College wants controlled mediumship, not hallucinatory visions. The medium decides we're sufficiently normal and we are allowed to enroll. We are now members of the Ivy Northage School of Mediumship. I mentally add "and ballroom dancing." It's that kind of a place.

We come back next week for the first class. The teacher is Janet Orman, a mild-mannered and encouraging lady. She settles down our nervous group of beginners. Chris looks on dubiously as Janet Orman draws the curtain and dims the lights. It's a bit different from management consultancy. We sit in a circle of chairs, trying to avoid eye contact but covertly checking each other out. There are more women than men, many of the men are gay, and we are the youngest attendees in "Beginners' Mediumship" by twenty years. I guess that people are more likely to take up mediumship when they have a hot-line to their personal dead. It is an autumn evening; outside it is dark. As we sit and concentrate, the street sounds of traffic and the voices of home-bound commuters seem to fade. The top-floor room has housed thousands of mediumship circles, decades of spirit vision. We slip into another world. Will my white-clad Indian lady turn up, I wonder? I'm unsure of this figure's status—spirit guide, image of a previous incarnation, a fantasy from my unconscious that mediums pick up? Whatever she is, she seems serene and peaceful. I must be the only person I know with a chalk portrait of a previous incarnation.

I am not at all sure how this is going to go, when Janet Orman teaches us an extremely useful exercise, "Opening the Chakras." Janet Orman talks us through the exercise and on this first occasion, I notice something right away. After we have completed the exercise and opened our eyes, the atmosphere in the room has changed. I can see halos of light around people's heads—auras. I run my eyes around the circle, checking it out. As we relax, the auras grow bigger and brighter—interesting.

◡

Chakras

I use the chakra exercise still, and will describe it in a moment, but what have chakras to do with mediumship? *Chakra* is a Sanskrit word that means "wheel," and they are considered energy centers in the physical body that interact with the aura—the body's energy field. No scientist has provided physical proof of their existence, but as a construct, they work. They have been widely used as a means of spiritual and psychic development since yoga was introduced into the West in the nineteenth century. Most of our knowledge of them comes from Indian tradition, but the idea of energy centers in the body is found in ancient Irish, Chinese, and other teachings from all over the world. As well as centering and balancing our energies, the exercise of opening our chakras increases our psychic sensitivity. When we open our chakras, we open the third eye, which helps us to see nonphysical energies. We also open the throat chakra, which enables us to speak directly from the unconscious and interpret what we see without the interference of the conscious mind, and we open the solar plexus chakra, which increases the sensitivity of the hands and allows us to detect and project energy. This simple exercise helps train us to do magic.

Each chakra has different functions and qualities and is associated with particular glands in the body's endocrine system. The glands of the endocrine system play an important role in maintaining the body's health by secreting into the bloodstream powerful hormones that maintain our autonomic functioning. Yoga postures stimulate different chakras and glands and help to keep the body healthy.

The colors follow the spectrum, with the chakras most closely associated with our physical selves being visualized at the red end of the spectrum. It is important to remember that the colors are imagery—a way for our minds to translate a particular concept. They are not absolutes. The colors listed here are those used in the

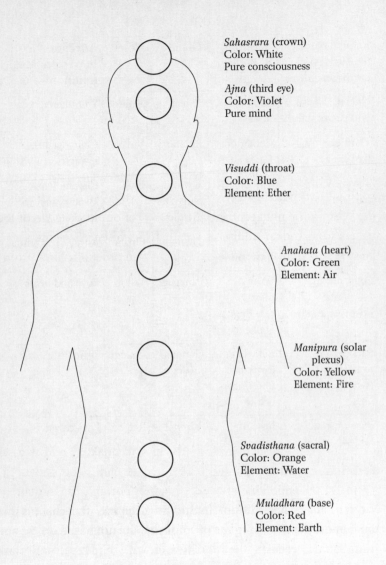

Sahasrara (crown)
Color: White
Pure consciousness

Ajna (third eye)
Color: Violet
Pure mind

Visuddi (throat)
Color: Blue
Element: Ether

Anahata (heart)
Color: Green
Element: Air

Manipura (solar
plexus)
Color: Yellow
Element: Fire

Svadisthana (sacral)
Color: Orange
Element: Water

Muladhara (base)
Color: Red
Element: Earth

CHAKRA DIAGRAM

CHAKRA SYSTEM

English Name, Sanskrit Name and Translation	Location in Body	Gland	Color	Attributes in Western Magical tradition
Crown: Sahasrara (thousandfold)	Top of head	Pineal	White	Spirituality
Third eye: Ajna (knowing)	Center of forehead	Pituitary	Violet	Clairvoyance, inspirational vision
Throat: Visuddi (purify)	Throat	Thyroid, parathyroid	Blue	Clairaudience, inspirational writing, speaking, channeling
Heart: Anahata (unstruck)	Center of breastbone	Thymus	Green	Altruistic, spiritual love
Solar plexus: Manipura (lustrous jewel)	Solar plexus, two fingers above navel	Pancreas	Yellow	Love and healing
Sacral: Svadisthana (sweetness)	Belly and lower back, four fingers below navel	Gonads, prostate	Orange	Sexuality
Base of spine: Muladhara (root support)	Base of spine	Adrenal	Red	Physical energy

Western magical tradition. In Indian teaching, the chakras have much more complex systems of color that are not based on the spectrum. Some teachers describe the crown, third eye, and throat chakras respectively as ultraviolet, indigo and blue, ultraviolet, blue, and turquoise, or other similar variations. Remember that color is subjective and one person's turquoise is another person's blue or green. If you are used to visualizing chakra colors in a slightly different way to the one I describe, you might like to experiment with a new color system to see how it works for you.

ⓔ
Chakra Exercise

To open the chakras, sit comfortably with your spine straight. Close your eyes and relax. If muscles in your legs or arms seem tense, flex them and then release them. Allow your breathing to become regular. When you feel relaxed and your breathing has become slow and steady, visualize a tiny round circle of pulsating red light at the base of your spine. Now imagine drawing a current of energy into the chakra so that it grows warm and begins to glow. The chakra energizes and begins to grow larger, becoming a spinning red disc of light. It pulsates with red energy and light. Visualize the base of spine chakra growing larger until it covers the whole of your lower spine.

Draw more and more energy into your base of spine chakra. Then, as the flow of energy comes into your body, allow it to fill your lower body with red light. Allow the light to rise, growing lighter, turning to orange. It reaches the level of your belly. As it does so, visualize the sacral chakra in the center of your belly activating. It begins to glow with orange light. Allow the orange circle to grow larger and larger, pulsating with energy. Draw more energy up the spine and into the sacral chakra, so that this too spins faster and grows wider, glowing with bright orange light. Allow the flow of energy to rise up through the center of your body, filling it and growing lighter. Orange lightens to golden yellow at the level of the solar plexus. Here it begins to activate the solar plexus chakra that starts to spin and glow with a golden yellow light. Focus on the base of the spine once more and draw more energy up the center of your body and into the solar plexus chakra. Allow it to open wider and wider. Allow the chakra to spin faster and faster until there is a golden spinning Sun at your solar plexus. Focus on the base of the spine again. Draw more energy in and up your body, past the spinning orange sacral chakra, past the golden-yellow solar plexus, up to the center of the breastbone, where there is the small green fiery glow of the heart chakra. Let the energy you have drawn upward feed the green fiery glow. Your heart chakra begins to grow, to spin faster and faster, growing larger and larger, until it covers the whole of your chest with green glowing light.

Focus on the base of the spine again and draw energy up through your body, past the heart chakra to the throat, where there is a small blue glow. Allow the energy to stream into your throat chakra and to spin the chakra faster and faster until there is a pulsating blue center at the throat. Go back to the base of the spine to renew your energy. Draw energy in through the base of spine chakra, up through the sacral chakra, through the solar plexus, through the heart chakra, to the throat. Then go back to the base of the spine again. Draw a current of energy right up through the body, up past the throat and into the third eye at the center of your forehead. Allow this energy to merge with the violet spot at the third eye and to spin the third eye energy faster and faster until there is a spinning violet center in the middle of your forehead. Focus on the base of your spine. Draw more energy into your body and up past the sacral chakra, past the solar plexus, past the heart, past the throat and into the third eye. Allow the violet glow to spin faster and faster. Then allow the current of energy to shoot up through the head and out of the crown. Allow the energy to cascade down your body, bathing it in light, light flowing down over your body to your feet in a white stream. Focus on the base of the spine. Draw more energy right up through the body, past the sacral chakra, past the solar plexus, past the heart, past the throat, past the third eye and out again through the crown chakra, and down the body to the feet. Repeat this a few times and then relax. Enjoy the feeling of having your chakras open and energized.

When you are ready to stop, it is important that you close your chakras again. When we first did this exercise, Janet Orman explained that two chakras are always open—the crown chakra at the top of the head, which connects us to spiritual energies, and the base of spine chakra, which connects us to the Earth. The other chakras should be closed in everyday life. The purpose of opening them is to increase our sensitivity to the energies of other people and to those of our environment. This must be done in controlled situations.

Closing your chakras can be done more quickly than opening them. One of the easiest ways is to imagine each chakra as a stained glass window of the appropriate color. Starting at the top, the crown chakra, visualize a fountain of white light spurting out of your crown chakra down the outside of your whole body. Let it flow over the third eye, closing the chakra completely as though a white shutter is being drawn over it. Then draw more white light down from the crown past the third eye to the throat chakra, and then over the throat, shutting the chakra. Draw more light from the crown down and over the heart chakra. Now draw more white light down over the top of the head, over the third eye, over the throat, over the heart chakra, and down over the solar plexus chakra. Then, from the crown of the head, draw more white light down past the solar plexus, past the sacral, and down to the base of the spine. Allow the crown chakra and base of spine chakra to remain slightly open. These are your links with the energies of the Divine and the energies of Earth.

Morning Meditation

Opening the chakras can be part of a good meditative exercise to start the day. Once our chakras are open, we can think about the day's priorities, what we need to do and get done, and ask for the insight, energy, and strength to do it. It's a form of praying, but not addressed to deity in human form. We send our thoughts out to the great mind of the universe and come into unity with it. Afterward, when we have closed our chakras again, we find that the visualization and regular breathing make us feel balanced and centered, but also energized. It's like the feeling you have when you've been leisurely swimming or doing some nonstrenuous exercise. Asking the universe to help us in what we do has another effect: we become less wrapped up in our personal concerns. We get them more into perspective and we become less egocentric. When you articulate your priorities to the universe, you become aware of being a player on a stage where the audience is the cosmos. We don't want to be totally bound up in our own trivialities, we want to live our lives in a better way. We begin to gain clarity.

POINTERS FOR PRACTICE

For magic, we need to develop our sensitivity to subtle energies. Practice opening your chakras to balance your energies and to make you hyperaware. You can open your chakras every morning as a meditative exercise, think about the day's priorities, and ask for the insight, energy, and strength to do them. Meditation makes us less egocentric and helps us to think more clearly and to discern fantasy from reality. Believe in reincarnation if you wish, but don't fantasize about a glamorous past; let magic help you improve the present.

CHAPTER FOUR

Energy 101

The Beginners' Mediumship classes went well. Our group grew used to one another. We began to practice on each other, seeing if we could identify dead relatives. Anyone can make up a spirit guide or a previous incarnation. Dead relatives are a more objective test. Being deficient in the dead relative department, I was not very useful to my mediumship colleagues. They scrutinized my aura enthusiastically, waiting to pick up something from the astral planes, but apart from a few incarnations, there wasn't much to go on. Instead, they started to see aspects of my everyday life. One woman described with great accuracy the inside of our house, which she had never visited. Others picked up people I knew. Our first experiments were usually highly accurate—the famous beginner's luck. Then there was a falling away. We got things wrong. If someone enthusiastically describes a dead relative whom you don't recognize, what do you do? Telling your mediumship colleagues that they are off-track can seem rude, discouraging, and difficult. We learn to find polite ways to convey that we haven't the faintest idea what someone is talking about. Then some of us began to move up a stage. There were moments of astonishing clairvoyance.

Auras

Mediumship classes develop people's ability to see auras, the energy fields around the body. The crown chakra is the origin of the idea of halos. People who are highly spiritually advanced have strong auras that can be seen as strong energy fields around their heads.

Aura Watching

Notice the area surrounding people's heads when you talk to them intimately, one-to-one. You may see an aura of light. Does it grow brighter and stronger as they talk about themselves?

When I see the aura grow bright and strong, I know that I have grown closer to that person's core self. When someone is withdrawn, mistrustful, or reluctant, there is barely any visible aura at all. The clearer and brighter the aura, the more positive is the person's state of mind. When we are ill, sad, or grieving, the aura is faded, dull, drab. We are taught that auras have different colors according to the dominant features in people's lives and personalities, but I never see colors. Auras look white to me—different shades of white, some brighter than others, but white. Many others in the mediumship class could not see color either, but we found that if we were asked to say what we thought the color of someone's aura was, as a group we were fairly unanimous. We were using color as imagery to interpret someone's personality.

Reading Auras in a Group

If you want to experiment with aura colors, get a group of people together. Ask them to sit in a circle with some paper and a pen to make

AURA COLORS

Aura Color	Attributes
Red	Energy, physical strength, in excess and when darkly colored
Pink	Altruistic love, healing
Apricot	A refined form of orange, intellect in the service of spirit
Orange	Warmth, honor, intellectual strength
Yellow	Balanced energy, engagement with the wider world
Green	Affinity with nature, creativity
Turquoise	Communication, writing, singing, inspirational use of voice and word
Blue	Healing, mediumship
Violet	Clairvoyance, psychic ability
White	Purity

notes. It is good to encourage people to write down what they see because they are more likely to give their real opinions rather than just agreeing with everyone else. Talk the group through the chakra opening exercise. Once you have opened your chakras, ask each participant to take turns, closing his or her eyes and for a few minutes breathing deeply, while drawing energy up through the chakras into the crown chakra. Ask people to watch for any changes they see around the person's head. In Buddhist iconography, it appears as the thousand-petaled lotus around the Buddha's head, site of the crown chakra. Ask people to write down what they see—any changes in the size or brightness of the person's aura, and the predominant color or colors in each person's aura. If people cannot "see" color as such, tell them to write down the color they think the aura would be if they could see it. This rather convoluted phrase is a way of bypassing the conscious mind, which might be telling you, "I can't do this, the whole idea is ridiculous." You know the kind of thing. Often we spend more energy telling ourselves that we cannot do something than it would take to just do it. Once everyone has looked at everyone else's aura, compare notes and see how much overlap you find. Encourage people to talk about whether they "saw" the auric color, sensed it, or "guessed," or "fantasized" what it might be.

Not Too Open

Opening the chakras is a way of increasing our sensitivity, and having chakras open feels good. You feel more aware of what is going on around you, more aware of emotions, energies, undercurrents. Especially if you are an emotionally closed person, the novelty of openness feels great; so good that you want to have your chakras open all the time. Don't. Chakra opening increases our sensitivity to energies of all kinds—good and bad. You do not want to be open to other people's negative energies or to negative atmospheres. It is a bad idea, for instance, to travel on public transport with your chakras open. You will sense the symptoms of other people's illnesses, which is unpleasant, and strange people will come to talk to you. Some people are magnets for the deranged. I didn't believe how bad it could be until I became friends with someone who was a psychic magnet for every lunatic in London. We would go into a pub, one I had been in scores of times without the slightest problem, and complete lunatics would sit down next to us and trap us in conversation. It was the same on the bus, on the train, in restaurants, in cinema entrances. There was something open about her, something that emanated, "Come and talk to me." This was great in social gatherings, at business networking conferences, on long plane journeys when she was getting bored. On the street, it was hell. She learned the chakra-closing technique and it made the crucial difference. We could go out in peace. This, by the way, is part of the secret of invisibility.

◎

Too Open? Try Closing your Chakras

If you are someone who is always being approached by peculiar people in public places, try closing down your chakras before going out.

Generating Energy

Beginners' Mediumship taught us how to open our chakras as a way of improving our mediumship and clairvoyance. In Intermediate Mediumship, we started to learn to use the chakra opening exercise as a way of generating energy.

◎

Exercise to Generate Energy

Sit with your spine straight and your hands on your thighs. Open all your chakras, then draw more energy up from your base of spine chakra to fill the whole center of your body, activating the solar plexus chakra and the whole area around the middle of your body. Allow energy to flow out from your trunk and into your lower arms. There is an intimate connection between the solar plexus chakra and your hands. Visualize your hands beginning to glow with golden light. Keep replenishing the energy by going back to your base of spine chakra and drawing more energy into the solar plexus and channeling it to your hands. Returning to the base of spine chakra for "top ups" will stop you from feeling depleted. Now close your eyes and slowly bring the palms of your hands together until you can feel the energy from one hand pressing against the other. Open your eyes and see how far apart your hands were when you began to sense your energy. If you do this exercise regularly, you will find that your ability to project energy from hand to hand will grow steadily stronger.

Psychometry

Learning to generate energy into our hands increases our psychic sensitivity to objects. Psychometry is the technique of sensing the energy field around something, usually objects that have been worn or are in some way strongly connected with someone. Professional mediums will sometimes use psychometry to start a private consultation. You give them a ring or other piece of jewelry and from this they can tell you what has happened to you in the past.

@

Psychometry Exercise

To try psychometry, you need other people to help you practice. You will need some jewelry or watches that people have worn, or other objects that have emotional resonance and that have been in close contact with them. Ask people to bring something that other people are unlikely to recognize. It can be something of their own or something they have borrowed from someone else. Have them slip the object under a black cloth on a tray when they arrive. Make sure no one peeks as they do it. Performance anxiety can make people want to cheat.

When it is time to begin, sit in a circle. Dim the lighting, light a candle, and open your chakras. Ask one person with a soothing voice to talk the rest of you through the chakra opening. Draw energy into your hands. Once people feel that their hands are energized, pass the tray around and ask everyone to take something out from underneath the cloth—not the object they brought. Take turns drawing energy into your hands and sensing the energies around the object. Don't spend too long sensing it because your conscious mind will kick in and start to weave a story around it. Instead, just open your mouth and describe the impressions you are getting. They may not be visual images. They are more likely at first to be sense impressions, emotions, a time period, colors. Start to talk about what emanates from the object—happiness, sadness? Is this a possession of someone now dead, someone living? Images may start to form in your mind, or names, of people connected with the object, or places where it has been. Often you will have auditory impressions. Isolated words, names, or phrases will come into your mind. They may mean nothing to you, but say them anyway. They may make perfect sense to the person who brought the object.

Don't let the person who brought the object give any feedback at this stage. Wait until the end. Once everyone has had their turn at the psychometry, go around the circle and ask people to identify the objects they brought and to comment on the accuracy of the feedback.

It is important that everyone takes a turn before any feedback is given because, until people are used to doing this kind of exercise together, there is a lot of performance anxiety. If the first bit of psychometry is way off-track, people will be put off and won't believe they can do it. It also means you won't feel like a complete failure if people before and after you are brilliant and you are hopeless. In the final feedback session, there are bound to be some other psychometry dunces.

Interpersonal sensitivity is important in the feedback process, so invite only sensible people to your psychometry experiments, not drama queens. It is important when doing psychometry, or any kind of psychic interpretation for people, not to be melodramatic or to say things that might worry them. If you sense negative energies from something, it does not mean that you should say nothing—the owner may be aware of it—but you should be careful how you say it. My friend Bridget visited a well-known medium and gave her a ring to psychometrize. The medium held the ring for about thirty seconds, then threw the ring on the floor and said that the ring had a horrible, negative energy. The owner was my friend. She might not be perfect, but . . . The ring was antique, so perhaps the previous owner was a negative person, but throwing the ring on the floor was not helpful.

Psychic Cleansing

Mediumship is a useful skill, but it goes only so far. Mediumship is about being a passive receptor and sensing energies. Magic is about changing energies. If the medium Bridget visited had been magically knowledgeable, she would have handled the situation differently. We are not victims of fate. We can take action. A helpful response would have been to advise my friend that there was past unhappiness associated with the ring but that it could be psychically cleansed, and to advise her how to do it—soak it in salted water for twenty-four hours and then rinse thoroughly. As it was, my friend, who was not very magically knowledgeable, thought that there must be something wrong with her. Was she emanating negative energy or something? What could have been an interesting experience turned into a source of unnecessary anxiety. How to change energies was one of the first things that I learned as a newly initiated Wiccan and I have described this experience as it occured below. My first psychic cleansing was both an exciting and nerve-racking event. It is important to practice with friends as you begin to learn these rituals.

◡

MY FIRST WICCAN RITUAL

The circle is cast, Goddess and God invoked, then Kim, the group leader that evening, explains the focus of our magic. "Tonight we are going to work on a psychic cleansing." I'm not sure what this is— some kind of astral shower? He explains. Sylvia, a woman who knows someone in the group, has asked us if we can help rid her house of negative energy. She has just moved in and feels there are unpleasant and aggressive energies there. She hadn't felt too positive about the house when she bought it, but it was cheap. It's beginning to sound a bit like a Hollywood horror movie, but it isn't that dramatic—there are no ghosts coming up through the floorboards. It's just that the place isn't making her feel good. She wonders, could we help?

We hold hands. We are told to visualize the negative energy leaving the house, but we are given no guidance on how to do it. People shut their eyes and enter what appears to be a light trance. I look around, not sure what to do. The others are much more experienced than I am. I'll have to use my intuition. I shut my eyes and start to visualize the house. We haven't been told what it looks like, but I see a terraced house, Victorian, a long narrow hallway, an old, brown-painted door with stained glass. Suddenly, I find myself on the first floor, looking down the stairs to the front door. The elongated corridor is dark, dismal, depressing. Regardless of any negative presences, this sight isn't going to fill anyone's heart with joy first thing in the morning. There is a thin strip of threadbare carpet going down the stairs—maroon held down with stair rods. I'm afraid to step on it. I feel old, unsteady. I feel as though I'm going to slip and fall down. I sense my mind is moving into something else. Is this a memory? Did an elderly person slip and suffer an injury, or even die on these stairs? I push this thought out of my mind. I'm not sure if this is real clairvoyance or an overactive imagination.

I turn away from the stairs along the landing. On the right is a decrepit bathroom with an old gas water heater. This doesn't look too safe either. Farther along are three doors to bedrooms, one to the left, one to the right, one straight ahead. I walk into the front bedroom—dire 1960s furniture: large wardrobe, ugly dressing table with medicine bottle and coffee mug stains, pink candlewick bedspread, dirty curtains, a place of illness and death. I examine the other two bedrooms. One, the end bedroom, seems light, much lighter than the rest of the house. There's no logical reason why—the windows are smaller, but I like this room. Maybe this is the bedroom to use. Another bedroom is tiny, and filled with clutter. I'm more confident in the house now. I go downstairs—carefully. The rest of the house seems much less "intense." I wonder, did someone spend a lot of time upstairs ill? I sense a distinct energy. I walk around the downstairs rooms—living room, dining room, kitchen—mentally opening the windows and circulating air. I mentally create a current of energy to push any negative energy out of the windows. My mind is getting tired. I want to stop. Kim senses that we are finishing and tells us to bring our visualizations to an end. We talk and compare notes. Most of us have seen the same kind of house and it does match the description Sylvia complained of. I am relieved I haven't made a total idiot of myself, but also intrigued. I know that my visualization wouldn't have been so accurate if I'd done this exercise on my own. What happens in a group? Do the less experienced somehow tap into the psyches of the more experienced? If some people who are magically experienced "see" something, can they take the others along? It seems they can.

☾

✦

POINTERS FOR PRACTICE

Magic involves visualization, sensitivity to subtle energies, and the ability to generate energy. Practice looking at people's auras when they talk enthusiastically and using the chakra opening exercise as a way of generating energy into your hands. Remember to close your chakras when you don't want to be invaded by other people's energies. Try practicing with friends. Groups are often more psychic and create stronger magical energy than individuals.

CHAPTER 5

Crystal Energies

$\mathcal{N}$atural magic uses the energies of our bodies, minds, and emotions, and the hidden properties of the natural world—stones, crystals, trees, plants, planetary and stellar influences. In my Wiccan training group, we were taught to use our abilities to sense the energies of natural objects. One evening, we were asked to bring some crystals to the training session. We performed the exercise described below to familarize ourselves with the energy of many kinds of crystals.

SENSING CRYSTAL ENERGIES

A few days before the exercise, I put some crystals in glasses of water with salt added and sit them on a south-facing windowsill to catch the Sun. I do this so that people will be able to sense the energies of the crystals unadulterated by my hopes, fears, and energies. One of us casts a circle. Then we spread a black cloth out on the floor and place candles on it for light. We get out our crystal treasures and pool them. We draw etheric energy into our hands, take a crystal each, and sense what we find. The crystals on the black cloth in the center of the candlelit circle are like children's treasures, the flickering contents of Aladdin's cave. I take a large piece of clear speckled amber, marked with the wings of insects captured in it when it formed millennia ago. I hold it up to the light, fascinated by its goldenness. I close my eyes and sense its energies. I see tropical trees. It seems to come from a far off place—Southeast Asia? This is not the Baltic amber that I am used to. It feels warm. I think of healing, warm energy loving and renewing the body. I am reluctant to let go of the amber, but I wipe it with a piece of silk and put it back in the pile for others to try. I watch the others communing with their stones. The atmosphere is peaceful, quiet, with gentle intensity. To remember this experience, I make notes about the amber in my magical diary.

I take a piece of clear quartz. While the amber was warm, this is cool and hard. It fits in my hand perfectly, like a miniature wand. I feel I could use it to project energy. I rub the stone on my third eye. It is soothing, clearing. I rub it on my heart chakra. It is cold and soothing here too. I think of a cold hand on a child's fevered brow. I rub my breastbone again and up over each lung. A clearing stone? To clear a fever, to clear the lungs? I feel it could also clear clutter in the mind—a stone of clear-seeing; not to aid clairvoyance as such, but to remove the barriers to clear sight. It's like a cold drink of water. Reluctantly, I clean it and put it back. I make my notes and look for something to contrast with the quartz—dark red carnelian. I sense deepness, thick red blood. I know that carnelian, like other reddish stones, was often called bloodstone and was used in ancient medicine to help reduce bleeding. I like the stone but am reluctant to hold it too long. This is not the right stone for me. My blood is already too thick. I put it back and take a piece of turquoise.

It reminds me of a turquoise piece I bought years ago from the Navajo. I think of it as the American Indian jewel. I love it but rarely wear it. It seems friendly, but it is not for me. I pick up a purple crystal, thinking it is amethyst, but one end is too dark and the other fades to crystal clear. This is a fluorite crystal. This stone feels mysterious, exciting. It seems hard and enduring, but I don't know whether this is literally true or if it has something to do with the energy of the stone. Fluorite scores four on the ten-point Mohs scale of gem hardness—above calcite, but way below diamond at ten and quartz at seven. I sense that fluorite has some energy that I lack, but

I do not know what it is. (Later I discover fluorite's attribute is to increase concentration. A friend gave me a piece that fits perfectly into the hand. I keep it by my computer and hold it when I'm trying to think through something complicated.) I put the fluorite back and take something that seems softer, though in reality it is not—rose quartz, one of my favorites. I sense soothing, calmness, balance. I like to keep rose quartz in the house, but I never wear it as jewelry. It feels wrong when close to me. I take a piece of amethyst, the stone of bishops' rings. I like to wear it. Its color reminds me of the third eye. I sometimes rub my third eye with it before healing to help me see clearly what I should do. Wearing it is supposed to stop you from getting drunk. Unfortunately, I've found that this isn't true.

Crystal Exercise

Like the ritual I performed, you can do this crystal exercise with friends or alone. Find, buy, or borrow six different crystals or select six pieces that you already possess. Don't worry about their ascribed properties. Use six different stones that appeal to you because of their color, shape, or consistency. Small, rough pieces of rock are fine. Once you have your six pieces of stone, cleanse them of any previous influences they may have picked up. Crystals are thought of as absorbers and transmitters of energies. You want the energies they absorb and transmit to be yours, not someone or something else's. You can cleanse them by placing each one in a separate glass of salted water for twenty-four hours. Rock salt or sea salt is usually the preferred choice for magical workings. You can buy this in supermarkets or health food stores. If you buy pure rock salt, you will notice that it has a grey color. Ordinary table salt is bleached white.

Once they have had their twenty-four hours of purification, take the crystals out of the salted water, rinse them, let them dry, and then place them on a piece of dark cloth. Do the chakra-opening exercise and energize your hands. Take each crystal in turn, hold it in your hands, shut your eyes, allow your mind to go blank. Focus on your fingers. Allow your fingers to sense the energy coming from the crystal. If your conscious mind says, "But how do I do that?" ignore it. Unconsciously your body will know. How does the crystal feel in your hands—hard, soft, brittle, strong, friendly, cool, restrained, pulsating with energy, warm, energizing, soothing? Note your reactions on a piece of paper. Try another crystal. What differences do you sense? When you have sensed all the stones, look at the traditional meanings given in the table below. Do your impressions match those of the standard interpretations? If you found you were drawn more to one crystal than another, look at its properties. Are you attracted to something that should traditionally rectify a physical or psychological imbalance that you have?

Color Symbolism

The attributions of crystals, herbs, and other substances used in natural magic evolved haphazardly. They are largely related to color. The ancients had no way of testing the chemical composition of different stones, so judged them on color, rarity, and hardness. Color seemed particularly salient. As children and as adults, we love rainbows—they seem to offer beauty and hope, and in many cultures are considered a bridge to the heavenly realm of the gods. Irish leprechauns buried their golden treasure at the rainbow's end. We love crystals that split light into the spectrum. Color fascinates us because it has a strong emotional impact and influences our moods. Some colors depress us; others energize or soothe us. Hospital emergency departments avoid red walls because they increase waiting patients' aggression. Our associations with color derive from our experiences of them in the natural world. Red and orange at one end of the spectrum are associated with warmth, fire, flames, and the emotions we feel when our skin reddens. We become red with

STONES AND THEIR PROPERTIES

Stone	Properties	Magical Attributions and Qualities
Agate	Banded variety of chalcedony, wide range of colors and shapes including moss agate and onyx	Mercury. Strength, protection
Amazonite	Deep green or greenish-blue feldspar	Bones, sense of self worth
Amber	Hardened tree resin. Usually gold but also red, green	Sun. Purify mind and body
Amethyst	Light to dark purple variety of quartz	Jupiter. Psychic awareness, use to treat addictions and alcoholism. Meditation, mental clarity, calmness
Aquamarine	Blue to blue-green variety of beryl	Courage
Aventurine	Usually green, but may be orange, brown, yellow. Small inclusions of shiny minerals create glistening effect	Calm and serenity
Azurite (Chessylite)	Blue to very dark blue copper carbonate	Creativity
Bloodstone	Dark green to greenish-blue chalcedony dotted with small, red, bloodlike spots	Mars. Use to counteract blood pressure and leg cramps. Carry to attract fame
Carnelian (Cornelian)	Reddish to reddish-brown, transparent to translucent chalcedony	Anger, physical energy, to counteract allergies
Celestine (Celestite)	Colorless, white, orange, orange-brown, light brown, yellow, greenish-blue, gray, blue, strontium sulphate	Dream recall

STONES AND THEIR PROPERTIES (CONTINUED)

Stone	Properties	Magical Attributions and Qualities
Citrine	Yellow, orange, orange-brown, or reddish-brown variety of quartz	Sun. Material gain, success in business, joy. Use to treat digestive system, blood and circulatory system
Diamond	Colorless, but also found with tinges of other colors	To purify mind and body, mental clarity, confidence
Emerald	Green variety of beryl	Venus. Love, kindness, calmness, good memory
Fluorite	Calcium fluoride. Range of colors, often green and purples. Can be multi-colored	Helps one's concentration
Garnet	Group of minerals with related physical and chemical properties including blood-red pyrope, carbuncle (deep-red pyrope), dark, blackish alamdine, rhodolite—rose-red to violet pyrope	Commitment, sexual attraction
Geode	Hollow rock with layer of agate surrounding crystalline quartz	Astral travel
Hematite	Iron oxide, sometimes with traces of titanium. Light to dark gray, black, brown and reddish-brown	Mars. Use to treat bloodstream, circulatory system, fever
Jade	Gem quality form of minerals jadeite and nephrite. Green is common but also found in other colors	Venus. For dream recall, to increase confidence, banish loneliness, protection for houses
Jasper	Opaque variety of chalcedony, many colors	Astral travel

Stone	Properties	Magical Attributions and Qualities
Labradorite	Sodium calcium aluminium silicate found in white, gray, light blue, light green, pale orange-red, black	Use to increase self-awareness and for extra-terrestrial energy/communication
Lapis lazuli	Deep blue lazurite (silicate family) with pyrite, calcite, and other minerals	Jupiter. Use to increase psychic awareness, boost immune system, lift depression, give vitality
Lepidolite	Violet to pink or white ore of lithium, a silicate	Combats stress, promotes sleep, calmness
Malachite	Light to dark-green copper carbonate	For alleviating arthritis, boosting immune system, encouraging luck and money
Moonstone	Feldspar, colorless through white to light blue. Also yellow, orange, and reddish varieties	Moon. Women's health matters
Obsidian	Black to dark green volcanic silica glass formed by hot lava and water	Saturn. Eases grief
Quartz (Rock crystal)	Colorless, transparent, well-crystalized variety of quartz	Meditation, mental clarity, energy, dispels negativity
Rose quartz	Pink quartz usually found in massive form and only rarely as crystals	Venus. Altruistic love, peace, and harmony
Ruby	Red variety of mineral corundum	Mars. Passion, power, energizing, bloodstream, circulatory system, headache, fever
Sapphire	Blue sapphire is blue corundum	For clarity and inspiration, especially of the voice and in public speaking. Good fortune

STONES AND THEIR PROPERTIES (CONTINUED)

Stone	Properties	Magical Attributions and Qualities
Smoky quartz	Black or dark brown variety of quartz	Mental clarity, use to gain cooperation, protection, meditation
Tiger's eye	Golden and brown pseudomorph of quartz	Confidence, sexual attraction
Topaz	Golden (imperial) topaz is the most valuable	Sun. Creativity and self-expression, antidote to depression and grief
Tourmaline	Red, green and multicolored are common. Group of minerals with related physical and chemical properties. Electrical properties—attracts dust and dirt particles when rubbed or heated	To alleviate nervousness
Turquoise	Blue-green. Hydrated copper aluminium phosphate	Healing, emotional stability, communication, friendship

anger and aflame with passion. We experience red and orange as energizing colors.

Blues and violets are tones we see at twilight and early morning, the beginning and end of the day. We associate them with coolness, quiet, resting. Green is the color of nature in spring. We associate it with fertility and things beginning anew. Yellow is flowers, sunlight, the color of noonday light and golden afternoon and early evening summer sun. It is bright and optimistic, but in large doses can overwhelm. Pink is soothing and is often associated with health and well-being. We talk about being "in the pink," of looking pink with health. Pink stones are thought of as creating calming environments. Pink is also associated with positive feelings. In the magical tradition, the color pink is associated with altruistic love; so rose quartz

is thought to encourage altruistic love. We think of the big cats—
lions, tigers—as having strength and sexual energy. The stone tiger's
eye becomes associated with sexuality. We associate sexuality with
red, the color of aroused sex organs, so deep-red garnet becomes a
stone of sexuality. Golden colors are associated with the Sun, positive energy. Golden topaz becomes an antidote to depression. Sometimes stones are treated as antidotes to conditions; sometimes the
connection is more homeopathic. Black is associated with mourning,
and obsidian is recommended for coming to terms with a death.

Placing crystals in key points of your home where you want to
encourage a particular energy works well. Partly the effect is psychological. It may also be due to the properties of the stones, but
that is questionable. Undoubtedly stones do have particular physical properties. Hematite, for instance, is an iron-based substance
that emits a low-grade magnetism. When I wore a hematite bracelet
for a television appearance, every time I touched a door or wall I got
an electric shock. The hematite was doing something to my energy
field. However, many attributions of crystals and minerals take no
account of their chemical composition. Many stones are varieties of
quartz or of chalcedony, a microcrystalline variety of quartz. Apart
from the color, their chemical composition is the same. Like all
magical law, don't accept this absolutely, just try it and see. You
will certainly find their color and beauty psychologically uplifting
and because you know what your intention was in placing the stone
in a particular place, it acts as a signal to your unconscious mind.
Here is the place of love, here the place of healing, here the place
of mental activity, here the place of sleep and dreams.

If you would like to have crystals and stones in your home, obtain a crystal or stone associated with the energy you want to manifest. Perhaps you would like rose quartz for love and harmony, clear
quartz for a clear-thinking environment, or jade for protection. Use
the feng shui diagram on page 65 to establish where might be a
good place to put your stone. Many crystals can now be bought to
hang in windows, but remember to treat natural objects with re-

spect. They may do things you are not anticipating. Clear crystals can be used to focus sunlight to start fires. Be wary of hanging quartz in a south-facing window in summer.

Crystal Energizing

Cleanse the stone by soaking it for twenty-four hours in salted water. Rinse off the salt and dry it. Find a quiet time, dim the lighting, and light a candle in the room where you want to place your crystal. Place the stone on a piece of dark cloth. Open your chakras and pour energy into your hands. Create a visual image of what you want your stone to bring you. If it is a happy harmonious home, imagine walking around each room, seeing it clean, orderly, warm, comfortable, emanating happiness. Once you have mentally walked around every room, focus on where you want to place your crystal. Pick up the crystal and generate energy from your hands, pouring into the crystal the energy you want it to emit—peace, energy, good fortune, love, harmony—whatever it is you are seeking. Once you have generated all the energy you can, place the stone back on the cloth and relax in silent contemplation for a while. Then close your chakras and put the stone in place. It is a good idea to recharge the stone about every three months.

Buying Crystals

Buying crystals can be difficult. Unscrupulous dealers often mislabel them. Rhodolite, a form of garnet, is sold as ruby. If lapis lazuli is at a price that you can afford, it is probably reconstituted and is not thought to have the same qualities as naturally formed stone. Some dealers dye stones to enhance their color. If colors are bizarrely vivid, they are probably dyed. Deep rose quartz is likely to be dyed. Natural rose quartz is usually pale pink. Turquoise is soft and easily dyed. Heat treatment is another method used to change the color of stones, and sometimes to pass them off as a different stone entirely. Green serpentine becomes jade. Obsidian is confused with smoky quartz. Citrine may be sold as topaz. Most blue topaz is heat-treated colorless or light topaz. Most pink topaz is heat-treated yellow or brownish topaz. Chrysocolla is often missold as turquoise.

Crystals are part of the Earth. Buy them from reputable dealers who guarantee that their products are from ethical suppliers. Crystals are often mined in developing countries and provide much-needed jobs and income, but many crystals are mined by indiscriminate blasting that destroys the local environment. Ethical mining is done by companies who restore worked-out mining areas and do not engage in large-scale blasting. This uses more local labor and is marginally more expensive—and well worth paying for. Crystal extraction should not leave a natural area stripped bare. Quartz crystals are often grown through a simple process that you may have tried in school chemistry lessons when learning to make crystal gardens. Laboratory crystals can be detected by their perfect shapes. Crystal purists decry laboratory-grown crystals, but while not formed by the Earth over millennia, laboratory crystals do not have the ethical mining problems of the "natural" product. Coral and pearl are stones that have magical attributions, but they are not listed in the table above because they were or are products of living creatures. Avoid buying coral. The destruction of coral reefs by pollution and souvenir hunters is a major environmental problem.

★

POINTERS FOR PRACTICE

Placing crystals in key points around your home can help create energy centers. Wear appropriate crystals to boost your personal energies in whatever you do. Crystals are gifts of the Earth. Buy them from reputable dealers who support ethical mining, or buy laboratory-grown specimens.

CHAPTER SIX

Magic Begins at Home

You, of the twisted trunk and the massive body,
with the dazzle and light of millions of suns;
lead me on a path that has no obstacles nor hindrances,
clearing the way in all that I do, ever, and always!

PRAYER TO GANESHA

In many cultures, sacred statues and shrines are set up in the home to bring positive energy and good fortune to the household. It is true that you can never have too much good fortune, but less can be more in deity statues. My friend Francesca, author of *Making Magic with Gaia,* sent me my very first Ganesha as a birthday gift from Boulder, Colorado. I'm grateful for the thought, but I was not immediately impressed by the little brass statue. He looked, well, ugly. Thank goodness, it was small! While I was sufficiently up on Eastern religious traditions to recognize Ganesha when I saw him, I could not think what he is for.

I discovered that Ganesha is the son of the Hindu goddess Parvati. While her husband Shiva is away fighting a monster, Parvati creates Ganesha by breathing life into a doll made of dough—so she says. Shiva returns from defeating the monster, bringing its head as a trophy. Young Ganesha is guarding the entrance to his home and challenges this warlike stranger. Shiva doesn't know about Ganesha.

Outraged at the impertinence—after all, Shiva is a god—he cuts off the boy's head. Having spun the dough story, a distraught Parvati begs Shiva to restore Ganesha to life. The problem is that Ganesha needs a head. Shiva gives him the spare head he has handy, that of the slain monster. Ganesha is restored to life, but his human body now bears an elephant's head. As a being who has died and resurrected, Ganesha has overcome the greatest trial of all and he is revered as a bringer of good luck, material fortune, and academic success. His image is placed by gates and at entrance doors to guard them and to block malevolent influences from entering. You can salute him before starting a journey or project and ask him to remove obstacles. He is one of the most worshipped of Indian deities. "He's great for projects that involve making money," explains the helpful friend.

Of course—money! Suddenly I understood—what a great gift. Ganesha suddenly looked wonderfully handsome, virile, and attractive. He has become one of my favorite deities. When you are sent a Ganesha by someone whose Boulderite international banker husband does something much more mysterious and esoteric with high finance than you have ever done with magic, it is a good idea to take it seriously. After consulting a feng shui diagram, I put Ganesha in the wealth corner of my London apartment to boost my finances. If you have a superficial knowledge of these things, this will seem logical. If you know a lot about them, this mixing of pantheons and spiritual philosophies will appall you. If you are a Chinese Taoist master, you'll mutter something oblique like, "When the water courser goes to the mountain, the mountain bows," leaving your bemused listeners to ponder the meaning and wait for enlightenment to come. If you know nothing about feng shui, I'll explain later.

Creating Energies

Why should a deity statue be magically helpful? We can think of deities as symbols that human beings have created to represent different aspects of cosmic energy. Wherever we travel in the world, we find human beings expressing one of their most natural instincts, which is to create sacred space. As soon as our earliest ancestors attained full human consciousness, they began to make shrines. They took the most powerful symbols they could find and arranged them in patterns in sacred places. Often these were hard to reach—deep, dark caves or tops of mountains. Sometimes they were at natural meeting points—at crossroads, or at the confluence of mighty rivers and streams. In India, two of the most sacred places are Hardwar and Rishikesh, where the sacred River Ganges first descends from the mountains to the plain. Our ancestors built altars and shrines as places of communication between the powers that lie behind the material world and us. At our sacred altars, we venerate the Divine and we ask for Divine energy and blessing to manifest in our lives.

When you install a deity statue, you are bringing new energy into your personal space, but before installing this new energy into your home, it is as well to sort out what you already have. Your environment is important if you want to bring magic into your life. If you read about magic, you may think it is all about cats, broomsticks, cauldrons, and strange diagrams, but the basis of magic is not material artifacts. It is imagery, sensitivity, and energy. To create magic, you must first create an environment that allows energy to flow.

Useful or Beautiful

If your energies are blocked, you cannot create magic. Your home is a reflection of you and your inner world. Reordering your home can help you reorder your inner world. Think about the atmospheres in the homes of people you know. Some homes are, well, homely. They are untidy, maybe none too clean, have ghastly décor, and are not situated in the best district in the world, but when you step inside you feel happy. There is a feeling of love and friendliness. You feel that the occupants like people. We like to visit, to hang loose, to be asked to dinner, or to stay over. Other homes are beautiful but cold, showpieces that you cannot imagine living in. And the occupants don't quite match. It's as though they are living in a house borrowed for a gossip magazine photo shoot, an environment that's designed to show how rich and successful they are and what good taste they have; except that the taste is not quite their own. Magical homes are both beautiful and welcoming. We go into them and the energy feels good. If we're buying a house, it's the one we want to buy. The décor is designed lovingly. It expresses the aesthetic sense and values of the people who created it. It belongs to them; it is not copied from a design catalog. The Victorian master craftsman William Morris once said that a golden rule for homemaking was to have nothing in your house that is neither useful nor beautiful. This is a good principle.

☺

Preparing Your Home for Magical Energies

Walk around your home and look at your possessions. Ask yourself, do I use this? Does it have a function in my life? If not, is it a beautiful object that enhances my environment? Look in your cupboards. Are they neatly arranged, or stacked with items you can hardly remember owning? How many possessions do you have that you never use—clothes, books, old magazines, CDs by a band you cannot bear to listen to now? Do you need all this stuff in your life? It accumulates dust, takes up storage space, and traps energy as well as dirt. If you made a list of everything you owned down to the last sock, how long would it be—one thousand, two thousand items? As a magical exercise, see how much you can slim down. A first rule of ventilating your possessions is that it is much easier to give things away than to throw them away.

Go around your home and find everything that you don't think you need. Divide everything into different categories. Make a pile for rubbish that can be thrown away and another pile for items that could go for recycling. Many recycling centers take clothes, shoes, old computers, newspapers, glass. Make separate piles for items that you could give to friends and items that could be given to a charity shop. Make a pile for items that you decide to keep because they have sentimental value. We can afford some useless or ugly objects in our lives, but let's make them objects that are meaningful.

If you own clothes that you have not worn for a year, ask yourself if you need them. If it is an item of sentimental value—a wedding dress, the suit you wore for your graduation—you might want to keep it. Normally, though, if you haven't worn a garment for a year, work on the premise that you don't need it. Don't worry if it's hardly worn. Fashion changes so quickly that you are unlikely to wear good quality clothes that no longer look right. Give them away to someone who can make better use of them. A good way of dealing with accumulating clothes is to throw away or give away a similar item whenever you buy a new one. If you have bought a pair of new jeans, do you need the old ones? If not, get rid of them.

What about items that need repairing? Lots of us have old electrical goods, chipped vases, and things that we mean to stick, glue, or fix, but we never get around to it. If something's been sitting there for two years and you've survived without it, maybe it's time it went. What about your kitchen? Take everything out of the cupboards. Are there faded old packages of food that you never quite got around to finishing? What is the sell-by date on that couscous? Throw away anything you haven't used for months. And what about those peculiar kitchen gadgets? The ones that well-meaning friends with greater culinary ambitions than yours give you for Christmas. Maybe they'd be of more use to a charity shop. Clean your cupboard shelves and put back only what you use and need. Get on top of your environment so you are in control of it, and not it of you. Once you've cleared things out, rearrange your furniture, rehang your pictures. If your environment becomes too familiar, you cease to notice it. Mov-

ing things around will help you see them again. It gives you new per-
spectives.

Geomancy

Geomancy is the art of understanding and aligning oneself to earth
energies. The ancient Chinese feng shui system is probably the
world's best-known form of geomancy, but all our ancestors practiced geomancy in the way they laid out their stone circles, temples,
cities, and other monuments. Feng shui means "wind and water,"
and a full-scale in-depth consultation with a feng shui professional
incorporates the layout and position of your home, and how this relates to your astrological makeup in the Chinese astrological system
and that of other people who live there. Feng shui uses principles derived from Taoism. It involves balancing active yang and passive yin
energies according to the different activities carried out in the house.
The idea is to create a layout that is both energizing and relaxing.
This means that energy must be encouraged to flow through your
home. Energy must not get stuck in one place, and it must not "leak"
out too quickly. The arrangement of our homes is becoming in-
creasingly important, and not just for aesthetic reasons. As home en-
tertainment facilities and computer systems become more complex,
we spend more and more time in our homes. Our home environments impact more and more on our psyches.

©
Aligning the Energy Flows in Your Home

Feng shui starts with your hallway, which is the first part of your
home that people will see. It should reflect your personality and how
you want to present yourself to the outside world. Is your hallway
warm and friendly, or is it cold and forbidding, dark and gloomy?

What colors would create the right mood, the mood that you want people to be in when they enter your home? Often, when we redecorate, we leave the hall until last, but it is the best place to begin. People may walk through your hallway without looking at it, but it creates an unconscious impression, and you want it to be the right one. If you put a deity statue in your hallway, the concepts and energy surrounding that deity are "circulated" around the house. They affect you and other people who come into the house and can unconsciously influence how you and they behave.

If, from your front door, visitors can see through the house, particularly straight through to the back door, this is seen as creating conduits that suck energy out of the house. On a practical level, this door position will create drafts. On a psychological level, the aligned doors will draw visitors' attention to what is beyond and outside the house, rather than drawing them into the house. Other than going over the top and rebuilding, what can you do? One solution is to keep any intervening doors between the front and back closed. This will stop the "out as soon as you are in" effect. Another trick is to hang small multifaceted crystals from hallway ceilings or lights to move energy around. Whether or not they are moving energy, the crystals move in the draft when you open the doors and they will act as slight distracters that focus our attention into the house rather than out of it. They are also fun.

Other Feng Shui Tips

Feng shui practitioners loathe en suite bathrooms. Western magicians adore en suite bathrooms; but there's the corruption of capitalism for you. Feng shui was devised, of course, before the era of flush toilets, when lavatories were simple buckets. No one wants this type of lavatory indoors and in the preplumbing West, toilet facilities were also kept outside, preferably in sheds at the bottom of the garden. Where West and East would agree is that it is a good idea to keep the bathroom door closed, even if for purely aesthetic reasons. The horror feng shui has for toilet lids left up is well known. In feng shui, when you flush the toilet, you are thought to be flushing away wealth. The gaping hole of the toilet is a void into which your wealth can fall. A Freudian, of course, would have lots to say about the association between wealth and anal retentiveness. Western magicians do not have the same phobias, but common sense will tell you that it is a good idea to put down toilet lids when they are not in use. Flushing distributes microscopic water droplets full of germs everywhere in a three-foot radius. Apologies for the sanitary digression, I'm not really obsessed with bathrooms, but it illustrates the point that even if the magical reasons for a practice are not obvious, think about why people have found it helpful before discarding it.

@

Switching Off and Tuning In

If you find it difficult to switch off and relax when you come home from work, make sure that you change out of your work clothes. Put on clothes that express your personality. Depending on what you wear at work, you might want to look smart and glamorous, or scruffy and laid back. Do what feels right for you, but make a conscious switch from work mode to home life.

Many people do at least part of their jobs at home. Some points to remember if you have a home office is that feng shui practitioners believe that you should be able to see your office door from your desk. You should not sit with your back to the door. This makes good psychological sense; our animal instinct is always to be able to see what is coming, so predators do not surprise us. Sitting with your back to the door may make you unconsciously insecure and tense. You should not sit directly opposite the door either. Your attention is being drawn out of the room rather than focusing on your work. Similarly, you will be distracted if you are aware of people constantly walking past the door. Feng shui practitioners recommend putting a crystal ball on your desk if you want success in careers in the media, education, writing, publishing, and communication. The crystal is thought to bring in work, wealth, and recognition. Quartz crystal in Western tradition is said to bring clarity of ideas and to dispel negativity. There are no particular wealth associations, but hey, it's a useful paperweight, so why not?

If you work at home, it is even more important to make a psychological transition when you come to the end of the day. Decide what time is the latest you should work and when you reach that time, stop. It is easy when self-employed to work fourteen hours a day and think that this is what you have to do. The longer we work the more our productivity per hour goes down and the staler our ideas become. Not relaxing and changing gear also damages our health. When you stop, put work away, tidy up. It will be that much easier to start with fresh energy in the morning if your workspace is highly organized when you start. Switch to home mode by going outside for a quick walk around the block, then come home and change your clothes. You are now officially off duty.

Bedrooms are for rest, so they need to be tidy and tranquil. Watching television in bed is fun in hotels but best avoided in your own home. It is brightly colored and will stimulate you rather than making you want to sleep. If you want to sleep well, it is a good idea to stop watching television at least half an hour before you go to bed.

Identifying Energy Centers

In feng shui, each part of your home is associated with a different aspect of life and different energies. To identify the location of the different energy centers in your home, work out the positions, of north, south, east, and west. You can do this with a cheap compass or you can make a rough guess. In the northern hemisphere, sunrise is due east around the Spring Equinox, March 21, and Autumn

Equinox, September 21. In summer, sunrise moves gradually to the north, reaching the northeast around Midsummer, June 21, and then moving back toward the east again. In winter, it creeps southward, reaching southeast around the shortest day, December 21. As the days get longer, sunrise moves back toward due east. Similarly, sunset is due west at the equinoxes, northwest at Midsummer and southwest at Winter Solstice.

Once you have identified where the four directions are, mentally superimpose the feng shui diagram on your home, seeing which area of life predominates in each of the rooms of your house. If your home is irregularly shaped, you may find that a particular energy center is missing. Chinese homes, like Breton farms and cottages, were usually built with their doors in the south wall. This means that the house is facing the sun most of the day and is warmed. The Chinese also preferred their houses to be the nice, solid, stable shape of a square. The part of the house marked "projects, journeys, recognition, and fame" is where the front door and hallway would be in a house built on the favored orientation of south. Your doorway may not be in the south, so your entrance point may be in a different area of life.

FENG SHUI DIAGRAM

Wealth, *Northwest*	Career *North*	Relationships *Northeast*
Parents, family, health *West*	Energy *Center*	Children, projects *East*
Wisdom, education, knowledge *Southwest*	Projects, journeys, fame, recognition *South*	Contacts, helpful people *Southeast*

There are expert ways of calculating your feng shui alignments using a feng shui compass. If you become more interested in feng shui, you can use these, but the diagram will serve as a simple way of introducing the concepts into your life. If you give a home to a deity statue, you are creating an energy center in your life, so it is important to decide which deity and where. What aspect of your life do you want to activate and emphasize? Here the feng shui diagram can help. You can also superimpose the diagram on each individual room in the house. This is helpful when deciding where to place beds, desks, dining tables, or shrines. You may not be able to have your home office in the career or wealth part of your home, but you may be able to place your desk in the career or wealth part of the room you use. Similarly, if putting a Kuan Yin statue in the relationships part of your home would mean trying to fit her into your tiny kitchen, you could instead put her in an appropriate part of the room.

Shrines

Natural magicians are eclectic about their gods. The famous British magician Dion Fortune once said that all Gods are one God and all Goddesses are one Goddess. In other words, all the different beautiful forms in which we venerate the Divine are just that, forms. They are symbols to help us understand Ultimate Reality. In natural magicians' homes, Ganeshas happily rub shoulders with Egyptian Basts, Madonnas of Guadalupe, and Buddhas. Gods and venerated beings are a tolerant bunch who have no problems getting along. It's their followers who mess it up.

Bring a Deity Statue into Your Home

If you want to bring prosperity and good fortune into your home, you could install a statue of the Indian wealth-bringing good fortune god Ganesha. If you prefer your good fortune to be the gift of a goddess, you could look for a statue of the beautiful Chinese goddess Kuan Yin. If you can, place the statue in the wealth corner of your home or room.

Deities

Kuan Yin (also spelled Guan Yin or Kwan Yin) is revered in Japan as Kwannon. Her full name is Kuan Shih Yin, which means "She who hearkens to the cries of the world and comes." She is the most famous Chinese goddess, considered in Chinese Buddhism to be a Bodhisattva, who out of compassion postponed her entry into nirvana to help humankind. The role of a Bodhisattva is to alleviate disease and suffering, so Kuan Yin is often represented holding a small vase filled with the tears of compassion in one hand, the other hand bestowing a blessing. Her Chinese titles include "Great Mercy, Great Pity," "Salvation from Misery," and "Salvation from Woe." She plays a similar role to the Virgin Mary in Catholicism. A popular image of Kuan Yin shows her poised riding on the back of a sea monster. The iconography hints at her nature. She is compassionate, gentle, able to ride serenely and with detachment over the stormy waters of life, yet also strong and powerful. Using feng shui principles, you could place her statue in the wealth corner of your home to bring financial stability and good fortune, or in the section for relationships, marriage, and friends to create harmony. In the center of your home, she would become a balancing influence and energy.

Another deity image that is highly popular in the twenty-first century is the ancient Egyptian cat goddess Bast. She has been worshipped for at least five thousand years. Her main cult center was in Bubastis in northern Egypt, where her annual festival attracted huge crowds. Her statues are made in the form of a seated black cat or as a standing woman with a cat's head. Bast is a good goddess for the home. Cats are great home lovers and fierce defenders of their personal space. Bast has the added bonus of being a goddess of love. If you have a cat and your Bast statue is cat-sized or larger, watch how your cat reacts. Beautiful, inexpensive Bast statues are readily available from museum shops and gift shops. Give Bast her own table, shelf, or mantel. Candles and flowers are particularly appreciated. Cats like lots of worship, so treat your patron deity as an honored guest. Flowers bring beauty into your home, and deities appreciate that kind of thing. Remember, you do not need to believe in the objective existence of great cats that stalk the skies in order to venerate Bast. You are venerating a concept and ideal, and by creating a sacred point in your home, you are saying something about how you regard your personal space and treating it with respect. This is a good starting point for magic.

Changing Atmosphere

When our Wiccan group did a psychic cleansing of Sylvia's home, we followed this up by asking Sylvia to help herself. Most people, when they ask for magical help, want you to wave your magic wand and solve their problem, but far too many people are ready to dump their problems on others. It is much better to help people to help themselves. People learn much more from discovering their own empowerment than from having someone trying to solve all their problems for them. It stops you from becoming the agony aunt or uncle for all your friends, and it helps you avoid falling into the ego trap of becoming the great magician or witch who can solve everyone's problems. People who go down this road are invariably looking for ways to avoid facing up to problems of their own. It was important that Sylvia took responsibility for creating the right atmosphere in her home. We advised her to open all the windows of the house for a day to air it and to clean the house thoroughly, preferably enlisting a gang of friends and turning it into a party. The support of other people is very powerful when changing atmospheres. Each evening for a month, we suggested that she burn a small amount of solar incense upstairs and downstairs, and play some peaceful but uplifting music, something to put her in a positive frame of mind. She adopted Bast as patron deity of the house and placed her on a table in the hall. Sylvia started a decorating program, beginning with that drab hall. The atmosphere in the whole house began to change. It was becoming a place that was loved and cared for, and a receptacle for positive energies.

✦

POINTERS FOR PRACTICE

If your energies are blocked, you cannot create magic. Your home is a reflection of you and your inner world. Reordering your home can help you reorder your inner world. Clear out what you no longer need and have nothing in your house that is neither useful nor beautiful. Place a statue of a deity of good fortune in your home to create positive energy. Use your magical knowledge to empower people to help themselves. Don't fall into the ego trap of trying to solve all their problems for them.

CHAPTER SEVEN

Magic and the Body

Magic begins at home, but magical and indigenous traditions worldwide also teach that magic begins in the body. Magic is something we experience and feel with flesh, bone, and sinew. It is a throbbing energy in our veins. It is the life force within us seeking to manifest new creativity and energy in the world. Magic makes the world a more exciting place, and that is good for us both psychologically and physically. Magic is about creating a certain environment around you, one that draws positive things to you and protects you from negative things, but magic can't protect us from inescapable realities of life—aging and death. I have met magicians who claimed to be immortal, but I didn't believe them, not even at my most teenage gullible. No magical or spiritual practice will overcome the inevitability of the decay of our material selves, but we can lessen the impact of this process by caring for ourselves physically and spiritually, and magic can help us feel healthy.

Many of the magical techniques I describe are ways of relaxing the body—something that reduces stress and ill health. Meditation, chakra-opening exercises, ritual, prayer, and invocation all lower the heart rate and produce relaxation. They are antidotes to the stress and tensions that plague contemporary society. The magical tradition sees incarnation in the body as a precious gift, one we should use wisely and well. We can best fulfill our destinies if our bodies function well. It is important to help them do just that. Caring for your physical self has enormous payoffs. Personal appearance is not the be-all and end-all that cosmetic surgeons would have us believe; but this doesn't mean that we can ignore it. Looking good is something we do not just for other people, but because it makes us feel better about ourselves. We don't all get equal shares in the glamour stakes, but we can make the most of what we've got. Magic is full of glamour spells to help us look our best. Of course, they work. They increase our self-confidence so that we have a charismatic glow. Magic generally, without any glamour spells, tends to make people seem physically more attractive. "You look so well," exclaim your friends. "Have you had your hair done?" Or, "You've lost weight." If you are working with cosmic energies, it's a bit like having regular good sex. It does leave an afterglow. In fact, praying, meditating, chanting, and fasting have a similar effect, and regular spiritual practice in all religious traditions is associated with increased health and well-being; but natural magic can be a lot more fun.

Practicing magic doesn't mean that we can ignore all the sensible stuff about taking care of our bodies. An important aspect of magical philosophy is to reclaim ownership of the body. If you have a house, you want it to be well maintained and nice looking. If you have a car, you want it to have great bodywork and a well-running engine. Since we live in bodies, we need to take account of that and enjoy having them at their best. And we have much more control over our bodies than we realize. We can exercise this in ways that enhance our health and well-being, or we can cause ourselves harm.

Invisible and Overvisible

I found out, as do many teenagers, that it is all too easy to control my body. When I was fourteen we had very little money, too little to eat three meals every day. I found there is a way to switch off brain signals; to turn off the signal for "hunger." I visualized it as a thermostat dial in the brain. I turned it down and found that I could function on much less food. My lack of hunger alleviated my mother's anxiety about the lack of food. She functioned through nicotine. She was addicted and couldn't stop smoking even though we didn't have enough to eat. And, of course, smoking suppresses hunger. I thought about it. If she didn't smoke, I could eat, but she couldn't not smoke. It was pointless to discuss it. Drawing attention to the reality would have made her miserable.

After fasting for a while, your skin feels smoother. You purge out toxins. Your stomach feels light, your body feels good. Sensations are enhanced. It brings a sense of power and control, and a lightness of being. It feels good to travel light, to have less to carry around. The feeling is addictive. When we started to have money again, I'd become used to not eating much. I had a certain curiosity about how much thinner I could get. I was taking the smallest size of clothes in the shop and still I was curious. How much could I disappear? Self-preservation kicked in. I called a halt to this form of invisibility magic, but some people can't. Media images encourage us to seek the sticklike figure. "You can never be too rich or too thin," said Wallis Simpson, whose engagement to King Edward VIII of Britain forced his abdication in the 1930s. Buffy and her friends look as though some vampire drains them nightly of flesh as well as blood. If we try to look like them, we have a problem because they are abnormal. Many of us go through phases of anorexia and bulimia (eating meals, then vomiting them up secretly afterward). We punish ourselves for not being the perfect beings of our magazine and silver screen idols. We suffer from paroxysms of guilt if we eat a normal meal. We have failed, we are unworthy—of love, of the universe, of anything. Conversely, when we can control what we eat, we are "in control," we have a sense of a "self" that has control over its outer casing, the body. We separate self from body. We are not our bodies but the voice of authority that has control over them and can manipulate them to our will.

If anorexia is about invisibility, obesity is about filling an inner void. Inside we are desperately hungry—and the hunger may be psychological or physical. You can read lots of psychotherapy books about obesity that tell you that you become obese because you have been deprived of love. Eating is a desperate attempt to provide love in the way that your earliest memories recall—the breast or bottle. We cry with hunger and are comforted, sheltered, a loving figure appears. So needing a loving figure, we cry out for food. The association is logical. It's just that the direction of causality is severely warped. And the thermostat may be too. Bodies hunger for more than calories. They need vitamins, minerals, a balance of protein, starch, fats, fiber. If we don't eat a wide-ranging diet that includes fresh fruit and vegetables, our bodies may signal to us that they are starved of essential vitamins and minerals, when we're eating more calories than we need. In the midst of conflicting signals, the body's thermostat does not know what to do. If in doubt, it signals "eat."

"Cogito ergo sum," said eighteenth-century French philosopher Descartes: "I think therefore I am." What he meant was that I am conscious, therefore I exist. Loosely translated, though, it's close to a magical truth, one once uttered by Henry Ford, founder of modern automobile production: "Whether you think you can or think you can't, you're right." Largely, but not entirely, you are what you think you are. If you want to look different, you need to think of yourself differently. If you don't change your image of yourself and your outlook, any dieting is likely to result in you binging your way back to your old image as soon as you can. Magic, like anorexia, is about control and will, but with more positive and constructive results.

Thinking Thin

If you want to be thin, our grannies told us, think thin. And, of course, since many grannies are witches in disguise, they were right. A 1999 study of just over three hundred Britons by James Levine of the Mayo Clinic in Rochester, Minneapolis, asked participants to visualize themselves as thinner and more attractive than they currently were. They were not asked to diet, but when we create a positive image of ourselves, it can become a self-fulfilling prophecy. A positive self-image enables you to feel better about your body, therefore you treat it better and you want to give it better-quality, healthier food. Thinking of how you want to be unconsciously influences your behavior to bring reality in line with the ideal. More than half the participants in the Mayo program achieved significant weight loss. The Mayo Clinic study was based on sound magical principles. It is yet another example of magic slipping into everyday life. If you are thinking magically, you will realize that you can take the exercise a little further.

☺

Thinking Thin — an Exercise

In the morning, just after you wake up, do the chakra-opening exercise. The chakra opening is a good way to begin because it makes you more open, and what you are going to do effectively is to practice a bit of self-hypnosis. You are going to reprogram your psyche. When your chakras are open and you feel relaxed and balanced, do this visualization.

On the right-hand side of your brain, inside your skull, there is a thermostat, a dial with figures around the edge from 0 to 200. Visualize the dial being set at just over halfway around at 120. Now turn it down to 95. Hold that image in your mind—the dial set at 95. Focus on visualizing the dial set at 95, while you slowly breathe in and out 95 times. What is this "thermostatic dial?" Just think of it as your body's food regulatory mechanism. You are adjusting the intake.

Now, create a second visualization. Visualize yourself as slim, fit, healthy, happy, and looking good. Visualize this "new you" for as long as you can hold the image. That's it. Close your chakras. The visualization bit is relatively simple. Where you will need a bit of persistence is to do the same thing every single morning for a month.

As a second stage of the "new me" process, you need to think about what you wear. Every evening before you go to bed, decide what you are going to wear the next morning. Get the clothes ready. If you leave it to a last-minute morning rush, you'll put on the same old things that you always wear. Only choose clothes that make you feel good about yourself. If you have clothes that make you look or feel drab, get rid of them. You don't want to wince every time you look in the mirror.

Stage three of the "new me" process is to become very interested in food. "What?" you cry, "I'm obsessed with food! That's the problem." It's highly unlikely that if you're really interested in food quality you are going to be fat. Gourmet eaters in countries like France do not suffer from the same weight problems as Americans and Brits. Food has become a major source of abuse. Advertising encourages us to eat trash that confuses the body's natural dietary signals of hungry or not hungry. We eat calorific content that isn't nutritionally satisfying, so we keep eating in order to get the essential nutrients—vitamins, minerals, etc.—that we need. For magic, we need our bodies to function well. Magic takes energy, and if your energy is depleted because your body isn't running as it should, then your magic will be depleted. Just try doing magic when you have raging flu—it's almost impossible. Magically, we need to eat the best-quality food we can afford. Find out about food quality and eat well, but don't eat synthetic rubbish. You deserve better, and your body deserves better. Magic teaches us that we should treat ourselves well, and we have access today to the knowledge we need to do so. Our knowledge of nutrition has improved enormously in recent years. Most of us know what is good for our bodies.

As well as eating the right way, we need to exercise our muscles. If you can't be bothered to do yoga or go to a gym, take dance lessons or play a sport. Walk instead of driving or riding in public transport. Walking saves money and makes you fit. If you bought a beautiful pedigree dog, you would be obsessed with keeping it healthy. Think of your body as a large pedigree dog that needs good food, exercise, love, attention, grooming, and companionship. Your body is more valuable than a dog. Treat it as though it is.

Healing of mind, body, and spirit as a holistic unity is an important theme for many people in contemporary societies. Religions that include healing services attract people in droves. We spend a fortune on complementary therapies, some of which are designed to address particular diseases, but many of which are designed to re-balance our energies and restore imbalances. In theory, we should be the healthiest we have ever been, but, in reality, we practice a large amount of bodily abuse. A bit of abuse is fun. If you do not suffer from alcohol addiction, then moderate drinking or even the occasional binge can be very enjoyable. Like heroin and cocaine, nicotine is physiologically addictive, which means that your brain chemistry is altered until you cannot function "normally" without having the drug in your system. It doesn't take much magical imagination to see that this is very bad news. "Soft" drugs are not necessarily addictive, but they all have their downsides. The bottom line is that if you lack the self-esteem and common sense to do something as simple as body maintenance, you won't be able to do something as extraordinary as magic.

Fertility Magic

Bodily magic is not just about maintaining health. One aspect of bodily magic that has always been an important part of the work of wise women, cunning men, shamans, and other traditional healers is fertility magic. For our ancestors, fertility problems were a mystery, so resorting to magic was as rational a choice as any. Today, in our high-tech medical age, it might seem that natural magic practitioners would no longer have a role to play when it comes to fertility problems, but they do. I discovered just how helpful magic could be when I was first asked to help with an infertility problem. I will describe healing techniques more fully in the next chapter, but the experience below was the first time I used magic to treat infertility.

○

A FERTILITY HEALING

My patient, Margaret, wants a child desperately but keeps having early miscarriages. Her doctor has told her there is nothing wrong, but early miscarriage usually means that there is something wrong with the fetus. I don't want to use healing to help her retain a fetus that nature wants to spontaneously abort.

I start healing her. I ask her to sit with her spine straight while I take her through a chakra-opening exercise, then I ask her to lie down and relax. I start to feel her aura with my hands, not actually touching her physical body at this stage, but just the energy field around her. Her head is buzzing and her womb is electric. As I approach it, I feel resistance, a force that wants to push my hand back. I go to her head and lightly touch her temples, synchronizing her erratic—perhaps even neurotic—rhythm with my own calmer one. I find myself going into a trance, taking her with me. As we go deeper, images and ideas come into my mind. I feel fear. What is she afraid of?

"Do you enjoy sex?"

Margaret flinches under my hands. And then she begins to tell me. She doesn't enjoy sex, not since she was raped—a classic date rape by someone she thought she could trust as a friend. Since then, sex has felt like a violation, even with her husband, whom she loves and who knows nothing about what happened at the party before he met her.

We talk, and much emotion is released—anger, grief, frustration at not knowing what to do, not wanting to make a fuss, a feeling of stupidity that she had allowed this to happen, that it must have been her fault. Then I try the healing again. This time there is no rejection. I channel energy into her body, healing the wounds, not of body but of spirit. She is absorbing so much that it comes to a point where I have to stop. I cannot channel any more energy. She has exhausted me.

The next time she ovulates, she becomes pregnant. After the first child, there is no difficulty. She becomes pregnant the second time with no healing interventions.

○

Conceiving

A third of couples who consult medical practitioners about fertility problems have nothing medically wrong with them, but something deep within them is preventing them from conceiving. Although consciously we may want to get pregnant, unconsciously we may not. Pregnancy means having trust in one's partner. It means limiting one's freedom. It may jeopardize one's career and severely dent the bank balance. Many people come from families where parents have left when children were young. The fear that one's own partner may do exactly the same thing may be strong; so too may be the fear that one may not be an ideal parent, or even a barely adequate one. If we are born into dysfunctional and fractured families, we may never have seen good parenting. We are full of unconscious fears— how will we manage when we become parents?

For women who have trouble conceiving, magic can be highly effective—so effective, in fact, that it was one of the best money spinners of village wise women and cunning men. If there is no physical reason why you should not conceive and you really want a child, then you need to reach deep within yourself to change that. It is your unconscious mind rather than your conscious mind that will determine whether you get pregnant. If you think of your psyche as an iceberg, 10 percent is the conscious mind. The other 90 percent is the unconscious—emotions, instincts, intuitions, sensations, hopes, and fears that we are not consciously aware of, but which strongly influence what we do. To change the way your unconscious mind has programmed your body, you need to communicate with the unconscious. A good way is to establish a meditative routine.

☺

Thinking Pregnant — for Women

Every morning when you have just awakened and are close to the unconscious world of sleep and dream, do the chakra-opening exercise. Focus particularly on opening your base of spine, sacral, solar plexus, and heart chakras. These chakras are linked to your womb and emotions. Once your chakras are open, visualize yourself with a round belly, pregnant and enjoying every moment of it. Visualize you and your partner having sex, loving and adoring one another. Bask in a golden glow of happiness for as long as you can. Then close your chakras from the third eye to the sacral chakra and, finally, visualize your body bathed in a golden healing light.

This is the starting point—changing the way your body is responding to the idea of becoming pregnant. At the same time, prepare your body for pregnancy—and your partner's body. Eat all the right foods, stop drinking alcohol, stop smoking, persuade your partner to smoke and drink less or stop entirely, and stuff yourself with folic acid. The advice to stop smoking and drinking is boring but essential. Both considerably cut down your chances of conceiving, regardless of any other health risks to you and a fetus. Chart your menstrual cycle and when you are most likely to ovulate. Keep this information to yourself. Don't tell your partner, "Today is baby-making day." Nothing is more likely to put a man off sex. Do seduce your man on the most appropriate days. Create a sensual, loving atmosphere so he's panting for sex. Make sure that you both enjoy the sex for its own sake. The more orgasms you have, the more likely you are to get pregnant, and once you are very pregnant it may be a while before you can enjoy such sex again, so go for it. Nature has also kindly ensured that orgasms help achieve pregnancy by encouraging the passage of sperm up the vagina and into the womb. Enjoy one another's bodies and giving one another pleasure. After sex, lie down. All those little sperm have only one goal in their brief existence, and that's to get to your egg, but swimming uphill is hard work. Horizontal tunnels are easier to negotiate. Lie in your loved one's arms, blissfully visualizing energetic sperm coursing their way up your insides, and await developments. As Nick says in the final scene of Joe Esterhas's screenplay for the movie *Basic Instinct,* "fuck like minks," "raise rugrats," and "live happily ever after."

POINTERS FOR PRACTICE

Magic takes energy, and if your energy is depleted because your body isn't running as it should, then your magic will be depleted. Meditation, chakra-opening exercises, ritual, prayer, and invocation are good for the body and for your energy levels. They lower your heart rate and make you relaxed, and you will look and feel better. If you want to look different, you need to think differently. Thinking of how you want to be unconsciously influences your behavior to bring reality in line with the ideal. If you are a woman with fertility problems that have no physiological cause, you can try magical techniques to help you.

CHAPTER EIGHT

Healing

In magic, we learn to sense energy and to project energy. We can use this to come into more harmonious relationship with our own bodies. We can also learn to use magical techniques to help others. Magical healing can be one of the most contentious uses of magic. Medical practitioners are naturally concerned that patients do not abandon tried and tested treatments in favor of miracle cures, but many refer patients to a range of complementary practitioners when they are known to have had proven success with particular ailments.

Healing is not a substitute for conventional allopathic medicine; rather, it forms part of complementary medicine. It is a way of boosting the body's healing processes. In Britain and some other countries, certified healers work in hospitals and other medical centers in conjunction with doctors and other specialists. In American hospitals, nurses can train as healers through taking recognized courses in Therapeutic Touch.

It is easy to dismiss magical healing as "purely psychological," but that misses the point. Magical healing is a way of teaching the mind to heal the body. And it is not mere human wishful thinking. I discovered in my healing practice that it works on animals too. In the late 1980s I was working as a psychologist, but two days a week were taken up with my healing practice. I found that as my practice grew, the speciality changed. At first, I had endless patients with bad backs, but then it became cancer. I found myself on a circuit, a recipient of recommendations passed by word of mouth by women at the local hairdresser's. Some men came of their own accord, but often they were dragged along, resisting, by their wives. The surface bravado doesn't inhibit the healing. Men just find it more difficult to admit they need help. I found I could relieve the pain of the dying. Less morphine is needed, and the quality of life for the final months is improved. I'm not afraid of death and don't mind going on the long tunnel out of the body with those who are at the end. It seems a familiar journey, one I've done many times before. What I had not done before was to heal a cat; as I describe below, a self-invited cat.

☽

A FELINE HEALING

A patient of mine, Shirley, lies on her back on the bed. The bed is covered with a white sheet. I wear a white coat, a requirement of the National Federation of Spiritual Healers to which I belong. The rationale is that the color white deflects negative energies. I suspect that the real reason is to make us seem more like medics. Shirley is the third patient I have seen this morning at the Saturday healing clinic I have in my home. It is near the end of Shirley's half-hour session. Then there will be a half-hour gap until the next patient—a chance for a break and a cup of tea. I'm looking forward to it. I start to close down the psychic and energy links between Shirley and me. I withdraw my aura from hers, disengaging gently. I hear a scratching at the door—I glance at my watch. It's too early for the next patient. I ignore the sound—more scratching. I apologize to Shirley and open the door. A large tabby cat stands on the landing outside. Two large amber eyes fix mine, "Meow," it cries. It wants something and it's highly intelligent. I know if I speak to it, it will understand. "Wait," I say and shut the door.

"It's a cat," I tell Shirley, and continue the closing-down process.

"I didn't know you had a cat."

"I don't."

Shirley makes another appointment and leaves. The cat comes

in, gets up on the couch, and lies down in her place. It stretches out and turns on its side, showing me a large lump. The cat lifts its head, looks at me to make sure that I have understood, and rests its head. I open my chakras cautiously and go into a light trance. I haven't healed a cat before and don't know what it will be like to contact its mind. There are no barriers. Images come into my mind, and smells. I push them aside. I don't need these, just a light contact, its psyche to mine. I touch the lump tentatively in case it causes pain. The cat relaxes and starts to draw energy from me. It knows what it wants and how to get it. I need only to act as a channel. Warm, golden energy flows from my hands into the tabby. It closes its eyes. I close mine.

"Meow!" it cries again, but this time more content. I come to and glance at my watch—fifteen minutes. The cat looks up at me, then licks my hand. It has broken the energy contact. It gets up, jumps off the couch, and meows for me to open the door. I let it out and go downstairs to see where it goes. The back door is open. It leaves, and there's still time for a cup of tea before the next patient. The cat comes three more Saturdays, at the same time, give or take ten minutes. Its body clock isn't perfect. I see it on the street some weeks later, after it stops coming to me, challenging a large dog that wants to pass it. The dog sensibly crosses to the other side of the road. It meows at me. I stroke it—no lump. It lived fives years longer.

☽

Healing Science

How did a neighbor's cat work out that I ran a healing clinic, find its way into the house, come upstairs, and demand healing? I haven't the faintest idea, but in magic odd things happen and we don't really question them because after a while you get used to unusual experiences and they cease to seem unusual. Every now and then you collide with the realities of other people whose lives don't include the magical dimension and you have to rein yourself in, censor what you talk about, and remember that your norm is not the same as other people's. My mother once said to me that everyone lives in their own reality and it is best left like that, that they are much happier that way. Some people's realities include magic and others' do not. Where they don't, people often prefer, as my mother hinted, to leave it that way.

If you need some science with your magic, though, there are a number of studies that indicate how healing works. Scientific evidence suggests that the healing process works through its effect on the body's magnetic fields, which in turn affect the body's immune system. Research by biochemist Dr. M. Justa-Smith* shows that magnetic fields affect the reactivity of certain enzymes in the body. These enzymes act as catalysts to speed up the body's natural healing processes. Justa-Smith's research showed that skilled healers can exert an effect on enzymes similar to that of a magnetic field. Using the wonderfully named SQID (Superconducting Quantum Interference Device), which detects infinitesimally weak magnetic fields, Dr. John Zimmerman showed that healers produce increased magnetic field emission from their hands during healing.† These results are consistent with other studies that show that healers can make UV-damaged enzymes reintegrate to their normal structure and function.

Healing and the Brain

Electromagnetic fields may be important in healing, but healing is also a function of the brain. I saw this for myself when, in the late

---

*M. Justa-Smith (1973), "The Influence on Enzyme Growth by the 'Laying on of Hands,'" in *Dimensions of Healing.* Los Altos, CA.: Academy of Parapsychology and Medicine.

†D. J. Benor (1990), "Survey on spiritual healing research," *Complementary Medicine Research* 4, 3: 9–33.

1980s, I was offered the opportunity by the National Federation of Spiritual Healers to participate in a "mind mirror" experiment, a form of biofeedback. Electrodes were fixed to my head with a greasy gel, and I was asked to heal someone while the "mind mirror" recorded my brain patterns. I began to heal, feeling my way into the aura of my volunteer patient, using my hands to sense the energy pattern down his spine. I felt drawn to certain areas of his body that seemed energy deficient. I focused on transmitting energy to these. There was a sudden high-pitched wailing—no, not the patient; a fire engine rushed by, siren blaring. The session ended and the results were played back. I saw the classic change found in experienced meditators during meditation and in healers during healing. There is a switch from there being greater activity in the left hemisphere than the right hemisphere to hemisphere synchronization—equal activity in both sides of the brain. The brain pattern changes too, from predominant beta waves to increased alpha, then theta, then delta. The final reading is highly anomalous—the hemispherical activity is perfectly balanced, showing equal amounts of beta, alpha, theta, and delta activity. At the point where the fire engine passed, I saw that my brain emitted a startled response—a surge in the beta waves, but no diminishing of alpha, theta, or delta. I had maintained the healing contact while noticing and responding to the outside stimulus.

I was surprised. I hadn't really believed that the physiological correlates of healing would be so distinctive and obvious. Whatever processes are involved in generating healing, they start in the brain. Healers are people who either naturally or through training can enter into altered states of consciousness in which they can exhibit paranormal powers. Further research on healers' brain patterns shows something else interesting: when someone is receiving healing, his or her brain pattern starts to synchronize with that of the healer—the "healing state" is "contagious." When one person enters into an altered state of consciousness, it facilitates someone else entering it too.

Skilled healers when healing are alert and aware of their surroundings, but also relaxed, receptive to dream-type images, and in a state of consciousness normally associated with the physiological repair that happens when we are asleep. Their brains are doing the things normally associated with being awake and the things normally associated with being asleep simultaneously. The presence of delta rhythm is interesting. When we are physically ill, the body tries to go into deep delta-type sleep for longer than usual. During delta sleep, hormones are released and the body carries out tissue-repair activities. So to summarize what we know so far about the healing process—and as yet we are only scratching the surface—healing involves the healer entering an unusual state of consciousness, and the person being healed mimics the healer's state of consciousness. The healing triggers the patient's body to heal itself. Healing involves learning to manipulate your brain patterns. The processes are the same as those involved in learning to meditate.

The scientific explanations for how healing works use a different language from magic. To explain how to heal, it is easier to work with magical language. When we heal, we communicate with someone. Some healers like to touch their patients. Others prefer to work solely on the aura. I prefer to touch. Touch is an important way of communicating. If we touch someone in a positive way, we are indicating, "I like you. I accept you." Healing is also an act of love. It is saying to another person, "I care about you and your pain and problem." This is the first stage of healing. When we are in pain or troubled, we are likely to feel better when someone reaches out to us and shows that they care and are willing to try to help.

@

Learning to Heal

As a preliminary to healing, do the chakra-opening exercise. This will help you deepen your state of consciousness and synchronize your brain hemispheres. If you have someone to practice on, ask her to sit on a stool or sideways on a chair so you can stand behind her. Relax and breathe rhythmically and ask her to do the same. Energize your hands. Draw energy from your base of spine chakra to your solar plexus chakra and channel it down your arms and into your hands. Once your hands are energized, feel the edge of her aura, around the head. If you have never felt an aura before don't worry. Gently move your hands toward her head. At a certain point, a few inches from her body, you will feel a slight resistance. You are touching the edge of her energy field. Pause for a few moments, re-energize your hands, then gently enter the aura and place your fingers on her shoulders. This is a nonintrusive place to touch someone and will not startle a nervous volunteer. Leave your hands on her shoulders for a while. You will start to get a sense of her "rhythm"—her breathing, her metabolic rate, whether her mind is racing or relaxed. After a few minutes, you will start to sense that your breathing is synchronizing with hers. Keep your hands within her auric field and move your hands from her shoulder to her spine. Move your hands down her spine, noticing if some areas seem to lack energy, and noticing any temperature changes.

Now place your hands on the sides of her head—never directly on her crown chakra. Focus on breathing slowly; slow down your brain and wait until you sense her rhythm is slowing too. When you feel that her brain rhythm is synchronized with yours, put your hands on any areas of the spine where you feel a different temperature or a lack of energy and channel energy to the spot. Draw energy up from your base of spine chakra, through the solar plexus chakra, and into your hands. Visualize this energy as golden light and allow it to flow from you into your patient. Maintain the energy flow for as long as you can, but no more than twenty minutes. Keep going back to your base of spine chakra and drawing in more energy, so you are acting as a conduit for the energy of the universe.

When you feel you want to stop, don't break the link with the patient suddenly. Go back to her head and give some last healing. Break contact by turning your attention away from her. Think about something else. Gently remove your hands from her head and step away from her. Now cleanse yourself by drawing white light down into your crown chakra, down your spine, and out of your base of spine chakra. Close your chakras from the third eye to the sacral chakra by drawing more white light down through the crown chakra and imagining the light closing the chakra as though a white blind is being drawn over it. Leave the crown and base of spine open because these connect you with the energies of the Earth and cosmos.

Share experiences with the person you were healing—what did she feel? Could she sense when your hands were in her aura? Did she have any experiences of cold, heat, or tingling when your hands touched her? How does she feel after the healing process? Did you do anything that seemed intrusive or too abrupt? Remember, healing should relax the person being healed.

Distance Healing

When healer and patient are in the physical presence of one another, the healing process does not require any complex metaphysical explanations. Many healers, myself included, touch the person they are healing. It is easy to see how this can result in two people entering the same altered state of consciousness. There is also evidence that healing can happen at a distance. People hundreds of miles apart can enter a simultaneous altered state, precipitated only by the healer visualizing the person receiving the healing and the person receiving the energy being willing to be healed. Here we have a telepathic process. We do not yet know how such processes work. Carl Jung's idea of the collective unconscious can be interpreted to mean that there are states of consciousness in which consciousness is not bound by the usual laws of time and space, so we can communicate with someone far away and enter into a deep communion with that person. Subjectively, this is how it feels. I feel as though my consciousness merges with that of the person I am healing, so I sense his or her thoughts and feelings. Whether this is a subjective impression or a scientific reality remains to be proven.

@

How to Heal at a Distance

Healing does not necessarily require the presence of the person being healed. Healing can be transmitted over a distance and can be done very effectively by a group. If you don't know the individual intimately, then a photograph can help you visualize him. To do distance healing, open your chakras and visualize the person you want to heal. Don't visualize him as sick, but as whole and well. You are using your visualization to create an image for the future, not an image of the present. Imagine the person walking around, looking happy and active and enjoying everyday activities. Next, direct energy into your hands. Imagine that you are reaching out and touching him, just as you would if he was present. Allow golden healing energy to flow from your hands into his aura and body. When you can direct no more energy, gently withdraw yourself from his energy field. For a final time, visualize the person as happy, well, and active. Let your vision fade and close down your chakras. Distance healing is best done over a period of time. The frequency will depend on how acute the problem is. Long-term chronic illnesses are more likely to respond to sustained healing over a period, say twice a week for four weeks. If, by then, you are not getting results, it is unlikely that you will get a response. If it is an emergency, then you might need to send healing every day for a week. If possible, arrange for your recipient to be in a quiet, relaxed state when you send the healing. This will help him receive it.

Barriers to Healing

Does healing always work? No. Sometimes the body damage is too great and sometimes people do not want to be healed. Curing people seems simple. Surely people want to be cured? Well, maybe; then again, maybe not. A friend of mine had serious asthma. The asthma was real but the attacks were stress-related. She became asthmatic after confrontations, before exams, and after visiting her mother. I heard that acupuncture could help and took her to see a famous Chinese physician at a London clinic. The sessions were expensive, but they worked wonderfully well. They also required regular follow ups, but she refused to go. The acupuncture was not painful or uncomfortable, but the asthma served a useful purpose. Whenever life got a bit too complicated, she could have an asthma attack and take to her bed. Removing the asthma removed the get-out clause that she had used throughout her life, and she was not yet ready for that.

Most people when they are sick want to get well, fast, but don't assume that this is always the case. When we first start to heal, we naively assume that everyone wants to get better and will be grateful that we've helped them, but human beings are much more complicated than that. If your instinct tells you that there may be more to someone's illness than the surface problem, try sensitively probing a little deeper. Does he or she really want to be cured, or does the illness serve a purpose? Is it a way of getting love and attention? Some parents lavish attention on sick children and ignore them when they're well. This sets up a pattern that the unconscious mind learns all too well: when I want attention, I need to get ill. Does the illness manifest when the person is particularly stressed? Is it caused by the stress, or is it a way of avoiding the stressful situation? "Sorry I can't do your presentation/come to my job appraisal interview/help you entertain your boring relatives (delete as applicable) because I'm ill." Migraine, asthma, eczema, psoriasis, influenza, and bronchitis are all illnesses that worsen with stress. Magic can help, but it is important to know what the problem is really about before trying to change the situation.

Healers and Healing

Healing can seem a nice safe outlet for one's magical powers—after all, what could be more altruistic than wanting to heal the sick? All spiritual traditions encourage members to help the sick. A danger is that wanting to heal can be an enormous ego trip. "Look at me," your psyche is saying, "aren't I good, wonderful, high-minded, pure?" This doesn't mean that other people can't benefit from healing. A lot of charitable work is done for not very creditable or charitable reasons. It doesn't mean that the recipients won't benefit, but if you are dishonest with yourself about your motives, your "do gooding" can corrupt you.

One of the archetypes of the healer is that of the wounded healer. In its best sense, this can mean that people who have suffered themselves can empathize with others and so become good healers. Going through psychotherapy is a prerequisite to training as a psychotherapist. Positively, this means that those who train as therapists are to some extent sorted out themselves. Negatively, it means that an awful lot of damaged people become psychotherapists. Psychotherapy and other healing professions, including conventional medicine, attract people who want to help others, but we can want to help for all kinds of reasons—some good and some bad. "Helping" puts you in a superior position and other people in a subordinate one. Being a magical helper can be even more of an ego trip than helping on a more mundane level—we can delude ourselves that we are special, "different," more "spiritual," "altruistic," "evolved," or whatever than other people. Truly spiritual people are truthful and simple and have a sense of humor. Ego trippers are full of self-deception and arcane jargon and have no sense of humor about themselves. If you meet anyone like that, take magical action—run swiftly in the opposite direction.

Healing can become teaching, showing people how to transcend the failure of the body. If you heal, heal with no expectations, and a process will take place whereby the energy change that you have helped generate will go where it wills—and sometimes it can do something that is beyond what you can envisage.

★

POINTERS FOR PRACTICE

Healing is not a substitute for conventional medicine, but complements it by boosting the body's healing processes and alleviating pain. If you want to heal others, it is important to understand the problem before trying to change the situation. Not everyone wants to be healed. Be aware that healing others can be an ego trip, a way of deluding ourselves that we are special. Heal without expectations, acting as a channel for a spiritual and magical process.

CHAPTER NINE

Intuition

The intuitive mind is a sacred gift and the rational mind is a faithful servant. We have created a society that honors the servant and has forgotten the gift.

ALBERT EINSTEIN, QUANTUM PHYSICIST

We are all aware of the operation of intuition in our lives. An important part of magic is learning to act upon it. Usually, this is important for ourselves. More rarely, we have intuitions that are important for other people. To give an example, in the mid-nineties, I read about near-death experiences and discovered that the tunnel experience that I had sensed when I was healing the terminally ill is a common one, often felt by people who almost die or who are pronounced clinically dead, but then resuscitated. I was then lecturing at a university and I had a strong intuition that I should tell my psychology students about these near-death experiences. So strong was the intuition that it drove me, mid-semester, to alter the syllabus and introduce the topic into a lecture. I described a near-death experience to my students. Typically, people hear themselves being pronounced dead by the medical staff. They may hear their friends and relatives grieving. Then suddenly they find themselves outside their bodies, viewing the scene from above. They are floating in midair. At first the sensation seems odd, but people become used to it and start to feel emotionally detached from what is happening. They can see their dead body lying below them, but there is no fear. Often at this point, they feel they are being drawn down a tunnel toward light. They emerge to be greeted by spirits of relatives and friends, or by a wise, loving being. This may be a deity, an angel, or simply a benevolent presence. The being often shows them a panoramic replay of their lives. They see everything that has ever happened to them, and it all makes sense. Everything is part of a coherent whole. At this point, if it is not yet time for people to die, they will be told or will sense that their task on Earth is not yet over. There is more to be done. They find themselves returning, but the return is hard. The afterlife seems so full of joy, love, and peace.

I asked my students if any of them had had such an experience. One person had been in a road accident and had experienced the detachment from the body stage and floating above the scene of the crash, but paramedics resuscitated her and she reentered her body. At the end of the class, when the students were filing out, one of the older students, who was in her fifties, came to talk to me. She told me shyly that she had had a near-death experience, but that it was too personal to speak about during class. She had nearly died when she gave birth to her first child. The experience had been terrifying. She found herself out of her body and panicked because she didn't know what to do. Well, perhaps the experience was good, I told her, because when she *did* die then she would know she should look for the tunnel. She wasn't at the next class. Three days after I spoke to her, she died of a heart attack. I hope that she knew what to do when the time came.

What Is Intuition?

Intuitions are ideas that slip in under the barrier that separates the conscious from the unconscious mind. Sometimes intuitions come to us when we are awake. An idea appears fully formed in our psyches and we have no idea where it came from. Sometimes it happens when we dream. All manner of material emerges in dreams: sexual fantasies, unconscious reactions to people and events of the day, and sometimes material with elements of precognition—an awareness of things that are going to happen in the future. For most people, there is a barrier between conscious and unconscious, and this is good. If too much material wells up from the unconscious, this leads to psychiatric illness. The aim of magic is to turn the barrier into a permeable membrane that allows ideas to come through from the unconscious, without overwhelming us. I wove the idea into a poem.

> In the silence that rings with sound,
> I am still and hear your voice.
> The transition of the formless into words—
> the mind a still, receptive pool.
> A thought drops in, disappearing—
> a stone without splashing,
> and rests in the depths,
> the waters digesting it—slowly.
> Is the stone a pearl?

Magic involves listening to intuition. Intuition comes from an older, more animalistic part of our brains than conscious rational thought. Before our early ancestors learned to think, they had to trust their five senses. They monitored sights, sounds, smells, taste, and touch to seek those things that they needed for survival and to avoid danger. It is likely that they also had instincts that we still do not know how to explain. If you have pets, you will notice that they have likes and dislikes. Some people have an aggressive or disorganized energy that animals find disturbing. Other people have a soothing energy that is like a magnet to cats. Animals sense negative energies in houses. If you are looking for a new house and the family dog refuses to cross the threshold, this is not the house to buy. We too have instinctual and intuitive reactions. If we learn to listen to them, they can guide us.

There is no point in having intuitions if you do not act upon them. In fact, if you are not willing to test your intuitions, you will become angry and frustrated. You "knew you shouldn't have done that"—take that job, ask that woman out, drive that way to work— and you did it anyway, out of laziness, force of habit, or because you didn't trust your inner judgment that "something" wasn't right. When you next have an intuition—that you should phone an old friend, take a different route to work, apply for a particular job—act on it. Try out your intuition and see how accurate it is.

Intuition is designed to help us. It may be part of a primitive survival instinct. This does not mean that intuition can protect us from everything; nothing can protect from harm all the time. Some people spend all their lives trying to ensure that nothing bad ever happens to them, and to them magic can seem the perfect panacea. There is a spell for everything. "Maybe with magic, I can protect myself against everything that might go wrong in my little world." Unfortunately, this is not true. A talisman will not stop a hurricane. However, it may give you the burning urge to go and pay that duty visit to Great-aunt Sally who lives two hundred miles away so you leave four hours before the hurricane starts. Magic helps us be in the right place at the right time—and not in the wrong place at the wrong time.

On Saturday, December 17, 1983, I was in the London underground traveling on a train to Knightsbridge. I was going to Harrods to do my Christmas shopping. The train pulled into the final interchange before Knightsbridge, South Kensington, and I had an overwhelming urge to get off the train and do my Christmas shopping in Oxford Street instead. I fought it. I did not want to go to Oxford Street in the Christmas shopping rush. No one in his or her right mind would want to go to Oxford Street a few days before Christmas. I glanced at the subway map. It meant two changes, struggling through the enormous crowds. I did not want to get off . . . my feet decided. The doors opened. I got off the train. Oxford Street—as badly crowded as I thought. Distantly, I heard a sound, like muffled thunder. I looked up at the sky; no sign of rain. Later I heard the news: the IRA had detonated a car bomb outside Harrods. Six people died and eighty were injured. Sometimes it's best just to follow your feet.

Magical Detachment

Intuition can convey important information. It is not always of the dramatic life or death variety, but it is information that can help in everyday life. However, if we want to develop and use our intuitions wisely and well, we need to learn to differentiate intuitions from hopes and fears. Intuitions are different and come from a deeper level of consciousness than everyday ego. To listen to the voice of intuition, we must detach ourselves from our egos. In fact, to do magic well, we have to learn to detach ourselves from what is traditionally called "lust for result." We do our magic, we visualize, we energize what we have visualized, and then we let go. The letting go is important. Magic does not work if we keep worrying away at it. We do the magic. We follow it up with whatever we need to do on the material plane and, having given it our best shot, we see what happens. This becomes easier with practice, and we can help achieve this state of consciousness by practicing ego detachment. This is an exercise to help you understand the concept of a state of detached consciousness. It involves saying an affirmation.

@

An Affirmation for Detachment

First, write or type the affirmation in large print so you can read it easily. Next, sit with your spine straight. Close your eyes and breathe regularly. When you are relaxed and have regulated your breathing, read the first line of the affirmation: "I have a body, but I am not my body." Close your eyes and say the first line to yourself. Now say it again, focusing on each word, giving it your full attention. Wait a few breaths, then continue with the remaining lines— read first, then close your eyes and say the line to yourself once and then a second time, focusing on the meaning of each word. Leave as long a gap as you wish between each line.

> I have a body, but I am not my body.
> I have desires, but I am not my desires.
> I have thoughts, but I am not my thoughts.
> I have feelings, but I am not my feelings.
> I have ideas, but I am not my ideas.
> I have fears, but I am not my fears.
> I have hopes, but I am not my hopes.
> I have knowledge, but I am not my knowledge.
> I have understanding, but I am not my understanding.
> I have wisdom, but I am not my wisdom.
> I am the One, who perceives these, but is not these.
> I was, I shall be, I am.

Rest for a while with the final words, "I am," breathing regularly. Then open your eyes.

This exercise teaches us that we have a core self that is different from all its attributes: we are greater than the sum of our parts. Incidentally, Western magical thinking is more similar to Hinduism here than Buddhism. As you go through the exercise you are likely to find that your spine becomes straighter, your breathing more regular, your body more balanced. You can use this exercise as a daily practice to center and still yourself. It is effective at the end of the day before sleep to help you relax and switch off. It can also help you in times of stress. Its focus is detachment, so it can also help you to clear your mind before making difficult decisions. You can also relate the exercise to the chakras.

Relating the Affirmation to the Chakras

CHAKRA AFFIRMATIONS

Chakra	Affirmation
Base of spine	I have a body, but I am not my body.
Sacral	I have desires, but I am not my desires.
Solar plexus	I have thoughts, but I am not my thoughts. I have feelings, but I am not my feelings. I have ideas, but I am not my ideas.
Heart	I have fears, but I am not my fears. I have hopes, but I am not my hopes.
Throat	I have knowledge, but I am not my knowledge.
Third eye	I have understanding, but I am not my understanding. I have wisdom, but I am not my wisdom.
Crown	I am the One who perceives these, but is not these. I was, I shall be, I am.

Try the exercise again, this time focusing on the associated part of the body as you say the affirmation. You may notice as you focus on the body region and say the affirmation the first time that there is muscle tension in that part of the body. As you say the affirmation the second time, allow the muscles to relax. You may also notice that your body is imbalanced, leaning to one side, or more tense on one side than the other. Allow the body to become centered as you work your way up the affirmation statements. When you have finished, continue breathing regularly for a few moments, poised and with your spine straight and eyes shut. You may notice that your eyes have focused toward the center, turning toward the third eye. This is a good starting point for any work of divination or clairvoyance. It will also help you as a morning exercise if you are going through a particularly stressful period in your life.

Moon Dreaming

Because dreams were seen in ancient times as powerful ways of receiving messages from the gods, all ancient spiritual traditions included methods for encouraging helpful dreams. Temples often had incubation rooms—places where someone could sleep overnight to receive a dream message. The Celts encouraged their bards to sleep in neolithic burial chambers, which were thought of as gateways to the Land of the Dead, the Otherworld, and the home of the Sidhe or Shee, the fairy people. In the dream, new songs, poems, and inspirations would come. Folk magic abounds with spells to have true dreams.

A Dream Spell

If you want to encourage dreams, buy a small pillow that you can put some drops of essential oil on. Paul Greenslade recommends a blend of one drop of rosemary to three drops of jasmine.

Jasmine is associated with the Moon, sleep, and the world of dream, and rosemary with remembering. Most people remember their dreams more in the five days around the full Moon. The Moon's light stimulates our psyches and we sleep less deeply. Sleep with a pad and pen close at hand, or if you are more technically minded, a laptop or a palm pilot, so you can record your dreams as soon as you wake up. Most people forget most of their dreams within a minute of waking, and it is very frustrating to have some brilliant insight during the night that you cannot remember once you have had a cup of coffee.

Interpreting Dreams

Solutions to problems often come in dreams. Sometimes these are dreams about important personal problems. We have no idea what to do about a situation. We go to sleep, and we wake up knowing the answer. Fiction writers frequently dream new scenes and developments of their plot. Scientists dream new formulas. Musicians wake in the night with complete new chart-busting singles in their heads. Sometimes we have trivial insights; we wake up knowing the solution to that final clue in the crossword that we just couldn't get.

Popular astrology magazines are full of columns about dream interpretation, and there are many slim volumes of symbols to help you interpret your dreams. Unfortunately, books cannot help you much because dream imagery is highly individual. If you kept a pet dog as a child, a large dog bouncing around in your dreams will mean something very different than it would for someone who was severely mauled by a neighbor's savage German Shepherd at the age of five. Our personal experiences and past associations determine the images and symbols that appear in our dreams, and our emotional associations are uniquely ours. Dreams do fall into different categories. Some dreams are rehashes of the day's events. Others convey unconscious emotions and feelings about our life situation. These are undercurrents that we are not consciously aware of, but are lurking away in the unconscious, giving us a sense of unease. Other dreams are "big" dreams, dreams that are about the future— where we should be going and what we should be doing. A small minority of dreams predict future events. By some mechanism that we do not yet fully understand, the unconscious mind, during sleep, can sometimes transcend the time/space boundaries that limit the conscious mind. Clairvoyant dreams are sometimes dramatic, fore-telling danger. In many families, people dream of the deaths of family members before they occur. My mother would dream her sister's illnesses, even though they lived many hundreds of miles apart and saw each other only rarely. However, they were physically very alike and even had similar accidents within a few days of each other. Sometimes we experience lucid dreams. We dream, and we know we are dreaming. Sometimes this happens when the dream is important and the unconscious mind is trying to communicate with the conscious mind, saying, "Wake up, listen, you need to know about this!"

Dreams can express all manner of unexpressed hopes and fears. In some indigenous communities it was recognized, thousands of years before Freud, that dreams were often about wish-fulfillment. Someone who had dreams that were unfulfilled was considered a source of danger and unrest in the community. Every effort would be made to show that person consideration, kindness, honor, and gifts, so that he or she felt cherished and valuable and no longer needed to fill the void with wish–fantasy dreams.

Some dreams reflect our fears. If you have frightening dreams, it is important to think about what you are frightened of. If you dream of a man chasing you, it may be that you live in a rough neighborhood and are worried about being mugged. If so, it might be time to move. However, the dream might also be symbolic. It could be that work pressures are getting to you and the man who is chasing you represents your boss. It could be that you are feeling guilty about something and are afraid of being caught. The chasing dream *does* have meaning, but a simple dream manual cannot tell you what it means for you. You need to sit down and review your life situation and see what might be worrying you because this dream is associated with anxiety. As a starting point, is there anything you are hiding? Is there something you might be afraid of people finding out about you? If there is something, think about how to deal with it. Are you doing something that makes your conscience uneasy? If so, you should stop. One part of your psyche is making judgments about what the other part is doing, and does not like it. We will not enjoy life with inner battles going on inside us.

A common dream is that we are in an everyday situation—driving to work, giving a presentation, or whatever—and we look down and find we are naked. Often these dreams happen in the morning, when we are trying to wake ourselves up for work, and they may be a confused mixture of dream and memory and not particularly significant. If you dream this in the middle of the night, however, it suggests that you have an underlying anxiety. When we are naked, we are exposed, literally. These dreams indicate a fear of "being exposed," of people discovering there is nothing behind the clothing, the veneer we are presenting to the world. If you are in a situation where you need to perform, this is a common anxiety. Or it may be that you are overperforming, that you are pretending to be something you are not and you are afraid of being found out. If you have a series of "exposure" dreams, think about what is going on. Are you in a situation that you find too stressful, or are you creating stress for yourself by putting on an act that is not really you? Are you afraid of people "seeing through" you?

What about the examination-room dream? Have you ever dreamed that you are sitting in front of an examination paper and cannot answer the questions? I used to have nightmares after my undergraduate finals of taking the finals again and getting a much lower grade. This "performance anxiety" dream came up often when I had to do something completely new or prove myself. Other people endlessly retake their driving test in their dreams. I used to have the naked lecturing dream until I started lecturing, then gradually I broke through the fear barrier and the dream stopped. Similarly, the examination dream stopped when I started academic teaching. Sometimes, to use Susan Jeffers's marvelous phrase, we just have to "feel the fear" and do it anyway.

Banishing Unpleasant Dreams

A classic way of finding out what is going on in your dreams is to talk to the dream figures you find there. Psychologist Carl Jung developed this as a tool in psychotherapy and called it Active Imagination. But dialoguing with images is an ancient magical technique and has long been used to assist in dream interpretation. You need to sit quietly with dimmed lighting, light a candle, and visualize the dream sequence. Now you are going to talk to something in your dream. It does not have to be a person. It might be a significant object or animal.

Suppose you have recurrent frightening dreams. If you are being chased, stop running, turn around, and ask the person or entity that is chasing you, "Why are you chasing me?" Then see what it says. Do not anticipate the answer because it may not be what you expect. The next stage in dealing with unpleasant dreams is to do exactly the same thing—but within the dream. The aim is to achieve a lucid dream, where you know you are dreaming and are in control. Tell yourself before you go to sleep that if you have the dream you are going to turn around and confront whoever or whatever is chasing you. The next time you have the dream, you may not succeed, but if you keep at it, you will. What typically happens is not that monsters eat you, but that whatever is chasing you shrinks in size, backs off, and retreats. The shrinking is significant. When we are afraid, our fears distort reality so that everything seems bigger and more threatening than it really is. Once we face our fears, we get them into perspective.

If you want a little more magical reinforcement, this is a multi-purpose earth-banishing pentagram to help you get rid of negative energies.

EARTH-BANISHING PENTAGRAM

Practice drawing it (see pages 150–51) and program your psyche so that if your entity appears in your dream, you are going to banish it. If you have the dream and haven't managed the banishing, do it when you wake up. Draw the pentagram in the air with your hand—think big here rather than small. Visualize it as a glowing bronze pentagram of protection, banishing monsters from your dreams. If your children are bothered by nightmares, they might enjoy banishing the ghoulies this way. It's more empowering than dreamcatchers.

POINTERS FOR PRACTICE

Magic involves listening to intuition. Intuition comes from an older, more animalistic part of our brains than conscious, rational thought. There is no point developing your intuition if you do not act on it. If you are not willing to test your intuition, you will become angry and frustrated. Intuition can make us more aware of danger, but we need to learn ego-detachment to differentiate intuition from hopes and fears. Learn to be aware of your dreams. They contain intuitions about present and future.

CHAPTER TEN

Divination

There are two types of aids to divination in the Western magical tradition. Scrying is a process of using a clear or black crystal ball or a bowl of darkened water to unfocus our vision, so that our brains spontaneously produce images. If our eyes have nothing to focus on, sensory deprivation will eventually ensure that the brain starts to create images of its own. If you are easily hypnotized, you may find scrying easy. If you're not, try it—it may work for you, but do not invest vast amounts of money in crystal balls, just in case it doesn't. Practice on a bowl of darkened water first. New age suppliers sell small crystal balls relatively cheaply, but my experience is that most people need a large surface for the vision defocusing effect to work. A small crystal ball is a nice decorative item and a great paperweight, and it may be good for energy boosting, but I have never seen a vision in one.

If you find that scrying does not work for you, don't worry. Other divination systems rely on intuition rather than on our ability to produce spontaneous images. These divination systems operate by offering us a set of symbols to interpret. The divinatory skill lies in knowing the symbol system well and then allowing the symbols to "play" in the unconscious and produce the grit in the oyster effect that results in a pearl. The symbol suddenly triggers ideas and associations that take us away from the symbol system itself and into the realm of clairvoyance. Reading an astrological chart works in a similar way. If you talk to good astrologers, you'll find that they know astrology inside out and backward, but their deepest insights spring from an "X" factor. They look at an astrological chart, and something in the shape and patterning triggers a string of ideas. When we use a symbol system such as astrology, the tarot, runes, or the I Ching, we interpret the symbols at three levels. Intellectually, we learn that the different symbols mean certain things. Intuition then allows us to read the combination of the symbols and draw them into holistic patterns with meaning. Finally, if we have the ability and inspiration, our minds will use the symbols as a springboard that enables us to see things beyond what the symbols show. This is true clairvoyance. People who are highly skilled clairvoyants can go straight to the final stage and do not need the divinatory system. But for most of us, the system, the "prop," is the best starting point.

Reading My Tarot

By my early twenties, my Waite tarot pack was already battered with overuse and now I needed another reading. I took it out of its wooden box together with a piece of black velvet. I sat cross-legged on the bed, spread out the black velvet in front of me, and selected a court card to act as "significator," the card that represents the questioner—in this case, me. I allowed my breathing to become regular, opened my chakras, and energized my hands. I took the cards and began to shuffle. I was contemplating giving up my well-paid job to return to the university. The job was good, but I was bored and my mind was hungry for new ideas and input. I formulated my question, "What will be the outcome if I return to the university to study another course?"

My hands were familiar with the tricky task of shuffling large tarot cards. They moved the cards as my mind held the question in consciousness, trying not to form any proliferating images, just holding the words as individual entities floating in my psyche. I got to a point where my hands seemed to stop of their own accord. I put the question out of my mind and dropped it into the well of the un-conscious as I cut the cards with my left hand into three piles. I took one of the piles at random and then placed the other two piles under it, putting the pack into one again. I repeated the cutting into three piles two more times to make three times three—the number so beloved of magic, riddle, and fairy tale. I laid out the cards on the black velvet, placing the first card on top of the significator to represent the central issue. I laid a second card across the first. The second card represents barriers and obstacles. The third I placed beneath the significator to represent what I had already achieved, and the fourth above the significator to represent what I could achieve. The fifth card, I placed to the left of my significator; this card represents past influences that I was leaving behind. The sixth I placed to the right, to represent future influences. The seventh card represents me, my attitude to the situation; the eighth represents my environment—what surrounds me. The ninth is my hopes or fears, and the tenth is the final outcome.

In this spread, I used a significator to represent me—the Queen of Wands. The first card to appear, the main issue, was the Page of Swords. In this context, I saw Swords as representing the intellect—here a part of myself that was not yet mature, that wanted to grow. But I also felt that this meant that I needed to assert myself. The reason was clear—the Knight of Cups crossing me. My then-fiancé did not want me to return to the university. He felt threatened by the idea. Beneath me was the four of Pentacles. Fours and earth can make for a desire for security, to cling to what we have. I was scared about giving up my income. It would be easier in so many ways to stay where I was, but behind me was the Hanged Man—someone in suspension. The Hanged Man can be a positive card. It can mean that we are going through an initiatory process, that outer life is on hold while we go through a period of great inner change. I felt that the spread indicated that my true path had been put on hold while I had a career job that I found unsatisfying. The Page of Swords is an action card—it was time to move on. Ahead of me was the eight of Cups, a journey, and one that would involve leaving behind things that I valued, but above me was what I could achieve—the Ace of Wands, the power of creative energy. The seventh card, my attitude toward the situation—the Ace of Swords—was a card of energy and power, but in the context in which I was asking the question, I felt it related to my need to use my mind and intellect, which were not utilized and "in suspension" in my current job. My environment was the eight of Pentacles—hard work, but with satisfactory results. Production is in progress. My hopes and my fears surprised me—the Knight of Wands, a fiery man. Was I unconsciously wanting, or fearing, to develop the masculine side of my psyche? The final outcome was a card of love, and possibly marriage. I breathed a sigh of relief. I was worried that going to the university would lead to the breakdown of my relationship with my fiancé—maybe things would be okay. I decided that I must take the opportunity of further study, whatever the consequences, and got my university place.

It was the right decision, but a lot of my tarot interpretation was wrong—not the reading, just my interpretation. When I told my watery Piscean fiancé (the Knight of Cups) that I was going back to the university he became very unhappy and after a few months we agreed the relationship should end. Meanwhile, my boss brought in my replacement. He was to shadow me for a month and then take over. My replacement was a fiery Aries male—a Knight of Wands. On the first day I met him, a voice in my head said, "That's the man I'm going to marry." And so it was. If I had not decided to go back to the university, I would have stayed in an unsatisfactory job and married the wrong man. As it was, I married the Knight of Wands.

Philosophy of Change

Tarot readings are most useful if you do them infrequently and only when you have serious decisions to make. The tarot is a way for us

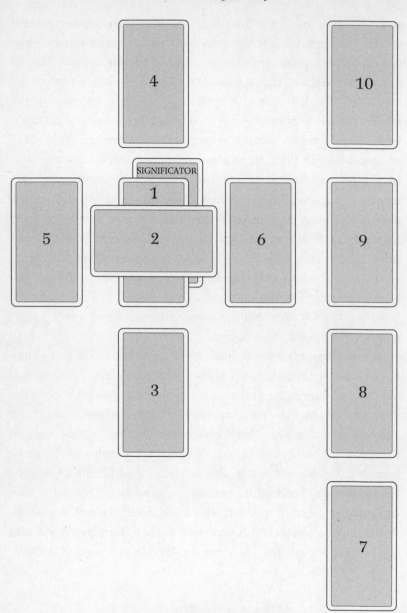

CELTIC CROSS TAROT SPREAD

to gain insight into our unconscious motives. The cards can provide a route for those unexpected and unaccountable bolts of clairvoyance that come like a spiritual grace to give us the insight that we need. Inherent in the tarot, and in all magical philosophy, is an idea similar to Chinese Taoism—an idea of impermanence. Nothing is static, or fixed. Everything is in a state of flux and in the process of leading to something else. Positively, however difficult or dark the situation seems, it will move on, evolve, the wheel of fortune will turn once more, and move us upward and outward from our difficulties. We can trust in the process of the universe. Its goals are not always the same as ours, and often our petty goals will be overturned by force of circumstances, but part of the art of the magician is to become a surfer of life's difficulties. When the great wave comes, we ride it and are not drowned.

When we do a divination, we do not really see the future as such. We see something from the timeless zone where all things are present simultaneously. In our linear, clock-driven world, it is hard to comprehend that time as we understand it applies only to material objects. At the extremes of time and space, the two concepts merge. This was the great insight of Einstein. We can think of the timeless zone as a state of consciousness, a state of existence beyond ordinary reality, where each atom has an infinite number of futures and can cause an infinite number of possibilities. Divination is like long-range weather forecasting. It can enable us to predict the trends. The unexpected can and will happen, but once we know the trends, we can plan how best to deal with them and, from our actions, the future is made. Weather is subject to chaos theory, which is misnamed. It is not really chaos but unpredictability. A slight change in one part of the complexity of life can lead to reverberations that alter destiny completely. In magic, the future is not seen as fixed. Magicians are change workers rather than fatalists. The pattern of the future is constantly being woven. At any point, there are numerous possibilities and ways in which things might go. If we can see the trends, take soundings, and look a little into the future, then we can influence where things are going. If you read any book about magic—fact or fiction—you will find that witches and magicians are consulted about two things: spells to fix things, to make them go the way that someone wants, and divination. Divination can be to find out what is happening in the present—where is the object that I lost yesterday? Or it can be about the future—what shall I do, which choice should I make, should I marry the maiden?

Tarot

Divination works on the hermetic principle of "as above, so below." The idea is that the pattern in the microcosm mimics the pattern in the macrocosm. The interaction that occurs between seeker and interpreter allows the symbolic representation of the seeker's situation to appear in symbols that the interpreter then interprets. Other than astrology, the major Western divination system is the tarot. The tarot first appeared in Europe in the late medieval period and draws on imagery that is thousands of years old. Since the appearance of the first packs, many different tarots have been devised, drawing on Celtic, Egyptian, Native American, and all manner of esoteric symbolism. Whatever the symbols used, the major arcana relate to qualities that are active or about to become active in the person's life. "Qualities" is really too weak a word. The major arcana are archetypal forces that are manifesting in the person's psyche and environment. The place in the spread where the card appears should indicate whether this force is present within the person or is impacting on him or her from outside, and in what area of life.

Tarot readers traditionally had different interpretations for the cards, depending on whether they were upright when laid out or upside down. Contemporary tarot readers usually read with all the cards upright. I find that the other cards in the spread can best determine each card's meaning, rather than whether it is upside down or not.

MAJOR ARCANA OF TAROT

Major Arcana	Attribution	Interpretation
0 Fool	Neptune	Beginning, youthful enthusiasm, unaware of obstacles
1 Magus	Mercury	Skill, initiative, ability to make things happen
2 High Priestess	Moon	Intuition, wisdom
3 Empress	Venus	Fertility, practicality, power to make joyful
4 Emperor	Aries	Leadership, management, guidance in worldly matters
5 Hierophant	Taurus	Spiritual leadership, teaching
6 Lovers	Gemini	Relationship, can be dilemma, decision between two equal goods
7 Chariot	Cancer	Movement, activity, travel, can have connotations of war chariot, in which case a triumphant outcome
8 Strength	Leo	Energy, courage, and strength
9 Hermit	Virgo	Discernment, good judgment, prudence, need for space and solitude
10 Wheel of Fortune	Jupiter	Change of fortune, surrounding cards will indicate whether good or bad
11 Justice	Libra	Judgment, decisions, the law
12 Hanged Man	Water	Suspended animation, time for turning inward, contemplation, wait
13 Death	Scorpio	End of one phase, time to begin another; literal death or an ending
14 Temperance	Sagittarius	Harmonious change, inner equilibrium, balance
15 Devil	Capricorn	Negative phase, feeling trapped, abuse of power, bullying

MAJOR ARCANA OF TAROT

Major Arcana	Attribution	Interpretation
16 Tower	Mars	Unexpected collapse of job, enterprise, life phase; coming as bolt from the blue
17 Star	Aquarius	Revelation, harmony with nature, hope
18 Moon	Pisces	Fear, anxiety
19 Sun	Sun	Positive energy, growth, good fortune
20 Judgment, Aeon	Fire	Renewal, awakening after sleep
21 World	Saturn	Culmination, bringing together of hopes and dreams and manifestation in reality, success

The minor arcana represent the interaction of the four elements with numbers. Wands are associated with fire, swords with air, cups with water, and pentacles with the element of earth. The interpretation of the numbers derives from the Jewish mystical and magical system of Kabbalah and the kabbalistic diagram that represents our cosmos, The Tree of Life. This has ten different sefiroth, or realms. The ten realms are associated with Earth, the seven magical planets, the zodiac, and the Divine. Our cosmos is considered an emanation of, rather than a creation of, the Divine. This subtle wording means that the cosmos is part of the fabric of the Divine. It is not fallen, corrupt, separate, or alienated from the Divine, but a manifestation of it. The implication is that we can find spiritual fulfillment in the study of nature and the cosmos, which is of course the aim of natural magic.

MINOR ARCANA OF TAROT

Suit	Wands/Fire	Cups/ Water	Swords/Air	Pentacles/ Earth
1 (Ace) Positive power of the element	Inspiration, creativity, enthusiasm, ambition, status	Love	Reason, intellect, justice, law	Material wealth and success, fertility
2 Uranus. Wisdom, duality, beginnings	New ventures	Loving relationship between two people	Negative energy in uneasy lull	Starting to make money
3 Saturn. Completion of a phase	New enterprises coming to fruition	Rejoicing, fertility, birth of a child	Sorrow	Money, wealth gained through enterprise
4 Jupiter. Creativity, joy, solidity	Joy from endeavors, completion of a task	Emotional indulgence, boredom	Peace after strife, rest, recovery	Wealth, security, time for investment
5 Mars. Destructive force at work	The rough and tumble of life, need to strive to attain goals	Emotional troubles, unhappiness	Battle of words or other battle, unpleasant- ness	Material misfortune, threat of poverty
6 Sun. Balance, harmony, success, altruism	Success in endeavors, public recognition	Success in relationships, solid friendship, teamwork	Moving on with some regrets, a necessary journey	Material success and time for altruism, giving away part of what is gained

MINOR ARCANA OF TAROT

Suit	Wands/Fire	Cups/ Water	Swords/Air	Pentacles/ Earth
7 Venus. Victory	Skill overcomes obstacles, positive for job interviews and other challenges	Overindulgence in emotions and fantasy, too much of a good thing	Intelligence overcomes a problem, cunning and strategy needed	Perseverance and hard work will prevail
8 Mercury. Solidity, but progress	Swift progress toward a successful conclusion. Generating ideas	Stagnation. Water must move. Time to move on	Solid obstacles, being hemmed in	Material rewards from work. Personal satisfaction, sense of achievement, jobs well done
9 Moon. Almost at the end	Position of strength. Past victories make the person a formidable opponent	Emotional strength. Time to enjoy the pleasures of life and relationships. Time to share	Anguish, anxiety, fear, paranoia. Real or imagined depending on surrounding cards	Time and space to enjoy fruits of past labors and material pleasures
10 Earth. End, completion, sometimes too much of a good thing	Too many burdens, something must be shed or energy will suffer. Time to pause, stop, slow down, reevaluate	Fulfillment and perfect happiness. As good as it gets	Culmination of a crisis. On the face of it a negative card. The worst it can get	Family support, inheritance. Culmination of wealth

In the tarot, aces are number one in a suit. They are positive influences, the energy of an element, undiluted, in its pure and original form. Two creates division and duality brings movement and action, usually positive. Twos are related to new beginnings. The number three is associated with Saturn and brings us into the three-dimensional world of form. Threes make energy manifest in the world. This is considered positive in all suits but swords. The number three and swords combine Saturn's tendency to melancholy with the aggression of swords, creating the "sword in the heart"—grief and sorrow. Four is considered a number of balance—the four elements working in harmony. Fours suggest "four-squareness," strong foundations, solidity. Fours are considered positive in all suits but cups. Why the exclusion of cups? Four is the number of the planet Jupiter and cups relate to watery emotion. Jupiter is a planet of enjoyment. In excess, Jupiter relates to overindulgence, so fours and cups combine as emotional indulgence. Five is the number of the planet Mars and Mars can be aggressive. Fives are considered negative in all suits. Six is considered a harmonious number, associated with the Sun. Sixes bring the solar quality of success to bear in all the suits. Seven is associated with Venus and considered positive in all suits but cups. As with fours, the beneficent pleasure-loving energy of Venus in the emotional sphere is considered too much of a good thing. There is a certain Puritanism in the tarot. Eight is the number of Mercury, and this double "fourness" is associated with stability. Stable water means stagnation; water is meant to move, so the eight of cups is considered a negative card. Swords are problems in the tarot, and eight means being stuck with them for a while—another combination that is considered negative. Nine is the number associated with the Moon, the Earth's satellite. At nine, things are almost at their peak—mainly for good, but in the case of swords, for bad. Ten, the final number, is associated with Earth and the fullest manifestation of the energy of a suit. Swords are considered more negative the further they progress into manifestation, so the ten of swords is a miserable card. The only consolation is that if this comes up in a tarot reading, this is as bad as it gets.

A word about swords: the sword suit is traditionally interpreted negatively in the tarot, but swords also represent thoughts and ideas. They convey what goes on in our heads. This can be anxiety, worries, fears, and phobias, but swords also represent the power of logical thought. Inherent in the problem, therefore, is the potential solution—to change the way we think. This is the principle of homeopathic medicine as opposed to allopathic medicine. By instinct, magicians lean toward the homeopathic.

Court Cards

The court cards in the tarot represent people with particular personality characteristics. If you are reading your own tarot or someone else's, you can select a court card as a "significator," to represent the person wanting the reading. This is not as easy as it sounds. We are complex creatures and take on different roles in different situations. The dreamy lover may be a practical businesswoman in the office. Someone who is impersonal and cold at work may have learned to "warm up" in a close, loving relationship. When I started reading the tarot, I found the significator useful, but I use it infrequently now. It is particularly useful if people ask you to read the tarot for them when they will not be present. A significator can help you focus on the person. A photograph, of course, will work even better. Kings in the tarot represent mature men, and queens mature women. Knights, called Princes in some tarots, are younger men, and Pages, sometimes called Princesses, are younger women.

COURT CARDS OF TAROT

Personality Qualities	Wands— Fiery	Cups— Watery	Swords— Airy	Pentacles— Earthy
Strengths	Creative, energetic, enthusiastic, inspirational	Imaginative, loving, psychic	Intelligent, just, rational	Practical, hardworking, sensual
Weaknesses	Aggressive, intolerant	Impractical, unreliable	Critical, insensitive	Unadventurous, boring

Traditional tarot books have sexist definitions of the court cards and limit you to the cards of your own gender, but women can appear as Kings or Knights, particularly in career situations where they are taking on traditionally male roles. I do not find that I appear as either a King or a Knight. I would like to be a Knight but never mind, I do have a subsidiary card that often appears, which is the Page of Swords. This is the Sword Princess—think Leia in Star Wars. It appears when I have to do battle.

℮
Three-Card Trick

Most books on divination will tell you not to attempt to do divination for yourself but, of course, everyone breaks the rule. There isn't always someone else to ask and we may not wish our nearest and dearest to have access to our secret thoughts. The reason why it's not considered a good idea to do divination for yourself is that it is almost impossible not to bias your reading. Until you become magically experienced, you are liable to see reflected there what you want or fear. You are bound to try, but be warned of the pitfalls. If you want to try, when you first learn the tarot, try a simple spread with three cards only. It is more difficult to deceive yourself, and much less confusing, if you keep the reading as simple as possible. As you become more familiar with the tarot—familiar enough not to need to look up the meanings when you do a reading—go on to a full Celtic Cross. Anyone who has used a divination system will know the temptation to try again if the first result is not what you want. Doing a follow-up question to clarify is fine, but trying to get a different answer is not. You will just go on until you get the answer you want—but it will reflect your dreams and not reality. Often, though, there is no need for follow-up questions. The first answer is remarkably clear.

I did a three-card tarot reading and drew the Ace of Wands, Strength card, and the Three of Cups.

The Ace of Wands is associated with fiery energy—something not too far removed from the process of controlling a combustion engine. Strength is someone composed and in control of something else—looks promising. The Three of Cups is a card associated with rejoicing. The omens looked good, but I was lucky—or the tarot was in a good mood that day. Suppose the reading had been disastrous? I would not have forfeited the test fee and not gone to the test. I would have gone to the test convinced I was going to fail. I could have made myself so unmotivated and anxious that the reading would become a self-fulfilling prophecy. As it was, the positive reading boosted my confidence; so much so that when I messed up reversing around a corner, I got frustrated and told the examiner that what I'd done was worthless. In fact, I was a lot more explicit than that. I asked the examiner if I could do it again. He said okay. I did it again and I passed. Now, with more experience of tarot reading, I would not ask the tarot if I was going to pass the test. I would ask, "What should I look out for when I take the test?" or "How can I best be prepared?" Don't paint yourself into a corner with divination. If you are going to do something anyway, asking what the outcome will be is pointless. Ask instead for guidance on how to achieve the outcome you want.

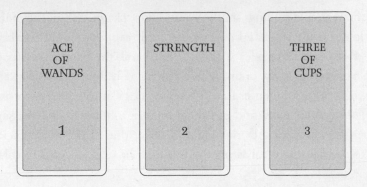

THREE-CARD TAROT SPREAD

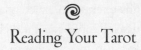

Reading Your Tarot

If you read the tarot for yourself, formulate your question, keep it simple, and before you do the reading, write the question down on a piece of paper so you can't cheat and reword the question if you don't like the answer. Ask simple, direct questions, but don't ask questions like, "Should I do such and such?" The tarot can show you trends that currently exist or the trends that will exist if you take a particular step. It is not there to tell you what to do. You are a free individual with the power of choice. What you need is guidance on how to exercise that choice. Don't ask, "Should I take the job?" Instead, ask, "What will happen if I take the job?" Often the answer will be clear, but if not, you could do a further three-card spread asking, "What will happen if I don't take the job?" The second question may be more important than the first. The first answer might make you think it was not worth pursuing the new job offer, but the alternative if you do not take it might be worse. Of course, if the first answer is direct and positive, do not confuse the issue by asking supplementary questions. It is never wise to tempt the patience of oracles.

For a simple reading, shuffle your tarot pack while thinking of the question you want to ask. Once the cards are thoroughly shuffled, cut them into three piles with your left hand, the hand that is controlled by your right brain, which thinks more holistically. Put the three piles back together in a different order. Cut the pack a second time into three piles, and put them back in a different order again. Then cut the pack a third time and select one of the three packs. Take the first three cards off the top of your selected pack and lay them out.

Look at the preceding tables to get your interpretation. As well as looking at the individual cards, look at the overall pattern. A preponderance of a particular suit means a preponderance of that element in the question. Pentacles indicate money matters, cups emotional matters, wands energy and success issues, and swords are barriers, obstacles, or ideas. People cards indicate that others are going to be part of the decision in one way or another. An Ace indicates that the power of the element is with you—a powerful force of inspirational, emotional, intellectual, or material energy is going to manifest in your life. The presence of two major arcana indicates that this may be a major turning point.

Significance of Significators

As your life journey unfolds, your significator may change. Throughout my teens, I was an introvert. In my early twenties, I decided to become an extrovert. Immediately, I stopped appearing in the tarot as the Queen of Cups—the receptive, archetypal mother type—and became the Queen of Wands. I also ended my relationship with a Piscean and married an Aries, went back to the university, and got a Ph.D. and a proper career. I had become active in the world in the way that I wanted, instead of being passive and a facilitator of other people's life journeys. For some people, becoming the Queen of Cups would have been the right direction in which to take their lives, but I needed to go out into the world, to engage with the world outside my head, in order to become myself. This did not mean that my dreamy watery side went away—I was still a writer and priestess—but I was now living out a side of myself that had previously been suppressed.

As I was writing this, I thought I would check what I am now. Maybe I have moved on? As a change from my battered old Waite pack, I took all the court cards out of a new tarot pack a friend has given me as a fun present. The Witches' Tarot was devised for the James Bond movie *Live and Let Die.* Many books are scornful about the Witches' Tarot, but it works perfectly well and is close in spirit to the original tarot cards in that it has no illustrations on the minor arcana, just the relevant number of each suit. This means that you have to rely on your own knowledge of the cards and your intuition, rather than pictures based on someone else's interpretation. I shuffled the sixteen court cards and took a card at random. It was the Queen of Wands. So today, I am still the Queen of Wands, but as someone with no earth in my astrological chart, I aspire to one day appear as the Queen of Pentacles. I keep gardening to develop my earthy side, but given the haphazard results I may have to wait until the next incarnation to live out my "earthy" self.

✦

POINTERS FOR PRACTICE

Divination is a way of tapping what is going on in your unconscious mind. Use divination as a guide, not a prop, and only when there is something you really want to know. Divination is like weather forecasting. It shows trends, not absolutes. Magicians are change workers, not fatalists. You are advised not to divine for yourself, but if you do, use a simple method where self-deception is more difficult. Don't try to predict the outcome of things you are going to do anyway. Instead, ask for guidance on how to achieve what you want.

CHAPTER ELEVEN

Waving a Magic Wand

. . . the true and absolute magical wand must be one perfectly straight branch of almond or hazel, cut at a single blow with the magical pruning-knife or golden sickle, before the rising of the Sun, at that moment when the tree is ready to blossom. It must be pierced through its whole length without splitting or breaking it, and a long needle of magnetized iron must occupy its entire length.

ELIPHAS LEVI, *TRANSCENDENTAL MAGIC*

You have seen it in the movies—the magician and his wand. Hollywood shows witches and wizards tapping objects with their wands and turning frogs into princes and princes into frogs. Unfortunately, magical wands do not have these powers. They are symbolic, an extension of your magical will. When we make magical objects ourselves, they become an extension of us. We put our energy, thought, and imagination into finding the materials, preparing them, and making something with them. In that preparatory process, the creative imagination is stimulated. We have already begun a magical process within ourselves. When we make something, we give birth to something new in the world. We are initiating a change. Magicians' grimoires are full of complex equipment—black-handled knives, white-handled knives, swords, sickles. These are a bit beyond most people's handicraft skills, but making a wand is a bit like making incense—relatively foolproof. Wands also have advantages over ritual daggers so beloved by witches for casting circles. They are airport friendly. My wands are well–traveled. Even pre-September 11 a ritual dagger in your hand luggage was considered a bit of a no-no. Security officials don't seem to mind a discreet wand or two.

As a budding teen witch eager to begin my magical career, I needed a wand. I checked out the instructions in Eliphas Levi's *Transcendental Magic*. They sounded tricky. Maybe a piece of hazel sawn off with a small handsaw in the morning would do? After all, it was August. Dawn is a bit early for a teen witch. According to Levi, August was the wrong time of year, but I was sure the gods wouldn't mind a bit of improvisation. As it was, I found a newly fallen hazel branch that seemed ideal. Though the branch was already discarded, mentally I thanked the tree for its gift. We should not take lightly the gift of trees that create oxygen for our planet. I whittled off the bark with a penknife. Eventually, a magician did make me the grimoire-authentic article, but it always felt dead compared with the wands I have collected and made myself. I keep the magician's wand as a curiosity.

Twenty years later, I feel I would like a new hazel wand; one made from the wood of my own Breton garden. I do it at the appropriate time. And here is how I made my wand.

○

MAKING A NEW WAND

On a morning in late January, getting up at dawn is not too much of a hardship. Spring has come early. Already there are bright yellow catkins on the hazel trees, streaks of golden dangling sunshine fluttering in the breeze. The woods are wet. Rain has tinged the hazel bark red. I take tree cutters and choose one of the straight upright coppiced shoots growing from the trunk of an elderly hazel. I cut straight and clean, just above a nodule, and dab the cut with a proprietary product for sealing pruned branches. I've cut the wand much longer than the standard ritual magician's length of elbow to palm of the hand. It feels more comfortable and balanced in the hand with a little more length and weight.

It's warm enough near noon to sit outside. I sit in the garden whittling the bark off the wand with a sharp knife. The wood is revealed as a dazzling white. By the time I have whittled down a few nodules, the wand has gotten thinner, but it's still substantial enough. I hollow out the top to make a hole for a beautiful slim amethyst crystal given to me by a friend. It's less easy than it sounds. The heartwood is soft but hollowing out the wand without going through the sides is tricky, and the slim crystal needs a surprisingly large hole to accommodate it. Finally, it slips neatly in, but hope alone won't keep it there. Quick drying adhesive doesn't sound exactly magical, but the stone won't stay in on its own. I smear the glue inside the hole and on the end of the crystal. It holds.

☾

Cutting a Wand

The traditional recommended time to cut a wand is at dawn, but you might want to give yourself some leeway. Another tradition is to cut the wood when the Moon is waxing, and some traditions favor as early as possible in the waxing phase—the new Moon. Cut a small branch or large twig from a tree. For holly and rowan, there are old traditions that say that you should tear off a twig or branch rather than cutting it, but a clean cut is less likely to damage the tree. Choose the tree with care. Find a place and a tree that attract you. Cut the wood cleanly, just above a nodule, as though you are pruning a rosebush. You could use a pair of large cutters, a small saw, or a

Swiss army penknife, and there are gardening products that seal cuts so they do not get diseased. If you want to leave the bark on your wand, then a branch about the width of your finger is fine. If you want to strip the bark or to insert a crystal at the end, start with something thicker. Grimoires tell you to make relatively short wands—the length of your elbow to the palm of your hand—but you may prefer something longer.

Choosing Your Wood

Grimoires often tell you to take living wood. Wood that has lain for a while and is starting to rot is unsuitable for a wand, which represents your will, inner strength, and determination, but newly fallen wood is as good as live wood. If your choice of time and place is right, you may find exactly the right piece of wood waiting on the ground right where you walk. As you learn more about trees, you may wish to make wands for different purposes. I have wands I have collected from different parts of the world—places where I have traveled, places with positive memories, and places of great beauty. When you make wands and choose places and trees to collect the wood that have emotional links for you, they have a resonance that items made by others lack. They will work more effectively for you because you have made them truly yours. Here are some trees that I have used for wands and for magical purposes.

Hazel

Hazel is a good all-purpose wood for a wand. To us it seems a prosaic enough tree, one we find growing in hedges, deciduous woodlands, and copses. Hazel's late summer and autumn nuts are a major bonus. Once the squirrels had competition—us. Our ances-

WOODS FOR WANDS

Tree	Latin Botanical Name	Element & Planet	Magical Qualities
Hazel	*Corylus avellana*	Air, Mercury	Divination, dowsing
Holly	*Ilex aquifolium*	Fire, Mars	Protection, courage, dream spells
Rowan or Mountain Ash Quickbeam, Witchwood, European Mountain Ash	*Sorbus aucuparia*	Fire, Sun	Healing, protection against harm, success
Eucalyptus incl. Tasmanian Blue Gum, Red River Gum, Cider Gum, Yellow Box	*Eucalyptus globules, E. camaldulensis, E. gunnii, E. melliodora*	Water, Moon, or Fire	Healing, protection
Willow	*Salix alba* (white willow), *Salix babylonica* (Weeping willow)	Water, Moon	Divination, protection, healing
Apple	*Pyrus malus* (crab apple or wild apple), *Malus domestica* (domesticated apple)	Water, Venus	Love, health
Oak	*Quercus robur*	Earth, Jupiter	Protection, strength, power
Yew	*Taxus baccata, Taxus fastigia* (Irish yew)	Earth, Saturn	Divination, dowsing

tors gathered hazelnuts as an important part of their winter diet, so nut trees featured greatly in ancient legend. In Irish myth, nuts bestow wisdom. By eating the nuts that fall into the sacred well of Connla, salmon gain the wisdom that enables them to perform the great migrations from fresh water to the sea and back again. The *Triads of Ireland* enjoined the death penalty for anyone who felled a hazel. For the Romans, the hazel was a magical tree, its nuts sacred to Mercury, messenger of the gods and patron of magic. In the magical tradition, it is sacred to Mercury and to the element of air. Perhaps because of its magical associations, hazel is also the dowser's wood. Forked "Y" shaped hazel twigs have been used since ancient times for "water witching," divining for underground water, and for finding seams of minerals. Archaeologists dowse to trace the outlines of ancient buildings.

☺

Dowsing Exercise

To try dowsing, cut a "Y" shaped hazel twig about a foot long. Hold the two prongs of the "Y" with the single arm straight out in front of you and walk over the ground you are surveying until you feel a "pull" and the twig starts to twitch, pointing up or down. Hazel is a traditional material, but if you want something more high tech, modern professional diviners often use two "L" shaped copper rods. You hold a rod in each hand and when you sense water, the rods will cross over.

Are the materials—hazel or copper—important? Probably not. Experienced dowsers often dispense with the rods. My father could find underground water sources just by walking over a field. He could also sense underground pipes in urban areas, a highly useful skill in old cities where the routes of underground streams and water pipes have been lost and forgotten. Good dowsers seem to sense the presence of water through sensations in their back and arm muscles, but the reactions are probably caused by sensations in the dowsers' legs. In the 1930s, experiments at Guy's Hospital in London showed that dowsers could *not* divine if their leg muscles were completely relaxed or if they were standing on a piece of metal or smooth glass rather than on the earth. The combination of standing on the ground plus being able to sense energies through their leg muscles produce optimum results for dowsers.

Holly

I have a favorite wand made of holly that is ideal for drawing magic circles for rites of protection. Today, we think of holly mainly as indoor decoration for Yule. Its evergreen leaves and mildly poisonous bright red berries make it a symbol of hope in the darkness of winter, a promise that the life force has not deserted us, that there are better times to come. Traditionally, though, holly is a warrior tree, associated with the planet Mars and with the element of fire. Its prickly leaves can hurt and fight back, and its wood was often used for spears. Warriors are guardians and protectors, but holly protects in another unusual way. The spikes of its leaves act as miniature lightning conductors, so hollies were planted near other trees to protect them. Miniaturized and variegated hollies abound in suburban gardens and gardeners make holly hedges, but to find a holly wand, you will need to find an older, larger tree. Try oak, beech, or other deciduous woodlands. In winter, you will find the holly easy to spot as one of the few green trees.

@

Growing Holly Trees

Holly can grow up to a height of thirty to forty feet with a spread of thirty to forty feet, but it grows slowly. If you have a garden, you might like to plant trees that have magical associations. Holly is suitable for small spaces and saplings can be found in pine forests, but they struggle for light under dark green canopies, so are often short-lived. If you want to rescue a holly tree to transplant it, it isn't easy—I've tried. You need to lift a very large clod of earth to keep the root ball intact. The soil often falls off as you try to put it into a container to transport it. When giving a holly sapling a home, remember that hollies like dry, sandy soil.

Warrior tree, protection tree, tree of hope, holly is also in folklore a love tree. Only female holly trees produce the distinctive red berries, and male and female hollies need one another to breed, so folklore has created links between sexuality and holly.

©

Love Spells, Dream Spells

If you are male, an old spell for success in love is to carry a holly berry in your pocket. Men have it easy; women's spells are more complicated. For women, a tradition to help you have a divinatory dream to show you your true love is to gather nine smooth "she-holly" leaves—that is nonprickly leaves of a female holly tree—at midnight on a Friday (the day of Venus). Wrap the leaves in a triangular handkerchief and tie the handkerchief into a bundle using nine knots. Put the bundle under your pillow and dream your dream. There is a similar holly spell to make dreams come true. Again, gather nine leaves. The day and time do not matter, but it is important to gather the leaves without speaking. Tie the leaves into a bundle of white cloth using nine knots and put it under your pillow.

Like all dream spells, this works not because of the properties of the materials used in the spell, in this case the holly. It works because the effort we have put into the spell impresses itself on our unconscious enough for it to provide what we want. You cannot use the true dream spell haphazardly. You need to know what you want to dream about and what you want to ask.

Rowan/European Mountain Ash

The deciduous rowan likes well-drained soil and thrives in mountainous, windy regions. Its slender branches and light-green compound leaves offer no resistance to heavy rain. Originally native to Europe, settlers transplanted rowan to North America, where it is known as European mountain ash, though it is not a true ash. You may spot rowan with other trees clustering beneath it. Rowan grows quickly and shelters slower growing saplings of other species. Its bright red berries, which come in late summer, are another way to identify it, and they give rowan its magical association with the element of fire and with the Sun and make it ideal for invoking successful creative energy. My friend Paul Greenslade once found an ideal branch and cut it for me. The bark is lovely and smooth, with horizontal markings not so different from silver birch, but reddish brown in color. It has become my favorite wand.

Folk tales speak of rowan as a protection against witches, but the stories are distorted. Rowan is a tree that protects those who honor it and was seen from ancient times as a protection against evil. In the north of England and Scotland small rowan twigs were tied with red thread and placed above the insides of front and back doors to stop evil from entering. Carrying a rowan twig would protect you while traveling, and keep this saying in mind:

> Rowan tree and red thread,
> Put the witches to their speed.

Willow

I have a long, white, thin, pliable, elegant willow wand that I use when I dedicate rituals to the Goddess and the Moon. It is a perfect representative of its source tree. You will find weeping willow trailing its elegant branches in rivers and streams, and at ornamental parks, a tree of grace. In the wind, you will see its narrow silver-green leaves shimmering and perhaps revealing their white undersides. In early spring, you can spot male willows by their yellow catkins and female willows by their gray catkins. The smaller goat willow has furry "pussy willow" catkins. "You remind me of the willow," my father-in-law said one day, surprisingly. He is not given to the poetic. "When the wind blows the willow bends and the oak stands tall. When the wind dies away, it is the oak that has fallen." The allusion is vaguely literary but I cannot remember—Aesop, Montaigne? Willow, the tree of the lady, the Goddess, the Moon, that which appears gentle but has great strength. Magically, the tree is related to water because of its water-loving qualities and the rippling effect of its branches when ruffled by the wind.

Willows feature often in traditional love magic. An Eastern European gypsy spell for a woman seeking to snare a husband is to wait until the ground is muddy, then to follow him and watch where he leaves footprints. She should then cut out a clear footprint from the earth, take it to a willow tree, and bury it beneath the tree, saying:

> Many earths on earth there be
> he whom I love my own shall be,
> grow, grow, willow tree!
> Sorrow none unto me!
> He the ax, I the helve,
> he the cock, I the hen,
> As I do will, so mote it be!

Country spells were straight to the point. "Mote" is an old word for "must."

Apple

Apples, like hazel trees, have long had magical associations. If we cut horizontally across an apple, we find hidden in the center a five-pointed star, the pentacle, a symbol of magic and healing. For our ancestors, a major problem through winter was storing foods that could provide a balanced diet. The apple was a true gift of the gods—hard, rich in vitamins, easily stored, brewable into cider, and suitable for bottling and sauces. Apples are associated in mythology with longevity, health, and beauty. In Roman myth, Pomona is goddess of apple trees and known as the Apple Mother who gives the apples of eternal life. In Celtic myth, three women take the wounded King Arthur to Avalon, Apple Island, to be healed and to await rebirth. In Irish myth, the source of apples is Emhain Abhlach, a place free of grief, sorrow, sickness, weakness, and death. In Roman mythology, their guardianship became Venus' honor. In Norse myth, it is the goddess Iduna, wife of Bragi, god of poetry, who is keeper of the apples. If the gods begin to age, she gives them an apple and their youth is restored. As well as providing healing, apples are associated with the feminine, the Goddess, and the powers of love. In Greek mythology, a golden apple was the fruit awarded as a prize to the most beautiful goddess—Aphrodite, goddess of love.

Apple trees' gnarled branches can provide short wands suitable for Venusian magic, but more often they are used to make a silver branch. The magical silver branch appears in Irish Myth. On it hung three or nine apples that played music to induce a bardic trance. The hero Bran of Irish myth was given a silver branch, and a silver branch belonged to the god Manannan mac Lir, who gives his name to the Isle of Man in the Irish Sea. Manannan's silver branch,

Craebh Ciuil, was endowed with powers to heal the sick, induce sleep or trance, and inspire joy.

◉

Making a Silver Branch

You can make your own silver branch by cutting a small gnarled apple branch, stripping it of bark, and painting it silver. Substitute nine golden bells for the magical apples and bind the bells onto the branch with silver, gold, or red thread. Ring it nine times before invoking deities, meditation, or divination, as a way of deepening your state of consciousness.

Eucalyptus

If the trees of your locality are not the traditional European trees of natural magic, use what is around you and find its associations in local myth and legend. In New South Wales, Australia, in the early '80s, we decide to make a eucalyptus wand. We have seen eucalyptus in our own northern hemisphere, as a foreign import that can have disastrous effects on ecosystems. Their root systems can cause buildings to subside. Eucalyptus's water-loving qualities mean that it can be used to drain marshes and destroy mosquito breeding grounds, but marsh drainage destroys a vast range of other wildlife habitat too. Tampering with nature is never without a price. Here in its Australian homeland, we can admire the hundreds of varieties of eucalyptus trees without these reservations. Magically, eucalyptus can be associated with the element of water, due to the soothing properties of eucalyptus oil, which is used to alleviate coughs. Conversely, eucalyptus can be associated with fire. Eucalyptus oil makes the trees highly flammable, and most varieties depend on fire to regenerate.

Oak

Australia's national tree is the eucalyptus. Britain's is the oak. Slow growing, durable, and large, oak is the tree of Zeus, Jupiter, Thor—male gods of great power. It is also a deeply rooted tree and associated with the element of earth. As a child, oak was one of my favorite trees to climb because it had low limbs ideal for children to reach. My friend Marilyn and I would sit in an oak to eat our lunch, hidden by the leaves from those who passed underneath. The oak was a playground for our cowboy and Indian fantasies. Oaks were security, continuity, and safety. It is a tree of longevity. Oak is a fertile tree that scatters acorns around it. Make an oak wand if you want stability, rootedness, and kingly strength.

Yew

Yew is another slow-growing tree, but its dark-green waxy needlelike leaves give it more solemn associations than the oak. Yews are associated with the planet Saturn, planet of old age. There are yew trees in Britain that are more than a thousand years old. Magically, yew is associated with seeing the future. Slips of yew wood were marked with ogham symbols and cast by druids for divination, in the same way that alder slips marked with runes were used further north, as yarrow stalks were used for Chinese I Ching divination. Yew would be a good wand for a Saturn rite, or any ritual where you need sobriety, longevity, maturity, age, and wisdom, but remember when collecting it that its leaves and fleshy red fruit are poisonous to young children and animals.

☻

Constructing Your Wand

Once you have your wood, you need to decide whether you want to scrape off the bark. If you take off the bark, you will see more of the grain of the wood, but the bark can be beautiful in itself. In any event, you will need to cut off any side twigs or nodules with a sharp blade. If you remove the bark, you can carve the wood with a pattern or symbols that appeal to you, or you can leave it bare. You can leave the ends of the wand as they are, or you can whittle the wand to a point or make a hole at the end to insert a crystal. Quartz is good and can be bought in the form of long, thin, symmetrical, laboratory-made crystals that are easy to insert, or you could choose another stone that appeals to you. The best way to fix the crystal is to have a piece of wood that is thick enough for you to hollow out one end to make a hole to sit the crystal in. Stick the crystal with a fast-acting glue, suitable for a wide variety of materials. Wood is absorbent but crystal is not, so you need a product suitable for both. When you are not using your wand, wrap it in a piece of silk. Traditionally, silk is thought to be a material that stops the "leakage" of magical energy. In any event, it's good to treat with respect and care items that we have set aside for magical use.

✦

POINTERS FOR PRACTICE

Wands are useful magical tools to focus our energy. Different woods have different traditional magical associations. Choose one that is right for your purpose. Making your own wands for ritual gives you an opportunity to learn to identify trees, relate to the countryside, and work with your hands. When we make a wand, we put something of ourselves and our creativity into it. It will be a more powerful focus for your magical energies than would a shop-bought product mass-produced by others. When you take wood, thank the tree for its gift. It is a way of reminding ourselves of trees' contribution to our biosphere by creating oxygen to ensure our survival.

CHAPTER TWELVE

Circle of Consecration

When you make a wand, it is traditional to do a ritual to consecrate it. To consecrate something is, from its very beginning, to dedicate it to a magical purpose and to use it for nothing else. This is done within a consecrated magical circle. Why do we create circle rituals? When we do magic, creating a ritual is a way of enhancing our concentration and focusing our energies on our magical intention. We can bless a candle for, say, a healing intention, but the effect of surrounding this with ritual is to strengthen what we do. We can create a circle to perform a specific magical act—to consecrate a candle to give to someone who is in need of a job or a change or fortune. It might be to consecrate a talisman—a magical object imbued with a specific magical intention. I will tell you more about these later. You might want to perform healing on someone within a circle to calm them if he or she is under great stress. For an important divination, you might want to create a circle as a place of calm and peace where you can be free of outside distractions. You might want simply to commune with Nature, to feel the power of the elements, to be revivified, entranced, energized.

Words are said, actions performed, certain implements used, and the space is transformed for a period from simple everyday reality to something that is "between the worlds."

Literally, of course, you are still in your living room, bedroom, the woods, or wherever. You are not somewhere in hyperspace. Psychologically, you make a shift. You create a microcosm, a miniature universe, in which different laws of time and space preside. To make magic, we enter a magical realm, create change, and step out of that magical realm again. Symbolically, the magic circle is a darkened pool, a womb, a place of incubation, the hermit's cavern of our spiritual journey. We come to the candlelit rite and if we take time to rest there, to be still within the sacred circle, we make space in our psyches for dream and vision to come.

Crystals and wood, gifts of earth; they are solid, tangible, yet their mystery takes us into other states of consciousness—from the solid to the ethereal, from present to past and future. Magicians seek the immanent energy of the Divine in Nature and are reborn into the otherworld of dreams that become truth; out of wood and tree and stone and leaf. The mediating space is the circle, the place of consecration.

Magic is often called the magical art, but magic is more than art. If you have watched performance art, dance, or live music, there can come a point when it is reaching transcendence. It touches something beyond itself, a deeper or higher part of our psyches. Ritual takes this experience one step further. It links us to the transcendent and immanent, that which lies beyond the everyday world that we see with our senses, and helps us to manifest the energies that we have created.

The magic circle is the place of transformation, the cauldron of change. We consecrate magical tools such as wands by blessing them with the four elements. The elements are the energies that are brought together to act as catalysts to precipitate change. The four elements are the way in which the ancient Greeks classified energy, probably deriving their ideas from ancient India. Air is energy in its least substantial and most mobile form. We can become aware of it through smells it carries or, in the form of wind, we can feel it, hear it, and see its effect on the world around us, but we cannot see air itself. Fire is more substantial; we can see it and feel its heat. Water is more solid. It takes on shape, molded by solid objects around it, and it can be tasted and touched. When it moves, it makes sound. Earth is solid matter, molecules adhering to one another to form semi-permanent shapes.

The elements are a basic structure that underlie the language of natural magic. Stones, planets, woods, zodiac signs can all be assigned to one of the four elements. Each quarter of the circle is dedicated to one of the four elements. At the center is the fifth element, the mysterious element of spirit. Spirit is shorthand for the nonmaterial realm, the realm of the gods, of nature spirits, of the Divine undying center of our being that in Indian tradition is called atman and, in the West, the self. Traditionally, the magical altar, the magician's laboratory bench or workstation, is placed at the center of the circle and is associated with the element of spirit. Symbolically, the magic circle shows that the creative force, which some might call Goddess or God, is at the center of material creation. If we contact that center, we change matter.

The best way of learning how to do ritual is to participate in ritual with other, more experienced people, observing what they do. The second Wiccan group that I joined was a long-established group of older people who had practiced Wicca for many decades. They gave no formal training, but I learned by watching and absorbing what they did. Not all of us want to do ritual with others, and it is perfectly possible to teach ourselves and to learn from books such as this.

To help, I will describe how I consecrated the hazel wand that I cut recently in January. I waited until the following October to perform the consecration. I was waiting for the time to feel right—and there is no need to rush in magic. One autumn day I felt, "This is the time," and this is what I did.

☽

CONSECRATING MY WAND

It is October and unseasonably warm. The leaves are still green, and butterflies flit between flowers. The weather pattern is altering. Starlings have laid a second clutch of eggs, confused by the late Sun into thinking it is spring. They have chosen to lay them in the roof, above our bed. Unlike the sparrows who preceded them, they are noisy sleepers. Chirpings, scratching, and the occasional sound of bird shit dropping incorporate themselves into our dreams. Wildlife is great, but not indoors. Once the young have flown, we will block up their entry point. Warm days and cloudless skies make for cold nights. Stars come out. The full Moon is in the fire sign of Aries, good symbolism for consecrating a wand, a channel for energy and will, associated magically with the element of fire. I lay a log fire in the granite hearth. We have other rooms we use for magical workings, but the thought of an open fire is inviting. I light the fire with a wax taper. The wood crackles slowly at first, then the kindling takes, then the first of the thicker sticks. The wood is from our land. Uprooted gorse bushes that we are trying to clear—gorse and broom grow like weeds here; a poplar tree blown down in a freak January storm—another effect of global warming; elm that has succumbed to Dutch Elm disease; a pine that has grown too near the house for the foundation's safety.

I set up an altar in the middle of the living room. The black coffee table on the black carpet serves well, but for the consecration of the wand, I cover it with a red cloth to emphasize the wand's connection with fire and add a red candle. I put a censer on the altar, and a fiery incense. Symbols of water and earth for the altar—water in a red glass bowl, earth dug up from the garden placed in an earthenware bowl, a chalice, and some plain Breton cake. I fill the chalice with Bordeaux Supérieur Appellation Controllé, mise en bouteille au château. Natural magic in France has advantages. I put the newly made wand on the altar, ready for consecration. I place four candles around the edge of the room, one in each of the four cardinal directions—east, south, west, north. East is associated with the element of air, south with fire, west with water, north with earth. I want to invoke the fiery aspect of each element. What would be fiery aspects of air, fire, water, and earth? I choose a yellow candle for the east, yellow for lightning; scarlet for the south, the fiery heart of the Sun; white for the west, steam; deep red for the north, molten lava.

My toes luxuriate in the thick black pile of the Chinese rug. Outdoor rituals in our stone circle in the garden are wonderfully magical, but not much fun mid-October. I go to the kitchen and turn down the oven. It is best not to eat before ritual. A full stomach is not conducive to psychic vision. Afterward, though, it is good. Eating earths us and brings the blood back to the stomach, away from the head-in-the-clouds world of ritual.

Time to begin. I switch off the electric lights, take a taper, light it from the fire, then light the candles from east to south to west to north, clockwise, and then the centered altar candle. I light charcoal by heating it on the grate. I wait until it glows red then extricate it and place it in the censer. I place incense grains to melt on the charcoal, releasing white perfumed smoke. Frankincense from the East mingles with burning pine resin and burning gorse wood from the fire. The smoke swirls up, aromatic, intoxicating. Outside in Nature, the elements are present around us. For an indoor magical circle, we rely heavily on symbolic representations. We build up through color, sound, symbol, and smell, a series of associations that trigger a change of consciousness that takes us for a while through the gates between the worlds.

I open my chakras and energize my hands. I bless salt and sprinkle it into the bowl of water to purify the water. By the usual synchronicity, the music playing in the background—Alain Stivell's Breton music *Renaissance of the Celtic Harp*—turns to the sound of waves, washing the coasts of Brittany's coastline, the *Armor,* the Land by the Sea. I sprinkle salt in the water. Salt is a natural sterilizing substance that symbolically cleanses and purifies the water. The music brings more sound of salty sea. I sprinkle the ritual space with the consecrated water then perfume the space with incense smoke.

Around the perimeter of the room, I draw a circle with my hand, separating a microcosmic world from the outer world. The circle is hallowed, made holy, set apart. The atmosphere changes, a subtle shift, as though the space around me is sparkling, energized. I face the first of the four directions—east, the direction of air. I fill my vision with airy images and air in different forms. I breathe regularly, deeply, breathing in the element of air, allowing it to enter the deepest recesses of my being, cleansing, clearing. I say what comes into my mind—an invocation that speaks aloud what I see.

I invoke air;
air of air, fire of air,
water of air, Earth of air;
sky, warm wind, mist, a sand storm—
blue, violet, white, yellow,
oxygen and hydrogen, spirit of air, source of life.
Eagle of the east, king of birds, come to me.

The incense flares up and the smoke billows eastward in response. I greet the east, "Hail and welcome," and turn to the south. Fiery images fill my vision.

I invoke fire;
air of fire, fire of fire,
water of fire, earth of fire;
spark, flame, hot springs, the Sun—
orange, red, white hot, gold,
and light, spirit of fire, that which brings life to the sleeping
land.
Enter my life, fill my psyche, grant me courage,
make my body strong,
spirit of fire be with me, in all that I do.
White mare of the south, magical horse of the Goddess, come
to me.

I wait until I sense a change in the atmosphere, "Hail and welcome."
I turn to the west. Listening to Alain Stivell's harping, I close my eyes
and imagine myself standing on a spray-splashed cliff top, looking
out to sea.

> I invoke water;
> air of water, fire of water,
> water of water, earth of water;
> cloud, steam, freshwater lake, salty sea—
> white, blue, blue green, green;
> shoals of silver fish, spirit of water.
> Silver salmon of knowledge, come to me.

I greet the west, "Hail and welcome," and turn to the north. I bring
to mind the smell of earth, newly dug, of the forest floor, of rich
earth in my hands.

> I invoke earth;
> air of earth, fire of earth,
> water of earth, earth of earth;
> dust, volcanic larva, mud, stone, rock and mountain—
> yellow sand, red molten lava, gray mud, brown soil;
> living garment of green vegetation, spirit of earth.
> Black bull of the north, come to me.
> Hail and welcome.

I return to the altar, take the wand, and pass it through the symbols
of the elements. I pass the wand through the incense smoke. "I consecrate you with air." Passing the wand swiftly through the candle
flame, "I consecrate you with fire." I sprinkle the wand with consecrated water. "I consecrate you with water." I press the wand against
a bowl of dark rich earth. "I consecrate you with earth." I take the
wand and present it to the four directions, then ask for a blessing for

the wand. I draw in the air a fire-invoking pentagram. A wand is associated in magic with the element of fire.

> By the power of fire,
> this wand inspire,
> so mote it be.

It's true: magicians have a weakness for rhyming doggerel. I open the window to look at the Moon, flooding the room with silver-blue light. It is almost bright enough to read. The Moon is white, proud, serene, floating on deep blue sky strewn with stars and an occasional passing cloud. I take the chalice. It is glass, painted with an image of Herne, the stag god of Britain, sent by post by a witch friend in Australia, miraculously without breaking. I hold up the chalice of wine, reflecting the silver disc of the Moon on its dark surface. This is the ancient art of drawing down the Moon—drawing down the silver light that energizes our psyches and increases our psychic powers. I ask a blessing on the wine from the Goddess and then drink of the dark liquid and the shimmering image. I close the window again and bless the Breton cake by energizing it with my hands. I ask a blessing of the Lady of the Earth, the goddess of fertility who brings life-giving food. The cake is hand baked at our local boulangerie and made with flour from the local mill five miles away. It is good to eat of the land when we celebrate our magical rites.

I sit for a while, sipping the wine, eating the cake, visualizing my fire pentacle. Then, remembering the First Law of Magic, I take the wand and draw over the pentagram of fire in the reverse order of invoking, "sucking back" the energy. I wrap the wand in black silk. Now the wand must be kept apart, used only in a magic circle. By consecrating something, we make it sacred and must treat it with respect. Silk is a traditional material for wrapping magical objects. It was once the most expensive material of all, an appropriate one to show that we are treating something as special, sacred, or magical. I bid farewell to the four directions, asking their powers to go, returning with my thanks to their airy, fiery, watery, and earthy realms. I tidy up, putting a morsel of cake and some drops of wine on the fire as libation. I throw the charcoal and incense into the fire. The consecrated water I pour outside on the land, giving it back to the earth. I extinguish the candles, snuffing them. The living room returns to normal.

☽

Consecrating Your Wand

You can create a similar rite to mine to consecrate your wand. Prepare an altar with incense, candles, water, salt, a bowl of earth if you are indoors, and the wand. You may wish to have an altar cloth, a deity statue, flowers, stones, and other items beautiful and precious to you to decorate your altar. If you would like to bless wine and cakes, you will need utensils for these. You may like to make your own fire incense, so here is a recipe.

Fire Incense*

- 2 teaspoons pine resin
- 1 teaspoon frankincense
- ½ teaspoon dragon's blood (see page 174)
- 3 drops juniper oil
- 2 drops cassia oil

Grind the pine resin and frankincense finely, stir in the dragon's blood, then add oils. Mix thoroughly.

*Recipe by Paul Kingsland

Consecration Rite

Center yourself to create an inner stillness—the right conditions for consciousness change. Opening the chakras is a good way of doing this; or, if your ritual is outside, you can just sit quietly for a while, listening to the sounds of nature.

Once you feel centered you are ready to begin. You might want to say something to state your purpose. You could say simply: I open this rite to consecrate and bless my magical wand.

Prepare your magical space. First, consecrate water. Channel power from your solar plexus chakra into your hands and place the tips of your fingers in the water, while visualizing power pouring from you into the water and filling it with magical energy. Draw more energy to flow down your hands into the salt, then sprinkle some salt in the water.

Take the water bowl around the edge of the circle, sprinkling the water on the ground to purify the ritual space. Start at the north and walk deosil (clockwise) around the circle until you come back to your starting point. Next, take your censer of incense and carry it around the perimeter of your sacred space, censing it with the sweet smoke. Start in the north and make your way back to north again.

Your ritual space is cleansed, purified. Now you must create a boundary between the space and the outside world. Go to the north of your circle. Draw energy into your base of spine chakra to replenish yourself. Channel energy into your preferred hand. You may find that even though you are right-handed, it feels appropriate to draw the circle with your left hand, the hand that is controlled by the right brain, which thinks holistically. Hold out your arm and visualize glowing light flowing from your hand. Now walk deosil around your circle, drawing a circle of light and energy around the edge of your ritual space. As you draw your circle, you could affirm your magical intention by saying something like:

I draw with my will the circle round,
to consecrate and bless my magical wand.
May the powers of the elements make sacred this space
and may it be blessed by the gods.

Next, call upon the elemental energies at the four quarters to guard
your rite. Before calling upon the quarters, you need to visualize a
scene appropriate to the element. Go to the east of the circle. Stand
facing outward. Visualize yourself in a high place looking into clear
blue sky, the wind blowing on your face. If you wish, imagine a gust
of wind lifting you up so you float on the wind. See, feel, and hear
the presence of the element of air, and then, when you are ready, say
an invocation similar to the one I created for my rite, but using your
own imagery and words. Once you sense the presence of the elemental forces, you may wish to say: "Welcome!" If you have made a
silver branch, you could welcome each element with three shakes of
the silver branch.

Walk deosil around the circle to the south. Stand facing outward.
Visualize a blazing Sun that grows larger and larger until it fills all
your vision. Feel its heat and flames that warm but do not burn. See
the flames and feel the heat of the element of fire, and when you are
ready say an invocation to fire. Once you sense the presence of the
elemental forces, you could bid them: "Welcome!"

Walk deosil around the circle to the west. Stand facing outward.
Visualize a blue-green sea. Waves crash against the shore, splashing
over you. Taste and smell the salt spray as it touches your lips. Invoke the west and welcome the Powers of Water.

Walk deosil around the circle to the north. Stand facing outward.
Visualize a standing stone within a clearing in an ancient forest. Feel
the rough, lichen-covered stone. Smell the musty, damp, rich smell of
earth. Invoke the north and the Powers of Earth and welcome them.

Take your wand and consecrate it by passing it through the four
elements. Pass it through the incense smoke, quickly through a candle

flame (if you do it quickly enough, the flame will not mark it), and finally sprinkle it with the consecrated water and lay it against the earth in your bowl, or the Earth itself, if you are outside. Say what it is that you wish from your wand. You could say something like:

> May my will be made stronger by you,
> my intentions made clearer,
> focus and direct my energies according to the will of the gods.
> So mote it be.

You may wish to offer your wand as a tool for the creative energy of your favorite deity or deities at this point and ask for his or her blessing.

Now energize your hands again and take the wand in both hands. Channel energy down the wand, uniting it with your current, your energy and power. You are imbuing it with your being, putting your imprint upon it, your sweat and will. Visualize energy glowing at the tip of the wand like a small flame. The wand becomes a torch. Now, using one or both hands, as you prefer, draw an invoking pentagram of fire in the air with the wand.

FIRE-INVOKING PENTAGRAM

Start at the apex and draw a line to the bottommost tip on the right-hand side, across the diagonal to the central left, across the center, down the diagonal to the bottom left, up to the apex, and then back once more to the bottom right point of the pentacle, associated in magical tradition with the element of fire. As you draw the pentagram in the air, visualize a flaming pentagram traced by the wand.

When you have finished, bless the cakes and wine, save some for libation, and consume the rest. Take your wand and draw over the pentagram of fire in the reverse order of invoking, "sucking back" the energy into the wand. When you are not using your wand, keep it wrapped in the piece of silk.

Then bid farewell to the quarters. We must remember that the elements are powerful forces. Whether we think of them as natural forces or as energy within the human psyche, it is important that you do not have an excess of this energy wandering around in your home.

Go to each of the quarters as before, starting in the east and finishing in the north. Face outward and address each quarter in turn, thanking the powers of air, fire, water, and earth for their presence. You could say something like:

> Powers of the East (South, West, North),
> Powers of Air (Fire, Water, Earth),
> thank you for attending my rite
> and granting me your energy and aid.

You might also like to thank the gods for their blessing and aid. A final stage is to close down your energy centers, the chakras. Within the circle, you want to be as open as possible to the energies you have raised. Outside the circle, you want to have control over what impinges on your psychic space.

To complete the process, take a little of your wine or other drink and cake or bread and pour it onto the earth as a libation. Also, pour your consecrated water onto the earth. You might like to say a few words of thanks as you return your offerings to the earth. Alternatively, if you have an open fire, you could give your offerings to the element of fire. If you do not have immediate access to outside space, keep a bowl of earth for this purpose. You can put the earth in a garden, yard, park or the countryside when you have the opportunity.

By returning a little of her gifts, we are acknowledging the Earth, the source of our being and that which gives us life. We pour consecrated water onto the earth rather than down the sink because it is important when we have set something aside for a special purpose to treat it with respect. This reminds us that magic touches on the sacred and holy. Symbolic actions like these are ways of reminding our unconscious psyches of important messages.

POINTERS FOR PRACTICE

Now that you have consecrated your wand, you can use a similar ritual format whenever you wish to create a circle. You can use your wand where before you used your hand to energize water and salt, and to draw the circle. You can create a circle for a specific magical intention, or simply to commune with Nature and the Divine. Use colors, sounds, symbols, and smells in your circle to create associations that trigger a change of consciousness. Keep special items such as wands wrapped in silk when not in use. Bless food and drink when you have done your magic to "earth" you. Return a little to the Earth to thank her for her gifts. Close down your chakras and bid farewell to elemental energies when you finish your rite, so you leave centered and balanced.

CHAPTER THIRTEEN

Powers of the Heavens

Seven wandering stars are there which move in spheres before Olympus' gate . . . To these stars the human race is committed: we have within us Mene (Moon), Zeus (Jupiter), Ares (Mars), Paphie (Venus), Kronos (Saturn), Helios (Sun), Hermes (Mercury). By this means are we destined to draw from the living aether of the Kosmos our tears, mirth, anger, our parenthood, our converse, our sleep and every desire.

EXCERPT 29, "ISIS TO HORUS," *WORKS OF HERMES TRISMEGISTUS*, GRAECO-EGYPTIAN, C. THIRD CENTURY

Much of natural magic involves using the mind, but equally important are the properties of natural things. Natural magic is the parent of natural science. Magic suggests ways of looking at things. Some of these are rejected as heretical and then later incorporated into mainstream thought. The borders of what is science and what is magic fluctuate. For thousands of years, the Moon, planets, and stars were considered major influences on life on Earth and on our individual lives. The heavens fascinated our ancestors from earliest times. In a world without electric light or atmospheric pollution, the stars were much clearer than in an urban environment today. When you go outside into the countryside at night, you notice the difference. If you go to the far north or elsewhere far away from civilization, the beauty of the stars in a clear sky is astounding. We are still fascinated by stellar phenomena. Millions of people watch when a comet approaches, when we have a solar eclipse, or if Mars or other planets are unusually bright. We sense that these events are not only beautiful but that somehow they have meaning.

Moon

One of the most beautiful aspects of our night sky is the Moon. Much of traditional magic takes place by the light of the Moon. In the night world we are closer to the unconscious, the hidden, that which has yet to be made manifest, that which is suppressed and as yet unrealized. Past, present, and future are simultaneously one in the realm of the unconscious. Night is when this world and the other world can meet. Moonlight is evocative. It inspires us to poetry, to go out and look at the night sky, and to marvel at the galaxies we see spread out before us. Images associated with the Moon are seas, tides, currents, women, menstruation, and the womb. The zodiac sign ruled by the Moon is Cancer, a sign associated with water and the sea. This is not just poetic metaphor. When the ancients created their astrological correspondences, they based them on what they observed, and they observed the Moon's power over liquids. The Moon affects ocean tides. We have high tides at the dark of the Moon and the full Moon, when Sun and Moon exert their strongest gravitational pull. Low or neap tides occur at first and last quarters, the waxing and the waning Moons. About 10 percent more rain and the heaviest rain occur in the days following the new Moon and the full Moon. Tropical storms are more likely to develop into hurricanes just after the new and full Moons. As I write this, with the full Moon in Leo, a 146 mph wind tears across Scotland.

An ancient idea is that the Moon affects plant growth by pulling moisture closer to the surface as the Moon waxes to full, and drawing the roots downward during the waning phase. The Roman writer Pliny, with characteristic Roman good business sense, recommended that farmers pick fruit for market just before the full Moon because it would contain more water and weigh more, but to pick fruit for their own stores at the new Moon because it would last better. Crops that grow above ground were planted during the waxing Moon and those that grow below ground—bulbs and root crops—during the waning Moon. The waning Moon is the time to transplant and to prune, with the last quarter being best for harvesting. All over the world and throughout history, lunar rhythms are systematically mentioned as influencing the growth, structures, characteristics, or properties of plants, and affecting their water content. This traditional knowledge was believed implicitly for centuries, scoffed at by nineteenth-century Western scientists, and then rehabilitated in the second half of the twentieth century. Not all traditional lore has been supported by research, but there is increasing evidence for the importance of the full Moon. In 1998, Professor Ernst Zürcher of the Department of Forest and Wood Sciences at the Swiss Federal Institute of Technology in Zürich reported on research carried out in Rwanda on the effect of lunar phases on the planting and harvesting of four different types of tree.* Sowing was carried out in all months of a year, two days before new Moon and again two days before full Moon. For all four tree types, seeds germinated much more quickly if they were planted just before full Moon than around new Moon. This effect was even more noticeable during the dry season, when water was scarce. This replicated results by Kolisko, in the 1920s and 1930s, who worked and who tested cereals, vegetables, herbs, and flowers. This and similar research on vegetable crops in Europe leads Professor Zürcher to conclude that the

*E. Zürcher (1998), "Chronobiology of Trees: Synthesis of traditional phytopractices and scientific research, as a tool of future forestry," paper presented at the *Third IUFRO Extension Working Party Symposium: Extension Forestry: Bridging the Gap Between Research and Application*, July 19–24, Blacksburg, Virginia, USA.

Moon affects growth because it affects seeds' ability to draw up water. Planting seeds just before the full Moon can give them an edge.

Magical power is also considered to be stronger on or near the full Moon. This is difficult to test empirically, but subjectively it matches the experience of those who practice magic. Magical energy is harder to generate at the dark of the Moon. The psyche feels sluggish, unwilling to cooperate. At full Moon, the psyche often feels hyperactive. Dreams are intense and it is harder to sleep. In many folk and indigenous traditions, each full Moon has its own name, derived from the agricultural and seasonal cycle. Hunger Moon and Wolf Moon are names for the full Moon in late January–February, when food was scarce and wolves would come closer to human habitation. Grass Moon was in April, when grass grows quickly, Rose Moon in June when the roses bloom, Frosty Moon in the long cold nights of November.

If you start to watch the Moon, you will notice that its color and height in the sky vary throughout the year. The August full Moon often has a glorious red glow. Harvest Moons are full and orange. Winter light gives the Moon a pearly iridescence. Often in winter, the Moon lingers all day in the sky, a pale shadow of itself against frosty blueness. In any year, one or occasionally two zodiac signs may have a second full Moon. Since the mid-twentieth century, the second full Moon has become known as a Blue Moon. In Shakespearean English, "Once in a Blue Moon" meant almost never. What we now call a Blue Moon occurs about once every two and a quarter years. Two Blue Moons in a year are more rare, occurring only around four times a century. The next double Blue Moons will be in 2018 and 2037. In some magical traditions, the second new Moon in a zodiac sign is considered special. These "extra Moons" are "bonus times," additional opportunities for magical working and are therefore lucky and powerful.

If you become used to working magical rituals on the full Moon, you will notice differences in energy at different times of the year. Is this due to how you are feeling at the time? Or do different full

Moons have different energies, perhaps due to either seasonal changes or the zodiac signs they occupy? You will have to decide. It is important in magic to observe things for yourself. Don't just accept old lore because it is traditional. Some traditional astrology, for instance, will tell you that when the Moon is in your birth sign, this is a time of inner tension. Maybe some of us need waking up with a bit of tension. As someone with a very passive natal chart, I find that the period of the full Moon in my birth sign of Scorpio, which occurs in April or May when the Sun is in Taurus, is good for me. I have passed a driving test, got a Ph.D., met my husband, and started a number of new jobs around the full Moon in Scorpio. The Moon is traditionally in astrology concerned with our image and self-expression, and for me, the full Moon in my birth sign is a good time to put myself forward and "shine."

Astrology

Thinking for yourself is important when it comes to astrology. One of the major ways in which people become aware of natural magic is through newspaper and magazine astrology columns. How many of us can resist a quick peek at the predictions for our star sign while filling in time in the hairdressers? Research on planetary relationships and weather patterns lends some support to the importance placed in traditional astrology on planetary configurations; so too does other research. The most famous and widely cited studies are those carried out by Michel Gauquelin, a French statistician, and his

NOTE: *Dates for zodiac signs are usual dates. Leap years mean that zodiac signs can start a day earlier or later than normal. If you are born at the beginning or end of a zodiac sign, you need to check the data for your year of birth to know which zodiac sign you are.

NAMES FOR FULL MOONS

Name of Moons	Alternative Names	Dates	Zodiac Sign	Full Moon In
Moon after Yule or Old Moon	Ice Moon, Wolf Moon	Dec 22–Jan 19	Capricorn	Cancer
Wolf Moon	Snow Moon, Hunger Moon	Jan 20–Feb 18	Aquarius	Leo
Lenten Moon	Sap Moon, Crow Moon, Worm Moon	Feb 19– March 20	Pisces	Virgo
Egg Moon	Grass Moon, Pink Moon	March 21– April 19	Aries	Libra
Milk Moon	Planting Moon, Flower Moon	April 20–May 20	Taurus	Scorpio
Flower Moon	Rose Moon, Strawberry Moon	May 21–June 20	Gemini	Sagittarius
Hay Moon	Thunder Moon, Buck Moon	June 21–July 22	Cancer	Capricorn
Grain Moon	Green Corn Moon, Sturgeon Moon	July 23– August 22	Leo	Aquarius
Fruit Moon	Harvest Moon	August 23– Sept 22	Virgo	Pisces
Harvest Moon	Hunter's Moon	Sept 23–Oct 22	Libra	Aries
Hunter's Moon	Frosty Moon, Tree Moon, Beaver Moon	Oct 23–Nov 21	Scorpio	Taurus
Moon before Yule	Long night Moon, Cold Moon	Nov 22–Dec 21	Sagittarius	Gemini
	Blue Moon		Second full Moon in a zodiac sign	

wife Françoise. The Gauquelins spent forty years conducting statistical analyses of the birth charts of twenty thousand people, examining correlations between planetary positions at birth and people's jobs, personalities, and hereditary traits. For people who were outstanding in their professions, they found significant relationships between their future occupations and the position of the planets when they were born. Outstanding sports champions are more likely to be born when the planet Mars is either rising (near the eastern horizon) or directly overhead. Jupiter was similarly prominent for actors and journalists, Saturn for scientists, and the Moon for writers. Both Mars and Saturn were prominent for famous doctors, and the doctors were much less likely than other people to have the planet Jupiter in prominent positions.* The Gauquelins also found correlations between specific character profiles and the positions of the Moon, Venus, Mars, Jupiter, and Saturn. Scientists in Belgium, the United States, and France carried out independent studies to debunk the Gauquelins' "Mars effect" for sports champions, only to find that their results confirmed the Gauquelins' findings.

More recently, research by Dr. Percy Seymour, astronomer at the University of Plymouth and director of the university's planetarium, leads him to conclude that astrology is neither mystical nor magical, but magnetic. It can be explained by the effect of sunspots on solar wind, which affects us via the Earth's magnetic field.† Dr. Seymour believes that infants in the womb are affected by magnetic stimuli and that the tendency to react to particular planets is hereditary. The planets do not influence personality directly, but do so via hereditary tendencies to respond to particular planetary energies.

Astrology is based on the idea of "as above, so below"; that events in the heavens trigger events on Earth. "As above so below" is the Hermetic maxim, "but after another fashion." Astrologers were delighted by the Gauquelins' endorsement of the importance of the

*Michel Gauquelin (1983), *Birthtimes*, p. 21.
†Dava Sobel (1989), "Dr Zodiac," *Omni*, December, p. 64.

planets, but the Gauquelins found no evidence that zodiac signs were predictors of people's personalities and futures. In fact, there are many reasons why traditional astrology is flawed. An important factor is the precession of the equinoxes. Our year now begins in January, but this is a relatively recent innovation. For two thousand years, the year began with the Spring Equinox, March 21, which is why Aries, which starts on March 21, is considered the first sign of the zodiac. Our zodiac is based on astronomical calculations that are now four thousand years out of date. The Earth's relationship to the twelve constellations that make up the zodiac has changed. In fact, there is no particular reason why certain sets of stars are clumped together as constellations at all. It is merely an arbitrary way of mapping the skies. We are currently in what is called the Age of Aquarius because on March 21, the astrological sign that is on the dawn horizon is no longer Aries but Aquarius. This turns all you fiery Ariens into supercool Aquarians and sinister Scorpios into vigilant Virgos.

If you are less than keen on this personality transformation, take heart. There may yet prove to be some basis for Sun-sign astrology. The sober, statistically driven, hard-headed world of insurance has done its own research. A 1995 study by the Zürich Municipal Insurance Company found that not only were Ariens (renowned for their love of fast cars and high-speed driving) involved in more accidents, they caused more expensive and serious accidents. Unfortunately, a British study produced different results. In 1996, the VELO group examined twenty-five thousand insurance claims and found that Taureans and Virgos were more likely to have accidents. Self-protective Scorpios were the safest sign of all. British Ariens are as safe as anyone else. It is difficult with such conflicting evidence to rely on Sun signs as a predictor of human behavior. Before you give up on Sun-sign astrology, on an anecdotal level, I expect many of you have the same experience as I do of a predominance of people with particular astrological characteristics in your life. There must be some explanation for my lifelong attraction to men with Mars in Aries, and the preponderance of Scorpio men in my magical group and their brilliance at magic. Or is it just that human beings are very adaptable? If we learn early on that we are proud Leos, do we begin to behave that way? Fortunately, natural magic does not work too much with the confusing world of Sun-sign astrology. Much more important for magic are the planets.

Planetary Magic

Walk into an occult or New Age shop and what do you see—crystals, incenses, aromatic oils, and candles. These are part of the paraphernalia of natural magic. Crystals relate in magic to the element of earth, incense and oils to air, and candles to fire. They can be used in ritual to enhance the atmosphere, to add to the sense that something unusual and different is happening. Their colors and smells have particular attributes. Medieval and Renaissance magicians devoted enormous energy to listing the attributes or correspondences of planets, plants, stones, animals—everything in the natural world you could think of. The planets provided the base scale, the spectrum of energies to which everything else was related. In the following chapters, you will see that planetary magic is a way of invoking the energies associated with a particular planet into your life.

Most magical practice revolves around those planets that could be observed with the human eye. Sir William Herschel did not discover Uranus until 1731. The discovery of Neptune followed in 1846, and Pluto was not discovered until 1930. These three planets have been incorporated into astrology as the rulers, respectively, of Aquarius, Pisces, and Scorpio, but they feature less than the nearer planets in magical thinking. The Sun is a star and the Moon a planetary satellite, but for magical purposes, the Sun, Moon, Earth, Mercury, Venus, Mars, and Jupiter are the "seven planets." The traditional associations with the planets derive from their appearance, the attributes of the deities whose names they bear, the pattern of their orbits, and their impact on the weather.

When we learn about magical correspondences—the attributions of what goes with what, such as hazel equating to the element of air—we are learning a new language, a picture alphabet. Do you remember learning in your childhood, "A is for apple, C is for cat?" This is a way of helping us to relate to the letters and remember them. We begin to create pathways in our neural circuits that connect one thing to another. Think about memory associations. If you think "rose," you can produce a whole string of associations with the word. These would be based on your memories and experiences, some of which will have emotional associations. For most people "rose" conjures up sweet smells, soft petals, summer gardens, maybe school holidays as a child, the garden of an elderly relative, a girl at school called Rose, maybe rosewood, rosy cheeks, rose of Sharon, and so on. One idea leads to another until you end up far from your starting point. Planetary correspondences are intricate embroidery in the psyche; a way of associating different concepts, categories, and ideas into a beautiful and harmonious whole. When we surround ourselves with a set of related symbols, they influence our unconscious minds and the way we respond to people and events. You are in effect reprogramming your psyche and filtering your perception through a particular lens. You become aware of opportunities that are associated with the energy you are seeking and open yourself to them.

The traditional correspondences are sets of associations built up from the collective experience of centuries of magical tradition. That doesn't mean that they should be followed blindly; some attributions are more useful than others. If you read a traditional book on magic, you will see that operations of Venus should be performed on the day of Venus, Friday. It can be psychologically helpful to do magical work associated with a particular planet on that planet's day. You can even, if you wish, divide each day and night into planetary hours and perform your magical workings on the day of Venus in the hour of Venus. If you think about it, though, you will realize that this is not important magically. The attribution of days of the week was altered completely in the sixteenth and seventeenth centuries when the Catholic Church adopted a new Gregorian calendar that meant moving calendars forward eleven days. Protestant countries did not embrace the new calendar immediately, which meant there was a period when it would be Wednesday January 9 in London and Sunday January 20 in Paris. As you can see, date and day allocation is purely arbitrary. They are not "real time." Animal associations with the planets derive from links with planetary deities or the behavior of the animal. The lion, with its tawny coat, love of basking in the Sun, dominance, and association with kingly imagery is attributed to the Sun. Night creatures are associated with the Moon. Owls fly at night, so they are associated with the Moon.

Sunpower

. . . if you would procure the solary vertue of any thing, this being wrapped up in bay leaves, or the skin of a Lion, hang it about thy neck with a golden thread, or a silken thread of a yallow color, whilest the Sun rules in the heaven: so thou shalt be endued with the Solary vertue of that thing.

HEINRICH CORNELIUS AGRIPPA (1651),
DE OCCULTA PHILOSOPHIA, BOOK I, PART 3

By associating a particular planet with certain colors, shapes, sounds, and smells, natural magicians build up an atmosphere that affects the unconscious mind, changing mood and behavior. This makes magic a kind of advanced mood music. By surrounding ourselves with, say, solar symbolism, we unconsciously absorb and imitate solar qualities. Other people react to us in different ways and our lives start to change. You can experiment with planetary magic by focusing on the energy of the Sun. Composed of helium and hydrogen and powered like a thermonuclear furnace, our Sun is hugely important to us and central to our existence. Without it, we die. Psychologically, it represents wealth (gold), energy, health, and the core of our being, the self, around which the rest of our psyche revolves. Magically, the Sun is associated with Sunday, solar deities, heat, warmth, and the colors gold and golden yellow. We associate these with summer, light, the times when we feel happiest and healthiest. The Sun creates a "feel good" factor. We associate the Sun's rays with physical well-being. On a sunny day, our mood is more optimistic. When we feel warm, we feel more relaxed and our muscles are less tense. We can wear fewer clothes so we feel less restricted.

@

Working With the Sun

Our unconscious minds are affected by our surroundings and by symbol and color. Supposing you wanted to bring solar influence into your life? You could start with you. Take the solar symbolism into what you wear. Buy a pendant of a solar-related jewel, such as amber or citrine. Wear a discreet gold bracelet. Try wearing a perfume that makes you think of summer sun. Bring solar symbolism into your surroundings by creating a home altar or shrine as a focus for its energy. Find a small table or shelf and cover it with a yellow or gold cloth. Place gold-colored candlesticks on it with golden candles. Add a vase of golden flowers. Burn some solar incense daily on your altar or use perfumed candles. Take a few moments each day to light your candles and/or incense and to meditate on the powerful energy of the Sun. Take the symbolism into your workplace. Your colleagues might balk at incense, but discreet touches of solar symbolism can go unnoticed. Place crystals associated with the Sun in your desk drawer, or on the desk as paperweights. Bring golden flowers to the office.

PLANETARY CORRESPONDENCES

Planet and Day	Number	Attributes	Goddesses	Gods	Color	Metals, Stones	Animal	Tree
Sun (Sunday)	6	Healing, health, wealth, success, physical energy	Sekhmet (Egyptian), Grainne (Irish)	Sol (Roman), Helios (Greek), Ra (Egyptian)	Gold, golden-yellow	Gold, topaz, citrine, amber	Lion	Rowan, mimosa
Moon (Monday)	9	Sleep, dreams, psychic powers, fertility, family harmony	Diana (Roman), Artemis (Greek), Selene (Greek), Yemaya (West Africa)	Nefertum (Egyptian), Sin (Babylonian)	Silver, violet, white	Silver, platinum, moonstone, pearl	Hare, owl, elephant, deer	Willow, euca-lyptus
Mars (Tuesday)	5	Courage, sexual vigor, physical energy, will	Athena (Greek), Sekhmet (Egyptian), Kali (Indian)	Mars (Roman), Ares (Greek), Ogun (West African)	Red	Iron, steel, ruby, bloodstone, hematite	Ram	Holly
Mercury (Wednesday)	8	Intelligence, eloquence, communication, study, self-improvement, breaking negative habits, travel	Minerva (Roman), Athena (Greek)	Mercury (Roman), Hermes (Greek), Thoth (Egyptian)	Yellow, orange	Mercury (quicksilver), fire opal, agate	Dog	Hazel

Planet and Day	Number	Attributes	Goddesses	Gods	Color	Metals, Stones	Animal	Tree
Jupiter (Thursday)	4	Positive outlook on life, business ventures, humor	Juno (Greek), Maat (Egyptian), Isis—as Queen Heaven (Egyptian), Kuan Yin (Chinese)	Jupiter (Roman), Zeus (Greek), Thor (Norse), Amoun-Ra (Egyptian), Ganesha (Indian), Brahma (Indian), Vishnu (Indian), Chango (West African)	Blue	Tin, amethyst, sapphire, lapis lazuli	Eagle, unicorn	Oak, cedar
Venus (Friday)	7	Love, joy, sensuality, sexual pleasure	Venus (Roman), Bast and Hathor (Egyptian), Aphrodite (Greek), Erzulie (West African), Lakshmi (Indian), Freya (Norse), Ishtar (Babylonian)	Cupid (Roman), Dionysos (Greek), Frey (Norse)	Emerald green	Copper, bronze, emerald, rose quartz, jade	Lynx	Apple
Saturn (Saturday)	3	Protection, longevity, long-term planning, endings	Rhea (Greek)	Saturn (Roman), Chronos (Greek)	Gray, black	Lead, jet, black onyx, obsidian, coal, slate	Goat; bat	Yew

✦

POINTERS FOR PRACTICE

Full Moon is a traditional time for doing magic and is a useful guide for gardening. Planting seeds two days before full Moon can give them an edge. There is some scientific evidence that the planets can influence our personalities, but there is less evidence for Sun-sign astrology, so don't accept traditional ideas simply because they are traditional. Check them out for yourself and see if they work for you. Planetary magic is at the heart of much traditional magic. Learn the traditional attributes of the planets as a basis for your magical practice.

CHAPTER FOURTEEN

Incenses and Oils

Oils

Our ancestors relied much more heavily than we do on their sense of smell. As hunter-gatherers, they needed to be able to follow a scent and to know which scents to avoid. A cave that smelled of tiger was not the best place for an overnight stay. Urban lifestyles have left us less aware of smell. We have become more attuned to visual stimuli, and tend to react on a conscious level to how things look—people, for instance—rather than how they smell. Unconsciously, though, the emotional and animalistic parts of our psyche react strongly to smell. Places and people smell good or bad to us and we react accordingly.

By deliberately manipulating our sense of smell, we can program the unconscious to react in certain ways. All magical and spiritual traditions use incense to stimulate the sense of smell and heighten psychic awareness. Incense is also burned as an offering to the gods. Smell stimulates memory. Photographs will bring back details of events but smells bring back the emotional tone. Burning incense is a good way to create a particular atmosphere in a room, to calm you before meditation, and as a way of stimulating your consciousness during ritual. If your magical consciousness has not developed as far as helping you kick the nicotine habit, incense can disguise your cigarette smell.

Most incenses and essential oils are made from plant products. In the magical tradition, the differing ingredients are associated with particular planets or elements. Planetary associations derive from smell and taste. Sweet-smelling substances, for instance, are associated with Venus and the Moon, unpleasant smells with the dour planet Saturn, and spicy and fiery tastes and smells with the element of fire and the planet Mars. Other associations derive from the shape of the plant, the color of its leaves, flowers, or fruit, or from myth and legend.

ⓔ
Burning Essential Oils

We can create a particular atmosphere in a room by evaporating essential oils on an oil burner. Put water in the bowl of the oil burner and a lighted night-light underneath. Add some drops of oil to the water and the smell will spread outward. You can add essential oils to bathwater. Use only a few drops and then disperse the oil with your hand. Oils are used in massage. Thin down the essential oil with a base oil, such as olive oil. Check the instructions of the essential oil carefully. Many oils can cause negative reactions if you are pregnant or breastfeeding, and some oils are not suitable for use on the skin. Oils can be inhaled by adding a few drops to very hot water. Put a towel over your head and the bowl and breathe in the vapor. Different oils produce different psychological and emotional reactions. Have a look at the table on pages 172–178 and select an oil that has the right properties for you.

ⓔ
Burning Incense

To burn incense, you will need to buy self-igniting charcoal blocks from a church or New Age supplier. "Self-igniting" means that if you put a hot flame to the edge of the charcoal, it will begin to spark and the sparks will spread through the charcoal until the whole block is hot. You can light the charcoal with a match, lighter, or candle flame. If you own a large lighter for lighting gas cookers or camping stoves, these are even better because you can keep the flame against the charcoal longer without burning your fingers. Once the charcoal is hot, place it in a bowl or a metal censer with earth or sand lining the bottom, so it does not get too hot. Place one or two teaspoons of incense on the charcoal block. The heat from the charcoal will melt the incense, and sweet aromatic smoke will rise.

Incense Making

You can buy incense ready-made from a New Age store or a church supplier, but it is easy and fun to make yourself. It is also highly satisfying if, like me, you are not very practical. I remember vividly my first experience of incense making; not so much the visual memories, but the smells. It was at my first Wiccan training group. We gathered around a table with jars and bottles of incense ingredients—resins, barks, oils, dried seeds. We opened the jars and bottles to smell them. The smells were exotic, overwhelming, like being in an Istanbul spice bazaar. We put ingredients in our mortars and pestles and experimented, pounding the harder ingredients and softening them with sticky oils to help them burn. We were given bowls of sand with round pieces of charcoal that reminded me of Catholic Masses and shown how to light the charcoal with cigarette lighters. The charcoal edges ignited and eventually glowed red like winter coal. Sparks flew across the surface of the charcoal, igniting the rest of the block, which then crackled into life. We placed our hot charcoals in the sand bowls and carefully put teaspoons of incense on the charcoal. Smoke and heady aromas rose into the summer air. We experimented with standard recipes, modifying them to find our own unique blends. We became incense makers.

This is a craft where you can't go too wrong. To pulverize the harder ingredients, you need a mortar and pestle—the kind you find in any kitchen shop. Simply pound and mix bark, gums, resins, and other ingredients such as dried leaves; mix in oil, and abracadabra, you have incense. The trick is to mix compatible ingredients in the right proportions. Incenses made with dried leaves can be harsh on the throat, much like tobacco. Oil added to a mixture makes it burn well. Gums and oils make a "smoother" blend. You need only make small quantities; four to five teaspoons is plenty for a ritual. You can buy ingredients for incense from a health-food store, herbalist, or esoteric supplier. Look one up in your telephone book or on the Internet.* Ingredients have become easier to obtain because many are now used in complementary therapies. Make sure you are buying the right ingredients. Oils labeled "perfume oils" may be chemical substitutes designed to mimic the smell of the natural product, but

*If you cannot find a local supplier, you can obtain products by mail order. European readers can try the famous herbalists Baldwins, founded in the nineteenth century, as a starting point: 171–3 Walworth Road, London SE17 1RW, 020-7703-5550, www.baldwins.co.uk. They can supply by mail order all over the world. Reading their catalog will give you an idea of the range of products available. Readers in the United States and Canada could try Richters Herb Specialists, Goodwood, Ontario, Canada, LOC 1AO, 905-640-6677, www.richters. com. Richters is an herb farm that can supply herbs to grow, essential oils, and a newsletter about herbs. Whole Spectrum, 8702 North Mobley Road, Odessa, FL 33556, 800-822-9698, www.aromatherapyproducts.com is a division of Essential Products of America Inc. and has an extensive range of oils. Azure Green is an esoteric supplier, recommended to me by friends: PO Box 48–WEB, Middlefield, MA 01243–0048, 413-623-2155, www.azuregreen.com. They supply oils, incense ingredients, ready-made incense, and other products. Pacific Botanicals, 4350 Fish Hatchery Road, Grant's Pass, Oregon 97527, 541-479-7777, www. pacificbotanicals.com, are an herb farm that supplies herbs in bulk. Blessed Herbs, 109 Barre Plains Road, Oakham, MA 01068, 800-489-4372, www.Blessedherbs.com. Devonshire Incense, 1026 Park Road 1–C, Smithville, TX 78957, 800-568-6242, www.devonshireincense.com supplies incense and incense ingredients such as gums and resins.

INCENSE INGREDIENTS AND OILS

Common Name	Latin/Botanical Plant Name	Smell	Element and/or Planet	Magical Properties	Health and Other Properties*
Acacia gum (gum arabic)	*Acacia nilotica, Acacia Senegal*	Sweet, grassy	Sun	Soothing, calming	Use to treat diarrhea and dysentery
Aloes gum (lignum aloe, agarwood)	*Aquilaria agallocha, Aquilaria malaccensis, Aquilaria sinensis*	Sweet, woody, balsamic	Venus	Protection, consecration, purification	Stimulant, used as erotic perfume in Eastern Mediterranean
Balsam of Peru	*Myroxylon balsamum var pereirae*	Sweet, flowery, like cinnamon when fresh, like vanilla when aged, balsamic	Water, Saturn, Earth	Strength and stability, healing	Antiseptic and antibacterial, oil can be used externally to treat skin conditions including wounds, eczema, scabies, ringworm, abscesses, and boils
Balsam of Tolu	*Myroxylon toluiferum*	Sweet, smoky, warm, vanilla-like balsamic	Air, Mercury	Purification, clearing the mind	Antiseptic, expectorant, anti-inflammatory, balsamic, oil can be used to treat skin problems, including cracked skin, ringworm, and frostbite; can also be rubbed on chest to treat respiratory infections

Common Name	Latin/Botanical Plant Name	Smell	Element and/or Planet	Magical Properties	Health and Other Properties*
Benzoin	*Styrax benzoin, Lindera benzoin*	Sweet, flowery, vanilla-like	Venus	Purification, prosperity, calming	Expectorant, antifungal, fumes from benzoin oil can be inhaled to alleviate mucus in the respiratory tract, applied externally protects chapped skin
Camphor	*Cinnamomum camphora*	Pungent, sharp, cool	Moon	Health, divination, intuition	Used to balance nervous system, reduce anxiety; alleviate panic and shock, inhalation aids breathing
Cassia oil	*Cinnamomum cassia, Cinn. zeylanicum, Cinn. Burmannii Blume*	Sweet, woody, spicy, warm	Air, Mercury	Clairvoyance, healing, love	Analgesic, antiseptic, aphrodisiac, stimulant, used to reduce anger and irritability, strengthens constitution and revitalize mind; add oil to a bath for nausea, faintness, and nervousness; tea may help ease colds and flu; can be used as cinnamon substitute
Cedar oil	*Cedrus atlantica*	Sweet, woody, balsamic	Jupiter	Healing, prosperity, sanctification, money, protection	Antiseptic, soothing for skin
Cinnamon	*Cinnamomum zeylanicum*	Sweet, woody, spicy, warm	Fire, Sun	Love, energy	Traditionally used to treat diarrhea and lack of appetite; now used mainly as food additive, but has antibacterial properties

Common Name	Latin/Botanical Plant Name	Smell	Element and/or Planet	Magical Properties	Health and Other Properties*
Clove	*Syzygium aromaticum*	Sweet, fragrant, vanilla-like, hot	Fire, Jupiter	Protection, love, Money	Antiseptic, stimulant, analgesic, aphrodisiac, antifungal; helps reduce flatulence, promotes digestion, restores appetite; mixed with a base oil, clove oil can be rubbed upon sore muscles, stiff joints
Copal gum (Mexican frankincense)	*Agathis coranthifolia*	Ethereal, clean	Fire	Energy, peace, meditation	Used mainly for incense
Cypress oil	*Cupressus sempervirens*	Spicy, woody, resinous	Saturn	Calm, peace, meditation	Astringent, can be used as antiperspirant; diluted with base oil can be used to massage varicose veins
Damar gum	*Shorea javanica Dipterocarpus*	Sweet	Mercury	Healing	Resin used in perfume, food gums, transparent varnishes and lacquers
Damiana	*Turnera aphrodisiaca*	Bittersweet, grassy	Venus	Love, sensuality	Traditional aphrodisiac, diuretic; leaf infusion can be used as tonic
Dragon's blood	*Daemomorops draco*	Ethereal	Mars, Fire	Strength, potency	Formerly used for treating diarrhea and syphilis but not now considered efficacious; main use is as red pigment

Common Name	Latin/Botanical Plant Name	Smell	Element and/or Planet	Magical Properties	Health and Other Properties*
Eucalyptus oil	*Eucalyptus globules*	Sweet, woody, balsamic	Water or Fire, Moon	Healing, protection	Analgesic, antibiotic, antiseptic, anti-inflammatory, stimulant, often used as a vapor rub to relieve coughs, colds, respiratory congestion; can be used as insect repellent
Frankincense	*Boswellia carteri, Boswellia tthurifera*	Rich, sweet, woody, balsamic	Sun	Consecration, divination, healing, spiritual purification	Uplifting, can enhance mental perception and consciousness; clears respiratory congestion when inhaled
Ginger oil	*Zingiber officinale*	Spicy, warm, stimulating	Fire, Mars	Passion, energy	Stimulant, used in Chinese medicine as antidote to prevent excessive mucus
Jasmine oil	*Jasmine grandiflorum, jasmine officinalis*	Sweet, floral	Moon	Relaxation, sleep, aphrodisiac	Mainly used in perfume
Juniper berries and oil	*Juniperus communis*	Sweet, woody, resinous	Fire, Jupiter	Healing, protection	Anti-rheumatic, antiseptic, diuretic, oil is used for flatulence and indigestion; infusion of berries can treat inflammation of urinary tract; a few drops in bathwater may relieve premenstrual bloating; for aching joints, mix oil with base oil and rub on

Common Name	Latin/Botanical Plant Name	Smell	Element and/or Planet	Magical Properties	Health and Other Properties*
Lavender oil	*Lavandula vera, lav. spica, lav. angustifolium*	Sweet, flowery	Air, Mercury	Mental clarity	Antiseptic, antispasmodic, aromatic, diuretic, sedative, stimulant; rub on temples for nervous headache; can kill many common bacteria—typhoid, diphtheria, streptococcus, and pneumococcus; useful for burns, sunburn, scalds, bites, vaginal discharge, anal fissure; inhibits scar tissue
Lemon oil	*Citrus limon*	Sharp, refreshing	Sun	Longevity, purification, love, friendship	Excellent preventative medicine rich in vitamin C to help body fight off infections; antiseptic, stimulant, antibacterial; drink juice diluted with hot water for sore throats; has been used as quinine substitute for malaria and other fevers
Myrrh	*Commiphora myrha*	Rubbery	Saturn	To bring something to an end	Stimulates immune system, under investigation as potential breast cancer remedy

Common Name	Latin/Botanical Plant Name	Smell	Element and/or Planet	Magical Properties	Health and Other Properties*
Oak bark	*Quercus robur*	Woody	Earth, Jupiter	Protection, strength, power	Young bark is anti-inflammatory, antiseptic, astringent, can be used externally to bathe wounds, treat frostbite, skin eruptions, sweaty feet, piles, and as vaginal douche for genital inflammations and discharge; internally can be used for chronic diarrhea, but in excess causes vomiting
Orange oil	*Citrus aurantium sinenis*	Sweet, refreshing	Sun	Wealth, good fortune	Controls cholesterol levels; limonene in oranges may have an effect on precancerous and cancerous cells
Pine resin (colophony)	*Pinus sylvestris*	Woody, balsamic, refreshing	Earth	Prosperity	Antiseptic, antibiotic
Rose oil	*Rosa centifolia, rosa damascena*	Sweet, flowery	Venus	Harmony, peace, love	Tea can increase appetite and alleviate premenstrual tension and menopausal symptoms
Rosemary oil	*Rosimarinus officinalis*	Sweet, herby, refreshing	Sun	Aids memory	Oil alleviates rheumatism and can be used as insect repellent

Common Name	Latin/Botanical Plant Name	Smell	Element and/or Planet	Magical Properties	Health and Other Properties*
Sandalwood oil	*Santalum album*	Sweet, woody, warm	Venus	Consecration, protection against negativity	Anti-inflammatory, antiseptic, aphrodisiac, used to treat insomnia, anxiety, tension; used in Tantra to awaken kundalini
Star aniseed (Chinese anise)	*Illicium verum*	Sweet, spicy	Mercury	Clairvoyance, psychic protection	Taken internally, oil can be used to treat indigestion
Willow	*Salix alba*	Sweet, woody	Water, Moon	Divination, protection, healing	Bark source of salicylic acid (precursor to aspirin), used internally to treat dyspepsia, rheumatism, arthritis, gout, inflammatory stages of autoimmune diseases, fever, neuralgia, headache; leaves useful for nervous insomnia

*Medical treatment with herbal and plant products is an exact science. They are best used under guidance of a qualified herbal practitioner or medical doctor. You may have allergies to particular products. Even in small doses, many products can be dangerous to fetuses, babies, and infants. Do not self-treat when breast feeding or pregnant.

they do not have the same properties. Essential oils are produced from the plant by steam distillation, which involves steaming the plant material, cooling the steam, and extracting the plant oil from the water, by expressing—pressing—the oil from the plant material, or by solvent extraction. Some ingredients, such as barks, you can collect yourself from beneath trees, where you will often find fallen bark, and from branches. You only need to scrape off a small amount. Do not, whatever you do, take a strip of bark from right around the trunk of a tree. This is called "ringing" and kills the tree. Juniper bushes are often found in parks and gardens. Cinnamon and clove can be found in supermarket spice racks. Incense is best when fresh, which is another reason for making your own, but if you find you have made more than you need, you can store it in clean glass jars with tight-fitting lids. It is best kept in a dark, dry place. Store incense out of the reach of small children reach so they won't mistake it for something interesting to eat.

Incense Recipes

Here are some recipes to get you started. As you become more familiar with the ingredients and their properties, you can experiment and make blends of your own.

Sun Incense*

This Sun incense uses plant products, gums, and oils from hot, sunny countries. Frankincense is the incense of kings, and Sun imagery is associated with royalty. Oranges rely on long hot sunny days to ripen, so they are solar linked. Cinnamon has a spicy, exotic, and stimulating smell. With this incense, we are creating a cocktail of

*Recipe by Paul Greenslade

smells that have associations that put us in mind of the Sun. The associations become stronger when you start to use an incense for a particular purpose and your memory links it to particular symbols, feelings, and thoughts.

> 2 teaspoons frankincense
> 1 teaspoon crushed cinnamon stick
> 1 drop cassia oil
> 3 drops orange oil

Crush the cinnamon. Pound the frankincense into small grains and mix. Add the oils and mix.

Moon Incense*

Moon incense is good to burn before divination, before visualization, or before making inner journeys. This Moon recipe contains camphor, eucalyptus, and willow bark, all of which are associated with the Moon. Both willow and eucalyptus trees are water-loving, and magically these tend to be related to the Moon, the planet that rules the tides. Copal, although associated with fire, is a good base gum to make the incense burn well.

> 3 teaspoons copal gum
> 1 teaspoon camphor
> ½ teaspoon willow bark
> 2 drops eucalyptus oil

Pound the copal gum and camphor with mortar and pestle. Add the crushed willow bark. Add the oil and mix.

*Recipe by Paul Greenslade

Mercury Incense*

This recipe is to clear the mind, and for all Mercurial purposes. It contains star aniseed and balsam of tolu, which are associated with Mercury and air. Cloves are often associated with fire, but they add a heady warmth and stimulate the sense of smell. Damar gum adds a sweetness without being overwhelming, which makes it a good base resin. It evaporates more cleanly on charcoal than frankincense, which tends to char.

- 1 teaspoon powdered clove
- 3 teaspoons crushed star aniseed
- 2 teaspoons damar gum
- 1 teaspoon balsam of tolu

Crush the ingredients finely and mix.

Venus Incense*

This Venus recipe uses acacia, benzoin, damiana, rose, and sandalwood—sweet smells traditionally associated with Venus. Lemon, as a yellow fruit from a hot climate, is traditionally associated with the Sun, but here it is used to offset the sweetness of the other smells.

- 2 teaspoons acacia gum
- 2 teaspoons benzoin
- 1 teaspoon crushed damiana
- 3 drops rose oil
- 2 drops sandalwood oil
- 1 drop lemon oil

*Recipe by Paul Greenslade

Pound the acacia and benzoin with mortar and pestle. Blend in crushed damiana. Then add oils one by one, mixing thoroughly.

Mars Incense*

In this Mars incense, the active Mars-related ingredients are the ginger and dragon's blood. Dragon's blood is not the blood of those creatures beloved of fairy tale, although dragons as fierce fire-breathing creatures seem ideal symbols of the warlike nature of Mars. Rather, dragon's blood is the powdered resin derived from the reddish, resinous substance that covers the ripe red berries of the *daemomorops draco* tree of Sumatra and similar trees. Ginger is a hot spice that relates to the fiery nature of Mars. It is recommended in Chinese Traditional Medicine for bronchial type people to "warm" them. Copal is associated with the element of fire. Benzoin has a sweetish smell and is used to make the mixture more pleasant to burn indoors. Some Mars incenses contain ingredients such as tobacco, iron filings, and sulfur. While these are substances traditionally associated with Mars, with the possible exception for some people of tobacco, they are not the most conducive concoctions for inducing a meditative state due to their acrid smell.

2 teaspoons benzoin
3 teaspoons copal
½ teaspoon dragon's blood
6 drops ginger oil

Using a mortar and pestle, grind the benzoin and copal finely. Blend in the dragon's blood powder. Then add ginger oil. Mix thoroughly.

*Recipe by Paul Kingsland

Jupiter Incense*

This Jupiter recipe uses oak bark. The oak tree is associated in mythology with thunder gods and, as one of the largest and longest-living of European trees, it is associated with kingship and stability.

1 teaspoon balsam of Peru
1 teaspoon pine resin
1 teaspoon oak bark
½ teaspoon crushed juniper berries
3 drops cedar oil
1 drop juniper oil

Mix the pine resin, usually sold ground, with the balsam of Peru, a thick liquid. Crush oak bark into small pieces with mortar and pestle and mix in. Mix in juniper berries. Add oils one by one, mixing thoroughly.

Saturn Incense*

Myrrh is a substance used in ancient embalming, hence the ominous significance of the gift of one of the three magicians to Mary, the mother of Jesus. This could be seen as emphasizing Saturn's sorrowful side but, more positively, it reflects Saturn's focus on long-term concerns. The cypress tree takes its name from Cyparissus, a figure in Greek mythology who could not be consoled after accidentally killing his favorite stag. The god Apollo allowed him to grieve forever and turned him into the cypress tree. Cypress is often sown near graveyards and is linked to Saturn's connection with melancholy and death. Cypress wood is very durable and was used by Ancient Egyp-

*Recipe by Paul Greenslade

tians for sarcophagi. The other ingredients are all associated traditionally with the planet Saturn, except for the cassia oil and aloes
gum, which "lighten" the mix. Aloes gum has Venusian associations.
It has been used as an erotic perfume for millennia, but in Far Eastern
medicine it is used in disease control, a more Saturnine activity. Cassia has Mercurial associations.

1 teaspoon aloes gum
2 teaspoons myrrh
½ teaspoon balsam of Peru
1 drop cypress oil
1 drop cassia oil

Crush the solid ingredients. Add the oils and mix.

Experimenting

You can experiment with making your own blends for particular
magical purposes. Suppose you wanted to do a prosperity ritual
with the idea that a business venture you are involved in would pros-
per and grow? The Sun and Jupiter might be good influences—Sun
for wealth and Jupiter for increase and growth. You would need to
balance oils and gums with other substances. If you look at the table
on pages 172–78, you might start to think about experimenting
with cedar, juniper, and oak, which are Jupiter-related. You would
also need some gums to give the mixture the right balance. Some
Sun-related gums are frankincense, which makes a beautiful base
smell for any incense; acacia; and benzoin. Experiment with the
right combinations, blending until you hit on something that seems
right to you. Remember, everyone's sense of smell is different—
hence the thousands of different perfumes for sale.

When you prepare your own ingredients for natural magic—
perhaps some obtained easily through an Internet order, others

gathered from a walk in the woods or from your own or your friends' gardens, other ingredients bought off a supermarket shelf— you are preparing not only the incense but your own psyche. You are opening yourself to the possibility of something magical happening. This is what natural magic is about. We create the right external environment to precipitate an inner shift, an inner change of consciousness. Inner change alters the way other people react to us, and this precipitates outer change. By synchronicity, the unexpected happens. It is just a matter of place, time, intention, and traveling hopefully.

★

POINTERS FOR PRACTICE

Planetary magic invokes the energies associated with a particular planet into your life. We associate a particular planet with certain qualities, colors, shapes, sounds, and smells to create an external environment that precipitates an inner change of consciousness. Inner change in turn precipitates outer change. Burning planetary incense can create a particular atmosphere in a room, calm you before meditation, or stimulate your psyche during ritual. Incense is easy and fun to make yourself, and is a craft where you can't go too wrong.

CHAPTER FIFTEEN

Sex and Love

> *To make a girl dance in the nude, write on virgin parchment the*
> *Character of Frutimière with the blood of a bat. Then put it on a*
> *blessed stone, over which a Mass has been said. After this when*
> *you want to use it, place the character under the sill or thresh-*
> *old of a door which she must pass.*
>
> THE GRIMORIUM VERUM

*A*ncient grimoires are full of spells that meet human weaknesses and needs. It seems that medieval priests were in urgent need of naked dancing girls and not at all bat-friendly. Another spell is to make three girls or three gentlemen appear in your room after supper. Unlike most of the spells, this one is for female magicians too. Not suffering from sexual frustration, I eschew the three gentlemen as a bit excessive, but it raises the question—how does magic view sex?

Venus

Sex and love in magical tradition is the province of the planet Venus. Venus is the "second rock from the Sun," the nearest planet to Earth. It appears at evening as the evening star and at dawn as the morning star, a bright shining star near the horizon. These beautiful stars capture human poetic imagination and seem somehow special, inspirational. Venus's brightness derives from its nearness but it is also a planet of intense heat with temperatures rising to 900°F. Like Earth, Venus may once have had large amounts of water, but it boiled away. The ancients may have sensed Venus's hotness, for Venus is a planet related in the magical tradition to the element of fire and the fires of sexual passion. Venus's fieriness is not wild and uncontrolled, but like the warmth of a summer's day. It is the feeling we have after a long lazy summer afternoon when heat has relaxed our muscles, our sensuality is aroused, stimulated by the Sun's effect on our pituitary glands; when we feel in harmony with the physical and animal aspects of ourselves.

The mythology of Venus is that she is the Roman goddess of love and sexual desire. Jupiter decreed that her husband should be the ugly smith god Vulcan, but he was not to her taste and she took what lovers she pleased, including the god most associated with male sexual virility—Mars. Venus and Mars's son Cupid is a god of love, depicted as a child with wings and a bow and arrow that could strike unsuspecting humans with passion's dart. Her day is Friday, which derives from the name of the goddess Freya, Venus's Norse equivalent. Venus's color is green, the color of growth and fertility. In Roman mythology, she was Lady of the gardens and vineyards, nature in cultivation. In medieval songs and in the Song of Songs in the Bible, to enter into a lady's garden is a metaphor for sex, an entry to the Garden of Delights.

@

Bringing Love into Your Life

If you want to bring love into your life, enhance your Venusian qualities. Start with your environment, your home. Our homes are like extensions of ourselves. They reflect our tastes, interests, and personalities. They also act as a mirror and reflect back to us what we think about ourselves. If we surround ourselves with drabness, we will think of ourselves as drab people and others will see us that way too. If we surround ourselves with beauty, then we will think better of ourselves. Are there ways you could bring more beauty into your home? This need not mean spending vast amounts of money on an interior designer's makeover. Plants, flowers, and burning incense or aromatic oils are inexpensive ways of making your home more beautiful. What about sound? What music do you find beautiful, and do you take enough time to listen and enjoy it? Play music more and watch the television less.

What about you? Look at what you wear and the colors that you wear. Do you wear color or are you colorless? Is your closet full of browns and grays? If you suffer from depression, do not wear depressing colors like brown or gray and avoid black. Do you know what colors suit you? Have you ever had a color consultation? Many people go through life wearing colors that do not enhance their skin tone. Color is not just for women. Male politicians and media personalities go to great lengths to use color to enhance their appearance and image. If you do not know your own personal color palette, consider going for a session with a color consultant. You can find addresses in lifestyle magazines and periodically department stores offer consultations as well. The cost of the consultation is more than offset by the amount of time it saves when it comes to choosing clothes.

Accepting Sensuality

In pre-Christian and magical tradition, Venus is a goddess, a deity to be worshipped. This indicates the magical traditions' attitude to sexual love. Magical teaching is that sex is a good thing. Past generations were in recovery from sexual repression and religious conditioning that taught them that sex was a morally dubious activity. If you were gay, it was a definite no-no. If monogamous marriage without birth control didn't appeal to you, you were on the road to hell. Today, you may be in recovery from your parents' sexual excesses. If your parents' sexual shenanigans led them to abandon their families, constantly change partners, and have children they could not afford, then celibacy may seem an attractive option. In the age of HIV, we cannot return to a Garden of Eden of sexual freedom and abandon. Sexuality needs to be enjoyed with responsible awareness, but sexuality is still one of the great pleasures and joys of human existence. Responsible sex means, of course, sex where the participants are fully consenting adults, don't cause unintended pregnancy, and don't give each other diseases. Irresponsible sex is an abuse of oneself and other people. Magic is about taking responsibility and taking control of one's life. When we take responsibility for what we do, we can enjoy the body better.

@

Creating a Romantic Atmosphere

Your sex life will be enhanced if you think of your bedroom as a Temple of Venus, which means it should have the qualities of a temple—beauty, cleanliness, order—as well as subtle Venusian signals that convey an atmosphere of sensuality. You can create a Venusian atmosphere by burning rose-scented candles and a rose essential oil in an oil burner. Place a vase of red roses, flowers associated magically with Venus, in the room, but check first that your partner does not suffer from hay fever. Throw a beautiful cover over anything that does not trigger associations of sensuality. Most people are not turned on by computer equipment. By introducing Venusian scents and symbols into your personal space, you are enhancing the unconscious triggers that encourage you and your partner to see your bedroom as a place of leisure and sensual delight.

Good sex depends on a partner that you respect and mutual trust. It also depends on being able to enjoy one's body—feeling comfortable about the way we look, being happy about taking our clothes off in front of someone else, feeling comfortable about having desires and being able to discuss them with our partners. It is easy for children and adolescents to absorb negative messages about their bodies and sexuality. To enjoy sex, we need to accept that we are sensual creatures and that this is okay.

Honoring the Body

This is an exercise to help appreciate the body. To do the exercise, you need quiet, privacy, warmth, and soft lighting. You may want to light a candle and to burn some incense or perfumed oil. The exercise is best done lying down. You might want to write or type the exercise in large print so that you can refer to the instructions as you go along. Alternatively, you could read the instructions onto a cassette so you can play them back. In this case, leave gaps for visualization between each instruction. You might like to precede your sensuality exercise with a bath, or you could do the exercise *in* the bath. To create Venus associations, add a few drops of rose essential oil to the bathwater. Light the bathroom with rose-perfumed candles. Float rose petals on the water if you want to feel really exotic. If you can hear your CD player when you are in the bath, play some sensuous music. Following is a version of an ancient invocation to Aphrodite, the Greek equivalent of Venus, attributed to the mythical musician Orpheus, whose singing and playing were so beautiful that all Nature would pause to listen to him. To attune yourself to the energy of Venus, say the invocation before your rose bath. Aphrodite was "foam-born." Born of the waves, she arrived in a shell at her island home of Cyprus.

Hymn to Aphrodite

Child of Ocean,
amazing beauty,
we honor you.
You rule deep Earth,
encircling heaven,
the stormy seas,
and everything in them.
Mother of sweet marriage,
you join the world together
with laughter and harmony,
even the Fates obey you.
Every eye seeks you.
Give us beauty and love.
Delighted by secrets
and lavish feasts
you are concord
and persuasion.
You are beautiful necessity,
even in the frenzy of the shark.
Delicate as sea foam of Cyprus,
fragrant as Syrian oils,
bright as golden chariots
on Egyptian plains
by the sandy bank
of the turquoise Nile,
a choir of the loveliest Nymphs
sings a hymn to your beauty.
With reverence we ask for the gift of grace.

To begin the exercise, relax and allow the tension in your body to seep away. Imagine you are swimming in a warm, clear blue sea. Above you, the Sun shines in a cloudless blue sky. You are naked. Water caresses your body as you swim through the waves. You are swimming toward a silvery white sandy shore. The water becomes shallow. You stand up and wade to the shore.

Beneath your bare feet, you feel hot sand. A gentle breeze caresses your body and the warm Sun dries your skin. There are no other footprints here. You are alone and there is nothing to fear.

Beyond the shore, sand gives way to lush green trees covered in fruit. Through the trees is a sandy path. You cross the beach and follow the path. Gradually, sand gives way to soft green grass. You feel a soft carpet of cool greenness beneath your feet. You find yourself approaching a temple. A sweet smell of incense wafts out through the open doors.

You enter the temple, naked and unafraid. In the center of the temple is an altar on which burns a vigil fire. All is light, warm, and joyful. You stand in front of the altar and commune with the vigil fire. The flames leap higher as though to greet you. A vision appears in the flames of the interior of another temple in a warm country long ago. There white-robed priestesses and priests came to tend the temple fire, but here there is only you. You are sad that so few come to tend the flame; for you sense that each of us has need of this vigil fire.

And then you sense in the temple a spiritual presence, the presence of the Divine. You stand before it naked and unashamed. Divine love flows over you, bathing your body in golden light, loving all of you—body, soul, mind, and spirit. You are a vessel of the Divine Spirit that watches over all. You sense that there is no shame in loving desire and no shame in the sexual love of another; for all love is a reflection of the love that the Divine has for us. You commune with this feeling for a while—a feeling of total acceptance of all that you are—beneath the loving gaze of the Divine Father and Mother of All.

Leave when you are ready. Follow the grassy path back through the trees. As the path approaches the sea, it becomes sandier, until it becomes a path of sand between scrubby bushes and emerges onto the shore. Go to the sea. Wade in. When the water is deep enough,

begin to swim. Turn on your back and float in the warm and welcoming sea. Float until you find yourself dreaming once more of your
room in your everyday world. You sense it is time to return.

Open your eyes. You are back in your bath once more. You are
alone, at peace, and with a memory of love and acceptance for your
body and yourself.

You will anchor the experience in your conscious mind and gain
more from it if you actualize it by making notes and drawing it.
Draw the temple—outside and inside. If any presences appeared to
you, draw them too.

Love Spells

Magic books, ancient and modern, reflect basic human preoccupations. Love and sex feature highly. As we've discussed, male grimoire
authors tend to emphasize sex—how to make a girl dance naked.
Modern girlie witchy books are full of soft-focus images and emphasize love. Love and sex spells reflect our anxieties about getting
a partner and are beloved of teen witches, but serious magicians do
not use spells to make individuals fall in love with them. Often such
spells do work—for a time. You can do some candle magic and
throw yourself at someone and they are likely to respond for a
while, but magic will not create the basis of a long-term relationship.
Lasting relationships depend on personal compatibility. It's there or
it's not. Magic may create the temporary illusion of it, but it will not
create the real thing.

Rather than doing a spell to make a particular person fall in love
with you, magic will work better if you do a spell to make yourself
attractive to others. This will give you self-confidence, and it's the
self-confident who win in the dating game. If you think about your
friends, you'll find loads of beautiful people who have bad relationships and loads of others who are a brilliant success on the dating
circuit simply because they ooze self-confidence and are fun to be

with. Neurotic people full of self-doubts are not much fun to be with. When we feel inwardly confident, we approach people. We make the first move and talk to them because we believe that people will like us and want to talk to us—and usually they do.

Creating a Rite to Venus

Upon this candle I will write
what I wish of thee tonight
O grant to me my secret boon
O lovely Goddess of the Moon.

TRADITIONAL CANDLE MAGIC SPELL

Love spells often involve candle magic, which is beautiful to do, and very easy. You can combine candle magic with a rite to Venus to draw love in your direction. You could also enhance the effect by using the rite to consecrate a Venus-related piece of jewelry that you can wear. A small piece of rose quartz on a chain would be ideal. If this isn't the kind of thing you can wear at work, then find something flat with a long chain that can slip under a shirt. Wearing it at work might be important. A high percentage of people meet future partners at work. If the rose quartz is not new or it has been handled in a shop, cleanse it of any influences it may have picked up by soaking it in salted water for twenty-four hours before your rite.

The Rite

For the magic rite, prepare a room with a Venusian altar. For the altar, you will need a green altar cloth, maybe something with flowers or birds, symbolizing the natural world. You will need a pink candle to consecrate and seven green candles (seven is the number of

Venus); three for the altar and four for the four directions. You will need some essential oil to anoint one of the pink candles. Choose a Venus-related oil such as rose. You will also need a Venus incense, red roses to decorate the altar, a bowl of water in a suitably Venusian color, a small bowl of earth, your wand, a chalice of sweet wine, and cake or sweet biscuits. A taper or thin candle that you can use to light the green candles is useful too. If you have a piece of jewelry to consecrate, put it on the altar. You might like to play some music during your rite. Choose something without words that could distract you—a gentle, soothing, harmonious music that makes you think of love and romance. Take a bath with added rose oil. Maybe you would like to say the Hymn to Aphrodite beforehand. Give your body a thorough scrub until your skin is pink and glowing. Most of us look quite good just after a bath. Put on a robe or some clothes that make you feel sensual.

To begin, light your candles for the four directions and your incense. Consecrate salt and water, sprinkle your circle space, cense your circle space, draw a circle with your wand, and call upon the elements at east, south, west, and north. Ceremonially light the three green candles on the altar. Now call upon the power of Venus. You could say something you have written yourself, whatever comes into your mind, or something like this:

Invocation to Venus

Venus, Evening Star, Lady of Love,
Queen of the Garden of Delights,
who blesses the body, love, and sexuality,
assist me to find a loving partner,
whom I can love and cherish and who can meet my needs.
Draw to me those whom I might love
and who might love me in return.
Lady of green magic,
power of all green and growing things,
beautiful one of the doves,

born of the sea,
come to me,
aid me.

Visualize a beautiful woman as you say the Invocation to Venus. Allow her image to build up in your mind. Let her presence draw close to you, so you are within the light of her aura. Open your chakras and draw in her energy so it fills every pore of your being. Now filled with the energy of love, take your pink candle and consecrate it with the four elements by quickly passing it through the incense smoke and an altar candle flame, sprinkling it with water and pressing it against the soil in your earth bowl. Put a small amount of oil on your fingers. Oil is a substance that is used in magic to carry energy. Use it to energize your base of spine chakra and draw energy into your hands. From the middle of the candle, smooth oil toward each end, focusing on your magical intention and avoiding putting oil on the wick of the candle. Think about you—happy, well, loved, in a loving relationship, fulfilled. Do not attempt to visualize what your lover might look like. When we meet someone we click with, often he or she looks nothing like our fantasy image of the perfect mate, but on a deep inner level we respond to one another. We know that this is the person for us. Once you have oiled your candle, light it from one of the altar candles and put it in its candlestick. Meditate on it for a while, drawing loving energy toward you.

Now consecrate your piece of jewelry. You need to bless it with the four elements. Next, hold the rose quartz in your hands and energize it, visualizing loving energy coming your way, then put the jewelry on.

Now bless the cup of wine. Ask Venus to imbue the wine with her very self, so that as you drink it, you drink of her essence. Hold up the cup and allow your hands to be energized to send energy into the cup and the wine. Then drink. Bless the cake or biscuits in a similar way. Keep a little wine and cake or biscuit to libate, to pour on the earth. Libation is an ancient way of honoring the Earth for what she has given us, by giving a little back. Say a thanksgiving to Venus as you do so. Pour your water from the rite on the earth also. Water that has been consecrated for ritual purposes should be treated as holy water, not just thrown down the sink.

Now there is a little more magical work to do. For seven consecutive nights (seven is the number of Venus), you should burn down roughly the same amount each night of your anointed candle. Each night as you light the candle, think about loving energy coming to you, becoming part of you, attracting others to you. Don't leave the flame unattended. Magic has a sense of humor and magical candles have a habit of catching things alight in ways that you don't want.

The most difficult part of candle magic is making yourself burn the candle when you should. It is amazing what excuses we can find not to do a simple thing like light a candle every night and sit in a room with it, but it is being willing to take care of the small things that makes great things happen.

Once you have found a lover—what then? How can magic help you enjoy a loving, sensual relationship? Here is an energy technique that you can use as a lead-in to sex. It is based on principles derived from the Eastern magical tradition of Tantra.

Sharing Energies

Teach your partner how to open his or her chakras (see Chapter 3) and practice a few times separately, until you can both do the exercise easily.

Before having sex, sit naked on your bed, back to back, your spines touching where possible. Relax and steady your breathing. When you are both ready, begin simultaneously to open your chakras. As you open your own chakras, visualize your chakra energies mingling with those of your partner. Sense where your partner has got to in the process, so you can keep together. You will find that you can sense where he or she is in the chakra-opening sequence, even if consciously you cannot explain why.

Visualize mutual spirals of energy rising, mingling, and activating one another as they surge up your bodies, so that you become two halves of a single whole—much like the beautiful conjoined images of the Indian goddess Shakti and her consort the God Shiva. Fusing your energies, you become one at a deep, unconscious level. Let this harmonious oneness become the starting point for your sexual union.

★

POINTERS FOR PRACTICE

Good sex depends on feeling comfortable with your body. Honor your body. Don't use magic to make someone fall in love with you. Good relationships are based on deep-seated compatibility, not superficial attraction. Sex and love are the province of the planet Venus. If you want to bring love into your life, enhance the Venusian qualities of your environment. "Like attracts like" is an age-old law of magic. If you want love, become someone others can love. Try mingling your chakra energies as a precursor to sex. If you and your partner enjoy this, buy a book about Tantra and learn more to make sex a sensual and spiritual exercise.

CHAPTER SIXTEEN

Travel and Other Mercury Magic

The objects that we use in magic—crystals, candles, etc.—help us focus our magical intentions. We can use simple methods or more elaborate ones. Candle magic is a simple method that is useful when we have a magical intention that has a clear, simple focus. It might be that we want to do well at a particular job interview, or on a particular examination. Candle magic would be appropriate here. Candle magic is also appropriate when there is a symbolic resonance between what we are seeking and the imagery of fire and flame. This is why candle magic is often used for love magic—to arouse flames of passion. If, as in the previous chapter, we use appropriate color symbolism and enhance the "specialness" of what we are doing by consecrating the candle in a ritual, our magic has a greater psychological impact on us, and the effect is enhanced.

Another major use of practical magic throughout the ages is for protection when traveling. You could use candle magic if you wanted to guard and protect someone on a short journey. Consecrate an orange candle—orange being the color associated magically with the god Mercury, patron of travelers—and burn it each evening while your loved one is away. For a long and more complex journey where you cannot be "on the case" all the time, you would need a different approach. For longer-term magic, talismans are useful. A talisman is a small consecrated object created for a specific magical purpose, often one that has to last for a few months or more. Talismans are like charged batteries that gradually use up their store of energy, after which they need recharging or replacing. Talismans often incorporate planetary symbolism, making it important to choose the right planet, so as to harness the most appropriate energy. If you look back at the Planetary Correspondence table in Chapter 13, you will find a useful source of ideas for which planet is appropriate for which magical intention. To help you understand how talismans are made, here is how, a few years ago, my husband and I made a talisman for a friend.

◡

MAKING A TRAVEL TALISMAN

One day our friend Rebecca calls, she says, "Everything's ready and I've got my place on the kibbutz. I was wondering . . ." She pauses, nervous, a little coy.

What does she want? I wonder.

"Would you make me a talisman? You know, a kind of protection talisman." My friend doesn't believe in magic. Would it be rude to point this out?

"You're worried about the trip."

"The kibbutz is quite near the occupied territories."

Thoughts go through my mind—sniper fire, suicide bombers, outraged ultra-Orthodoxists.

"Yes, of course. But you mustn't just rely on the talisman. Don't do anything silly."

Do you have a friend like Rebecca? She is the kind of person who always gets into trouble. If there's an unpopular cause, she feels compelled to support it. And despite being Jewish and going to work on a kibbutz, she's not a Zionist. If fact, she's a fairly right-on, hip, left-wing feminist. I'm not sure how it's going to work. And she's tactless. With every planet under the Sun in Sagittarius, she's never shy about telling people her views.

"When do you leave?"

The next Wednesday evening, my husband sits, drawing on an octagonal piece of orange card. He's drawing a square two inches by two inches, divided into eight columns and eight rows, the format for the magical square of Mercury, Kokab in Hebrew. Rebecca is Jewish and going to Israel, so a planetary talisman using principles derived from the Jewish mystical and magical tradition of Kabbalah seems like a good choice. Mercury in the Kabbalistic Tree of Life is associated with the eighth sefira, or realm. In magic, every possible piece of symbolism is harnessed to intensify the impact of the talisman on the unconscious. Since Mercury's magical number is eight, there are sixty-four numbers in a Mercury talisman, 1–64 arranged in an eight-by-eight square. The numbers appear to be arranged randomly at first, but they are not. They are cleverly arranged so that every row and every column adds up to the same number, symbolizing a solid, compact mass of focused energy.

PLANETARY SQUARE OF MERCURY

8	58	59	5	4	62	63	1
49	15	14	52	53	11	10	56
41	23	22	44	45	19	18	48
32	34	35	29	28	38	39	25
40	26	27	37	36	30	31	33
17	47	46	20	21	43	42	24
9	55	54	12	13	51	50	16
64	2	3	61	60	6	7	57

Planetary squares require concentration. The numbers are not written onto the square row by row or column by column. They must be written in order from one through to sixty-four. Chris writes in the numbers with an italic fountain pen. As he writes each number, we say an affirmation.

"Keep Rebecca while traveling safe and well."

We focus on Rebecca and all that we wish for her—safe travel, health, good luck, a safe place to stay, and safe friends. The planetary square is complete. Chris turns over the orange octagon and on the reverse side draws the symbol for Mercury.

We have focused on Rebecca, on the intention, on drawing symbols that relate to safety in travel. Now we must fuse the two together. We set up an altar to Mercury. Mercury's main color in the magical tradition is orange. A secondary color is yellow. We place a small table in the center of the room and cover it with an orange cloth. We place four orange candles on the altar and four more candles at the directions—east, south, west, and north. We place a bowl of pure spring water on the altar. Clean, pure springs of running water are one of the primary sources of healing and are associated with Mercury's patronage of medicine. We add a terra-cotta vase with eight yellow lilies. We set up a censer and some Mercury incense. We have symbols of air, fire, and water. We add a bowl of earth, a stone, a piece of black and white agate, a stone of Mercury, and a tiny dish of salt to symbolize the earth element. We bathe to honor the cleanliness aspect of Mercury and then enter the room in white robes with orange cords around our waists. For some magical rituals, a special robe feels appropriate. We light the candles at the four quarters with a taper and put out the electric lights. We light the incense. A sweet, fascinating aroma fills the room. Then we light the altar candles.

SYMBOL OF MERCURY

> Blessed be the light throughout the heavens,
> Blessed be the light beyond the worlds,
> Blessed be the light ascending,
> Blessed be the light descending,
> Blessed be the light in space,
> Blessed Be.

The flickering candlelight reflects on the brass candlesticks. The incense smoke rises, entwining itself with the flowers and rising high into the room. The candlelight and incense have already changed the atmosphere. We consecrate the water, add a little salt for purification, and then sprinkle the room with it. We cense the room so the aromatic smoke is spread through it. We draw a circle with a hazel wand and call upon the four directions, asking for blessing for the talisman. From the east, the realm of air, we ask that Rebecca may have wisdom on her journey. From the fiery south, we ask for energy and strength. From the watery west, we ask that she may meet friends, perhaps even find love. From the earthy north, we ask for down-to-earth common sense—after all, this is Rebecca.

We take the talisman and consecrate it with the four elements. We waft it through the incense smoke, flash it through a candle flame, sprinkle it with the consecrated spring water, and press it against the earth. We visualize Rebecca. We visualize her in Israel. "Keep Rebecca while traveling safe and well." We hold the talisman between our hands, energizing it while visualizing her well and happy. Finally, we call on Mercury.

"Mercury, Mercury, Mercury, grant her your aid. So mote it be."

We place the talisman in a leather pouch with a long drawstring, so she can wear it around her neck. We sit and bless white wine and eat orange fruit. The incense is dying down. The eating and drinking help us to change our rhythm, bringing us back from the heady Mercurial realm to the everyday world. We thank the beneficent energies of Mercury for their presence and bid farewell to the four directions. We put on the electric light. The room returns to normal, but seems somehow enhanced. The sweet aroma of the incense lingers for days, reminding us of magic.

Six months later, we get a letter from Rebecca. She went for a Saturday picnic with some friends. This would not be a major news point in most people's lives, but in her part of Israel driving on the Sabbath just about equates to infant slaughter. She and her friends are attacked by ultra-Orthodox men throwing stones. Dogs are set on them. One leaps for her throat. Her friends are terrified. The dog's teeth fix on the talisman in its leather pouch around her neck. The leather string holding it snaps and the dog stands back, clutching it between its teeth. Then it drops the pouch and walks calmly away. Rebecca grabs the pouch, and she and her friends run for their cars and drive away fast. Her friends had scoffed at her talisman, which went everywhere with her. Now they didn't. When she comes back to England, we tell her to dispose of the talisman. Once a talisman has done its work you should give it to the elements. Bury it, burn it, or throw it into the sea or running water.

◯

Thoughts About Magic

Mercury is a planet that is connected with thinking, so at this point, let's think a little about magic. When Chris and I made a talisman for Rebecca, we used two symbols on the talisman. On one side, we put the symbol for the planet Mercury, and on the other the planetary square of Mercury. Planetary squares were devised in medieval Europe by Kabbalistic magicians who loved mathematics. They were the kind of guys who would have been mathematics professors, computer specialists, or rocket scientists if they lived today. We could, of course, just write the word "Mercury" on one side of the talisman and leave it at that. Why don't we? Symbols speak to the unconscious mind, the older, more archaic part of the brain that thinks in pictures, not words. When we work with planetary symbols, we are in effect programming the unconscious mind—both our own and, if we are making the talisman for someone else, that of our recipient—to have a certain set of expectations. When it comes to planetary squares, we are enhancing the programming effect by making our brains perform an act of concentration while we focus on writing the numbers in the correct order.

Why did we choose to make the talisman on a Wednesday? If you look at the Planetary Correspondences table in Chapter 13, you will see that Mercury is the god in the Roman calendar who gave his name to the day we call Wednesday in English. In practice, the day seems to make little difference to the effectiveness of magical workings, but as we were free on a Wednesday, we did it then. Traditionally, it is considered that planets should not be retrograde when you are trying to use their energies. Retrograde means that the planet's orbit in the sky appears to be going backward rather than in its usual direction. We checked the planetary influences in an astrological ephemeris, which gives information about when planets enter different astrological signs, moon phases, etc. You can buy these in esoteric bookstores, but you can also find astrological information by looking on the Internet or buying an astrological magazine.

Why is Mercury associated with travel? The ancients spent much time observing the night sky and planetary movements. The heavens were the equivalent of television. People would sit outside to see what was "on" each night. They didn't know what we know about the cosmos, so some of their ideas were wrong; for instance they thought that the Sun orbited the Earth, rather than the other way around, but they could see that the small planet Mercury was fast-moving. It orbits the Sun in only eighty-eight days. Speed and fast movement became associated with Mercury; another name for the metal mercury is quicksilver. When the Romans began to create a complex pantheon of gods, they thought of Mercury as the messenger of the gods, so the Roman god Mercury was depicted wearing winged sandals and a winged helmet and zooming around the world like a modern-day FedEx courier. He became patron of communications and travel.

Jobs, Examinations, and Other Mercury Magic

Other myths grew up around Mercury. In his infancy, he was a bit of a delinquent. He stole the cows belonging to the god Apollo and almost got away with his precocious act of cattle rustling. He was discovered when Apollo noticed that Mercury had made himself a new musical instrument, the lyre, and that the instrument was strung with cow gut. The new instrument sounded wonderful, so much so that Apollo's pleasure was stronger than his wrath. He allowed Mercury to keep the cattle, if he could have the lyre. Mercury's cleverness as an inventor meant that he became associated with high intelligence and became a patron of all matters intellectual. Mercury was ever the inventor. Later he invented magic. Over time, he become the patron of learning, magic, and medicine, and of commerce and other transactions including theft, which might say something about how the Romans regarded the business world and doctors. In today's world, he has become patron of computer specialists. Mercury is often shown with a moneybag. His other distinctive symbol is his caduceus, a wand wrapped with two twisted snakes. The caduceus symbol later became the symbol of many medical organizations. Mercury's festival was celebrated on May 15, just before the start of the zodiac sign he now rules, Gemini. Mercury does not bring prosperity directly, but if you want to initiate a business venture, then Mercurial energy is a good force to invoke. Mercury is versatile. If you know anything about metallurgy, you will know that mercury is a fluid metal—it does not take a fixed shape. If you know anything about astrology, just think Gemini and you will have an idea of Mercury's nature. Gemini's color is yellow. Orange and yellow are colors that are bright, energizing, and designed to stimulate the mind rather than the emotions. Mercury's associated with the qualities of clear thinking, clarity of mind, and meditation.

I find Mercury energy helpful for examinations. It can improve your concentration, your motivation to revise, and your sense of what questions are likely to be asked. It's great for driving tests, setting up new computer systems, job interviews, communicating about money matters, and selling yourself. To engage the power of Mercury for help with something specific, consecrate a candle using a similar ritual to the Venus ritual in the previous chapter. For something more complex, create a talisman. Before doing Mercury magic, clear physical and psychological clutter out of your life. Mercury is associated with mathematics and order and requires cleanliness and order to do its work. Don't invoke Mercury into a disordered environment or you will invoke the negative side of Mercury, the patron of tricksters and thieves. Tidy your home, throw out any rubbish, clean the room where you are going to perform your rite. Before you start, sort out any financial records and tax returns. If your financial dealings aren't completely honest, do not invoke Mercury, as you may invoke the revenue service.

Mercury Insurance

A Mercury travel talisman is the astral equivalent of an annual travel insurance policy. If you travel a lot, both kinds of insurance are useful. Make your own Mercury talisman to protect you whenever traveling. Use the circle ritual format described for consecrating a wand and the processes we described for Rebecca's rite. Consecrate your talisman with the intention that it will work for a year and then recharge it.

Another useful form of travel protection uses as its basis the chakra exercise you learned earlier in Chapter 4 to protect you from being approached by strange people. If you are in a foreign city and want to be unobtrusive, try the technique below. It is unlikely to fool the average Jaipur hotel tout or Luxor amber salesmen, but it can help you blend into the crowd elsewhere.

Reducing your Visibility

Close your chakras, except for the top and bottom, and visualize three parallel blue rings around your body—one around your head, one around your trunk, and one around your legs. Still your mind and think about nothing, so no one picks up your thought pattern. Walk straight by.

It is easy to understand on a psychological level how we program our psyches to have a certain set of expectations when we do magic for ourselves. What happens when we do magic for someone else? By creating a talisman for another person, we are giving him or her a particular set of expectations. These will affect the way the recipient behaves, and his or her behavior will, in turn, affect other people's responses. Again, it is easy to understand how this works on a psychological level, but magic makes a leap beyond the psychological. Why was a vicious dog stopped in its tracks by Rebecca's "keep safe while traveling" talisman? Here we get into the realm of metaphysics. Magic works on the premise that symbolic human actions and thought processes can influence how the cosmos responds to us. We can devise many spiritual and scientific rationales as to why this might be so. We can construct just as many or more rationales to convince ourselves that this is not true. The Golden Rule in magic is to try things for yourself and to see if they work. Other people's anecdotes may hint that they do, but only you can decide.

✦

POINTERS FOR PRACTICE

Traditionally, Mercury energy is good for business ventures, travel, communications, and examinations. Work with the energy of Mercury for these intentions by making and empowering a Mercury talisman for long-term projects, or by consecrating a candle for a one-off event. As added protection when traveling, try the technique for reducing your visibility if you want to be less conspicuous.

CHAPTER SEVENTEEN

Prosperity Consciousness

"I've been rich and I've been poor. Believe me, rich is better!"

MAE WEST

There is an old saying in magic: be careful what you ask for because you will receive. King Midas, the fabulously wealthy king of Phrygia in what is now Turkey, is offered a gift by the god Dionysos. "Anything you like, my son," says Dionysos. Now if a god asks you what you want, asking for something material is dumb. Gods aren't much into materiality, but they are into practical jokes. King Midas asks that everything he touches will turn to gold. "Fine," replies Dionysos; the subtext being, "You jerk." Then Dionysos pirouettes and disappears in a puff of smoke, steam, or whatever, and everything King Midas touches starts to turn to gold—his food, furniture, clothes, and then most tragically his beloved daughter. Too late, he realizes the folly of what he has asked.

Money is good, but Gordon Gekko's 1980s *Wall Street* mantra of "Greed is good" is not. Greed is an attempt to fill an inner void. We are greedy when we lack something, but that something is usually a sense of being loved and a sense of our own self-worth rather than what our greed fixes on—wealth, power, cars, food, clothes, sex. We find ourselves in a trap. However much we have of whatever it is our obsession has fixed on, it will never be enough because it is not the real need. The real need is hidden from us, festering away in the unconscious. If we pursue money for its own sake, we will make ourselves miserable. Not that poverty is much fun either. I have had two periods in my life when I didn't have enough money to eat, and one period, when pursuing a conventional career, when I was relatively wealthy. Now, I'm okay. Like most people, I would like to be wealthier, but it only takes something like the World Trade Center disaster to make me realize that I am in a privileged minority. I live in the West, in a democratic society where everyone has some kind of political voice. I am free to choose where I live, what work I do. I do not have to cover my face in order to walk in the street. I am an individual and not a breeding machine to be used by men as they will. I am alive, reasonably healthy, and educated. I ceased long ago to have dreams of winning a lot of money on a lottery because I realized that if I was very rich I wouldn't feel the urge to work, and some of the greatest satisfactions in my life come from writing, which is harder work than it looks.

Don't think that winning a lot of money will solve all your problems. The old adage that money can't buy happiness is true; there are some very miserable rich people. If you don't have a talent for happiness, it's unlikely that money will make you happy. However, it will make misery more comfortable. What we need is to have sufficient money to be able to live healthy and productive lives without too much financial anxiety. Magic can help.

Money arouses all manner of psychological reactions. We are anxious if we do not have money. We may be afraid of having too much money. If we start to earn more than those around us—family, friends, partner—will they grow jealous, envious, rejecting? For many people, the more money they have, the more scared they are of losing it. Conversely, many of us never realize our full earning potential because we need to feel safe. We stay in jobs that are below our capabilities because we are afraid to look stupid by aiming for something better and failing. The amount we feel we should be paid is based on an unconscious evaluation of what we feel we deserve. If we have low self-esteem, we won't feel that is very much. Some job interviewers are geniuses at spotting those of us who have low self-esteem and who place a low value on ourselves. They reward us by meeting our expectations. In order to succeed in the world of work, we need a sensible evaluation of our market worth and soundly based self-esteem. Forget Midas; think Jupiter.

Jupiter

Jupiter is the planet associated in the Western magical tradition with prosperity. Jupiter was king of the gods in Roman mythology and is connected with enjoyment of material things, as well as with thunder, lightning, creativity, benevolence, and good humor. The word jovial comes from Jove, a form of Jupiter's name. As befits a king, Jupiter is the largest planet in our solar system, two and a half times the combined size of the other planets, with enormous curtains of lightning crackling in its hydrogen-filled atmosphere. Its interior is hot and it is a creator of energy, radiating more energy than it receives from the Sun. Interestingly, given its role in mythology as a parent of the gods, Jupiter is about 90 percent hydrogen and 10 per cent helium with traces of methane, water, and ammonia. This is close to the composition of the primordial solar nebula from which the entire solar system was formed. Jupiter equates to Thor in Norse mythology and is associated with Thursday. Although it is far away from us, Jupiter is often the brightest star in the night sky. With a strong pair of binoculars you can see its four largest Moons—Io, Europa, Ganymede, and Callisto.

Jupiterian qualities in the human psyche are those related to expansion and extraversion. Jupiter is about saying "yes" rather than "no," "I can" rather than "I can't." It is about engaging with the world rather than retreating from it. It is a fearless energy imbued with optimism. It's a favorite of motivational sales trainers. It has self-confidence, the blithe unquestioning self-confidence you get if you've been brought up by a rich family, been sent to the best schools, nothing bad has happened to you, and you're used to doing and getting what you want. Jupiter's energy can help us when we embark on new enterprises, have to move to a new environment, or start a new job. It is a leader's energy. You can help bring this energy into your psyche by surrounding yourself with things that trigger Jupiterian associations. Jupiter is a sky god who lives on the top of Mount Olympus in Greece. His color is blue, like a clear Mediterranean summer sky. The semiprecious stone associated with Jupiter is amethyst. Wear amethyst when you are starting out on a new venture or when you want confidence and good luck. Wear amethyst to job interviews, or put a piece in your pocket.

Jupiter's energy can attract prosperity, but it is pointless invoking Jupiter, then sitting back and waiting for something to happen. If you want prosperity, you will have to work for it, so you need a route that can bring it to you, whether it's getting promoted, starting a business, applying for a new job, or getting a qualification that improves your status and income. You can try doing magic to win a lottery if you like, but you are probably wasting your time. There are millions of other people out there praying, magicing, crossing their fingers, and rubbing their lucky Ganeshas to achieve exactly the same thing. You need to find a way that prosperity can come into your life through slightly more prosaic channels. Once you find a sensible route, you can do a ritual to Jupiter to help you.

Below, I describe a rite to invoke the energy of Jupiter. I suggest that you use a talisman as a focus for your magical intention because this is something that you want to last for a long time, and to work in all the different circumstances in which you find yourself. It is also portable; you can take it with you wherever you go. The talisman incorporates a planetary square, which is constructed in a way similar

to that in which the Mercury one that we used for Rebecca was constructed. Magically, Jupiter is associated with the number four, so
this time the numbers on the talisman are four by four, the numbers
one through sixteen.

@

A Prosperity Rite

How would you create a prosperity rite? First, obtain a small square
of blue card and make a Jupiter talisman incorporating the planetary
square of Jupiter. Draw on one side a square divided into sixteen
equal squares. A square one inch by one inch will divide easily into a
four-by-four square.

PLANETARY SQUARE OF JUPITER

4	14	15	1
9	7	6	12
5	11	10	8
16	2	3	13

What the square is doing is symbolically invoking the essence of
Jupiterian energy. By linking it to yourself, you then link it to your
life. You can integrate yourself with the talisman a little more by
making a personal symbol from the symbol of Jupiter and your initials.

SYMBOL OF JUPITER

If I intertwine this with my initials I could make the following symbol.

PERSONAL SYMBOL FOR PROSPERITY

Take a practice sheet of paper and work out your personal design. What you are doing is attempting to encapsulate your intention in a symbol made of letters, a symbol that only you can understand. You are allowing your unconscious mind and creativity to take over to turn what is a left-brain-manufactured conscious thought into a right-brain visual symbol. Once you have a symbol you are happy with, transfer it to the talisman.

Now that you have prepared your Jupiter talisman, you need a ritual to charge it with energy and get it working. It's a bit like charging up your mobile phone battery. If you wish, you could make a special wand for the occasion from a Jupiter-related wood such as oak. When we make things for ritual, we add our energy and creativity to them. The more of ourselves we put into a ritual, the more likely it is to work.

Set up a Jupiter altar with a bowl of earth, water, censer, candles—lots of blue, some purple, Jupiter incense, Jupiter-colored flowers, cakes and wine or juice to bless. Since Jupiter is associated with opulence, choose something rich to eat and a dark-reddish-purple wine or fruit juice. Jupiter is more Bordeaux Supérieur or Rioja D.O.C. than the cheapest red you can find on the supermarket shelf. Set out candles for the four directions. If you have any deity images, such as Kuan Yin or Ganesha, that relate to good fortune, you could put them on your altar. For the rite itself, cast a circle and invoke the four directions. Sit or kneel in front of your altar and consecrate your talisman with the four elements. Open your chakras, and draw energy into your hands. Call upon the power of Jupiter. You could say whatever you feel, or something like the invocation that follows.

Invocation to Jupiter

Jupiter, Divine one,
spirit of good fortune, positive energy, and worldly power,
fill my being with your strength,
manifest within me the power to create,
that I may bring the positive energy of wealth
into my life and the lives of those around me.

Or, as the Renaissance magician Heinrich Cornelius Agrippa saluted him:

Helping Father, King of heaven,
Magnanimous, thundering, lightning, unconquered,
high and mighty, great and mighty,
good, fortunate, sweet, mild,
of good will, honest, pure,
walking well, and in honor,
the Lord of joy and of judgements,
wise, true, the shewer of truth,
judge of all things, excelling all in goodness,
Lord of riches, and wisdom.

Visualize Jupiter's energy entering into your crown chakra, pouring down through all your chakras and becoming part of you. Now take your Jupiter talisman and draw energy into your hands. Allow the energy to pour from your hands into your talisman, filling it with energy, light, and power. Hold the talisman to your heart chakra and focus on your intention, while visualizing it coming about. Visualize yourself wealthy, prosperous, enjoying the fruits of your labors. Stop visualizing and channeling when you are ready. Thank the powers of Jupiter for their assistance and wrap your talisman in a piece of silk. At the end of your ritual, bless cakes and wine, then make a small offering to Jupiter. Sprinkle a few drops of wine and a few crumbs on the charcoal in your censer, then eat and drink. The Roman writer Cato in his book *De Agricultura* gives these words as an offering blessing:

> Jupiter, in making this offering to you,
> I entreat with goodly prayers,
> that you watch over me and all my household,
> may this offering be a comfort to you.*

When you are ready to close your ritual, thank Jupiter once more, bid farewell to the four directions, and close your ritual. Dispose of the consecrated water respectfully. You can burn the Jupiterian candles you have used in your rite when you are having dinner, or at any time. They will remind you of your ritual purpose. You can expect the talisman to last for about a year or so. You need to keep it in contact with you. You could carry it on your person, keep it under your pillow, or put it in a special place in your bedroom. After a year, you should either recharge the talisman with a similar ritual or, if it has done all it needs to do, destroy it by burning it in a candle flame while thanking Jupiter for his assistance.

*In Latin: *Iuppiter, te hoc ferto obmovendo bonas preces precor, uti sies volens propitius mihi liberisque meis domo familiaeque meae mactus hoc ferto.*

Jupiter and Leadership

We must not forget when thinking about Jupiter's association with prosperity and good fortune that his symbolism is wider and deeper than simple moneymaking. Jupiter as king of the Roman gods is associated with all the positive qualities of good kingship. The spiritual nature of Jupiter is conveyed by the taboos that had to be respected by the Roman *flamen Dialis,* the priest of Jupiter. He was forbidden to engage in any secular work or to observe other people doing so, he could not ride a horse, see an army dressed for battle, use an iron blade to cut his fingernails, or eat she-goat, dog, ivy, raw meat, or beans. The Roman prohibitions separated the priest of Jupiter from associations with the opposite energy of Mars—war and iron. If you think of the Dalai Lama—spiritual, dedicated to peace, and set apart since his childhood from everyday life—and then think about his mountainous kingdom of Tibet, cut off for so long from the outside world, then you have a sense of the essence of Jupiterian spirituality. The mountain symbolism is also important in that Jupiter is a sky god, associated with higher faculties of the intellect, relating through his rulership of the astrological sign Sagittarius to philosophical thought and inspired intuition. Before choosing medicines to treat a patient, a seventeenth-century physician would draw the symbol for Jupiter at the top of his piece of paper. He would in effect be invoking Jupiter to inspire his diagnosis and to guide him to the right treatment. One of the effects of a Jupiter prosperity ritual is to inspire us to find ways of making our fortune. The ritual will not work for us if we wait in passive expectation for someone else to do the work for us.

Magical Altruism

Invoking Jupiter energy is not just about bringing money to us; it is about achieving the right relationship with money. Jupiter as king of the gods is the beneficent distributor of his people's wealth. He is the resource to which people turn in their hour of need. To bring Jupiter's positive qualities into your life, you need to become Jupiter. By invoking Jupiter, you are bringing into your psyche an energy that is wise, caring, concerned with issues beyond oneself, charitable, and giving.

Magically, money will come to us more easily if we give some away. Think of it as a form of astral cash flow. There is an old magical law that whatever we give out in terms of energy, positive or negative, returns to us threefold. Some people attempt to reduce this to a kind of karmic banking system, whereby you stash away good deeds to outweigh your bad ones. Rather, it works on the same principle as sowing a crop. We throw tiny seeds into fertile soil and a crop emerges that gives us nourishment, plus the seed corn for the next crop. Giving also works on the psychological level. If you are generous enough to give to others, people perceive you as the kind of person they want to know and help. You create certain psychological and magical conditions around yourself, and other people respond accordingly.

Invoking Jupiter

If you want to create positive magical energy, you can do it on two levels. First, you can donate small regular amounts of time and/or money to charitable causes. Second, you can donate some of your magical energies to helping others. Magic can be used to help others, and natural magicians and magical groups usually put a great deal of effort into altruistic magic for individuals and communities, and today, in our environmentally beleaguered planet, into positive magic to help conserve our mother the Earth.

If you want to develop magical powers, then you need to decide what you want to use them for. "Power, money, wealth, complete happiness, and a sexy partner who adores me," might be your instant reaction, but it is not a particularly good one. We don't find happiness from what we have. What we have can go a long way to making us happy, but it isn't enough. We are happy or not happy because of what we are. Altruism involves doing things for other people without expectation of direct reward. It doesn't mean that there is no reward—of course there is. We are rewarded when we do things that make us feel better about ourselves. With a bit of luck, we may even be rewarded by feedback from others, but there is no guarantee. However, we may get feedback through seeing another's smile, through the knowledge that we are contributing to society, that we have given something back to the world. Make magical altruism part of your life. Do not use magic solely for your own concerns. And don't think that because you practice magical altruism, you don't need to do anything for others on the material plane. People cannot be fed on magic alone.

POINTERS FOR PRACTICE

Jupiter is the planet to invoke for prosperity, but don't sit back and wait for something to happen. If you want prosperity, you need a route that can bring it to you. Remember that like attracts like. If you want people to be generous toward you, be generous toward others. Human beings have an innate sense of justice. If we want good things to happen to us, then we need to give to feel good about ourselves and the world.

CHAPTER EIGHTEEN

Control and Goal

*J*upiter emerges as a benevolent force in mythology, but we first hear of him as a rebel against his father, Saturn, the first king of the gods. In a myth that surely gladdened the heart of Sigmund Freud, Jupiter carries out a primeval boardroom coup. Helped by his brothers Neptune and Pluto, Jupiter overthrows his father and marries his sister Juno. Jupiter takes over control of the Upperworld of sky and land, Pluto gets the Underworld, and Neptune the Sea. Jupiter's sister Ceres becomes goddess of cereals and grain—essential foodstuffs for humankind. Saturn's fate, though, is not so bad. Saturn flees to Italy, where he rules over a Golden Age of peace and prosperity for humankind. His festival, the Saturnalia, commemorates this happy period. The Saturnalia was a weeklong festival around the Winter Solstice in December that was later absorbed into Christian festivities.

In traditional astrology, Saturn has a bad reputation as a planet of melancholy, and the planet Saturn is an inhospitable place. It is a large yellowish planet with 1,000 mph winds, surrounded by eighteen named satellites, plus twelve recently discovered ones, and by rings of water, ice, and rock particles with ice coatings—not a cheerful prospect. Magically, however, Saturn's negative reputation is undeserved. All the planets have positive and negative characteristics. In magical tradition, Saturn is more positive. He is depicted as an old man who is careful, cautious, and conservative. He is also known as Old Father Time and is patron of old age. His colors are

dark and earthy—brown and black. He is like the classic govern-
ment official—a responsible steward of other people's resources.
Saturn is the ideal planet for bankers and accountants, and an essential force in monetary affairs. The energy of Saturn is negatively
that of the miser. Its positive aspect is planning for the future. It is
carefully guarding resources in order to make them grow—slowly.
Environmentalism could find Saturn, whose reign over Earth
brought peace and prosperity, an ideal patron.

Saturn and Debt

Many of us worry about money. In the West, the level of individual
debt is enormous. Much of this is managed cash flow. It is easier to
pay for purchases on a credit card than by using cash. Much of our
debt lies in mortgage repayments; but there is a lot more still unac-
counted for. A lot of debt is unnecessary debt for consumer products
we don't need. Magically, it is important that we arrive at a balance
with regard to money. We need to balance inputs with outputs, out-
goings with income. In order to become prosperous, we need the
energy of Saturn—constraint—as well as that of luck-bringing
Jupiter. There is little point in making money if we don't know how
to keep it. If you are poor because you are a shopaholic with enormous credit cards bills, Jupiter energy is likely to put you into the
optimistic, bouncy frame of mind that makes you feel like spending
more. If you are a compulsive spender, Saturn may be just what you
need.

☉

Working with Saturn

Here is a simple rite you can do to honor Saturn. First, find every
credit card, store card, and bank card that you own. Next, find a cal-
culator and gather the statements of your card accounts. Add them

up to find exactly how much you owe. If the result is making you have a heart attack, collapse in tears, or feel very, very sick, unless you are a member of Alcoholics Anonymous, have one glass of wine, or one beer. If you are a member of AA, pat yourself on the back. You have already made a good start in tackling your problems. Right, so far so good. Now engage your brain, invoke Mercury if necessary. It is almost impossible to manage life without a credit card and a bank card, but you don't need the rest. Take a pair of scissors and cut up all the store cards. "What?" you scream. Yes, seriously. If you can't manage money well, you'll never cope with lots of different credit bills. They just help you deceive yourself about the extent of your problem. Chop the excess cards up. If you are starting to ask, "Where's the magic in this?" just keep going. It is a magical act, an act of magical will. Get chopping.

Next, phone a friend or a relative, your bank, a debt counselor, or your accountant. You need some good advice about how on Earth you are going to pay everything off. Be totally honest about the mess that you are in. Don't talk it down or pretend that your debts are less than they are. Magical thinking is about seeing things exactly as they are. If you are prepared to do that, then you can ask for help. If you borrow money from relatives, agree on a monthly repayment schedule, set up a monthly payment from your bank account, and start on the road to magical money management. Don't, whatever you do, borrow money from anyone, even a parent, with the vague agreement that you'll pay it back "sometime." If you are a walking financial disaster area, then all you'll do is start spending money again and never pay back the loan, and you'll damage a relationship. No relatives who can help? Go to your bank. The solution is probably going to be to arrange a loan from your bank to pay off your credit debts. This will be at a lower interest rate than store or credit cards and will leave you with only one loan to find the monthly payment for. Remember, Mercury is the patron of communication and business. You may need some Mercury candle magic to help you communicate well. You will need to convince someone that your previous total financial incompetence was merely a passing phase and that you are on the road to recovery. Then you'll need some Saturn magic to help you keep to that. You may also need a second part-time evening job. Saturn is the planet of hard work and a good energy to invoke if you need a job to bail you out of financial trouble.

Once you've started to deal with your debts, you need to get control of your future spending, which takes us back to our friend Saturn. Saturn is about careful use of resources—your careful use of your resources.

℮

Saturn Talisman

A good way to bring Saturn energy into your life to ground you and to help you conserve your money is to make a Saturn talisman to carry in your purse or wallet. Before making the talisman, you need to make clear to your unconscious the nature of your magical intention. Your intention could be something like, "I enjoy spending less than I earn." This is better than "I will not spend money." Our unconscious minds work better with positive statements than negative ones. Negative statements arouse all kinds of childish resistances. Telling yourself not to do something puts part of your psyche in the position of patrolling, parenting, and disciplining the rest. This creates internal stress. Think of all the good resolutions you have ever broken and you'll know what I mean. Instead, take a positive step to a new future and tell your unconscious what it will do, rather than what it will not do. You want to harness your unconscious in a cooperative effort.

PLANETARY SQUARE OF SATURN

4	9	2
3	5	7
8	1	6

Make the talisman on a card—maybe brown card, with the squares and numbers in black. Black card with silver squares and numbers could be an alternative. The geometric form associated with Saturn is the triangle. The triangle symbolizes the three dimensions, the world of form. If you make your talisman in the shape of an equilateral triangle, you are signaling to your unconscious that you want to bring Saturn energy into your material circumstances. Sitting your planetary square into a triangle means that you will have to be precise. This is good. Neatness, precision, and care are qualities that you want to manifest in your financial life. Make the talisman small enough to slip in next to your credit card (not credit cards—remember you are cutting your cards down to one). Think about this as you make your Saturn talisman—marking out the square, writing the numbers. Say the intention aloud as you fill in each number, remembering that you must write in the numbers in their numerical order.

SYMBOL OF SATURN

On the reverse side of the talisman, make a sigil for your intention, using your initials in the same process as for the Jupiter sigil.

SPENDING LESS SYMBOL

Saturn Ritual

For the ritual, set up a Saturn altar. Saturn's colors are brown and black, but that makes for a depressing combination. Remember the Saturn myth of his beneficent rule over Earth add some green. You now have "earthy" colors that focus on practical, earthy qualities in your psyche rather than spendthrift fire "I want it now!"; water, "I'm a bit depressed today so I'll spend some money to cheer myself up," or air, "I'll think about debts tomorrow; something's bound to turn up." Put candles on the altar, make a Saturn incense, and decorate the altar with bronze or orange, earthy-colored chrysanthemums or other flowers, with some evergreen foliage. A few nice rocks would be a good addition, plus a bowl of earth and anything else that makes you think "Earth" and "Nature." The symbolism will remind you that you want to be earthed, focused in the here and now and in material reality.

If you have a tarot pack, you could put some tarot cards on the altar. In the major arcana, the card of the World or Universe is associated with Saturn. The World is a beautiful card of fulfillment. The classic imagery is that of a naked woman or androgynous figure dancing, surrounded by the four elements. In the minor arcana, the threes are associated with Saturn as the parent of form, the God that made the Gods, the force behind the creation of matter. What you are trying to do with your Saturn rite is to get control of your own personal world of form, your material life, in order to get it on a sound foundation. The three of pentacles is about money gained through enterprise, the three of wands is about completion of a particular phase, and the three of cups is about rejoicing. These threes and the World would be fine to represent positive Saturn energy. Leave out the three of swords, which is a card often depicted as three swords plunging through a heart, and which represents sorrow. It might be what you feel, but it's not what you need to focus on.

Create a ritual using the same structure as the Jupiter ritual, and create an invocation to Saturn. After your ritual, arrange it so that every time you reach for the credit card, you encounter the talisman beaming at you, "Just say no! You enjoy spending less than you earn." Take pride in your new ambition—to be a brilliant financial manager.

Goals

Jupiter's energy is about expansion, saying yes, taking up opportunities. In excess, Jupiter's energy is associated with greed, wanting too much, trying to have it all. The problem with trying to have it all is that we can end up with nothing. In the end, we have to refine, make choices. We have to discard some career and life paths and relationships in order to cultivate those that are most important to us. One of Saturn's magical images is of an elderly gardener, patiently planting and waiting for plants to flourish, pruning trees as necessary so they put their growth into the most productive directions. Saturn is an energy that can help us consolidate our goals. Saturn, remember, is the planet of long-range planning.

Why do some people succeed in life and others fail? Birth,

money, intelligence, good looks, talent—these all help, but some people have all these and fail; others have none of them and make it. Successful people are persistent, determined, and committed. They work hard. They try and keep on trying. They have the energy of Mars, the optimism of Jupiter, the clear-thinking of Mercury, and the persistence of Saturn. Faced with obstacles, they just keep going. They have a clear image of what they want, they sense instinctively who will help them and who will not, they persuade others that their ideas are good, and they create an atmosphere that makes others believe in them. Above all, they understand energy—when to go for their goal, when to wait, when to push and when to give way, without ever losing sight of their objective.

Psychological research shows that twenty years later, people who as students had a clear vision of what they wanted to achieve with their lives had generally done so. They also earned more and were more successful than those who had no clear goals. Obvious though it sounds, we cannot achieve anything if we do not know what we want to achieve. If we learn to listen to the inner guiding voice of the self, we find that we are given clues that help us find our goals. We get a sudden sense of "this is it"; we *know* we are on the right track. We have a sense of consolidation, that we have a firm foundation. People can be triggers, as can a chance word, a line from a song, a visual image. Suddenly the mind achieves closure. A solution to a problem that has been niggling away in the unconscious suddenly comes into consciousness—complete with solution.

A problem that was niggling me in my late teens was, "What do I want to do with my life?" I had been initiated as a Wiccan priest-ess, but I did not want a full-time career as a tarot reader, a healer, or any of the other "witchy" occupations. I was happy to do these things on a part-time basis, but I also needed an intellectual chal-lenge. But doing what? I took some time out and went to Paris. In an art gallery, I found myself standing in front of a painting by Rus-sian abstract painter Wassily Kandinsky, founder of the influential Blue Rider group of artists. Looking at the painting, I had a "bolt from the blue." I knew that I did not want to study English at the university as I had planned. Instead, I would study psychology. At that point, I knew next to nothing about psychology. Years later, I discovered that Kandinsky was a musician as well as an artist. He aimed to create art that would have the same emotional impact as music and that would cause people to have instantaneous revelations.

Armed with my instantaneous revelation, I returned to London to apply for a university place in psychology. In the meantime, I needed to earn some money. I registered with a temporary agency for a job. They had only one vacancy—would I be interested? It was to act as secretary and assistant to a psychologist. Of course I was interested. The job taught me about applied psychology. This confirmed my desire to become a psychologist. Before taking my university place, I took a holiday in the Greek islands, ending up on the beautiful island of Paxi, off Corfu. There I met a wonderful middle-aged French couple who sat with me under the olive trees, giving me the benefit of their experience of life, the universe, and the philosophy of everything, in a way that the French do so well. Their lifestyle seemed to me ideal. In the winter, they lived in Paris, where he taught at the Sorbonne University. In summer, they lived in a tent on Paxi, where they wrote books. Now I had a second goal. I would become a psychologist, but when I was old enough to have something to write about, I would become a writer and have two homes, one for the summer and one for the winter. I could have dismissed these ideas as daydreams, but because I had learned through my magical training to notice the ideas that flash briefly through our consciousness to guide us, I noticed and remembered them and they became my guiding vision. Once we find our vision, we can begin to fulfill it.

✦

POINTERS FOR PRACTICE

There is little point in making money if we don't know how to keep it. The positive aspect of Saturn is planning for the future and carefully

guarding resources in order to make them grow. Magically, it is im-
portant that we arrive at a balance with regard to money and learn
once we have acquired it how to keep it. A good way to bring Saturn
energy into your life is to make a Saturn talisman to carry with you.
Though it may sound obvious, the only way to achieve success is to
know what we want. We must always work to focus our goals.

CHAPTER NINETEEN

Will and Power

We constrain ye yet again by the Seal of the Sun
which is the Word of God;
and by the Seal of the Moon and of the Stars we bind ye;
and by the other Animals and Creatures which are in Heaven,
by whose wings Heaven cleanseth itself,
we force and attract ye imperiously
to execute our will without failure.

CLAVICULA SALOMONIS *(KEY OF SOLOMON THE KING)*

*T*raditional ritual magic is full of magicians summoning angels and demons to do their bidding and execute their will. This makes "will" sound like something we impose on the outer universe, but the ancient grimoires got it wrong. True will is something quite different. It is discovering who and what we truly are, for only then can we manifest what we truly want. In magic, the change agents are visualization, concentration, the ability to manipulate energy, and decisiveness. Decisiveness may seem an odd requirement for magic, but if you want to do magic, you need to know what you want, which is often more difficult than it seems. Suppose you decide you would like to get a fabulous new job in another city. You do some magic, you are offered a job that is exactly what you asked for, and you panic. You have a boyfriend. How will a long-distance relationship work? Your mother is getting divorced for the third time, so it is a bad time for you to be away. What about your years-old network of friends? Sometimes we find that getting what we want has too high a price. We want other things more. There is no point in doing magic to get something and then deciding you don't want it. For most people there are conflicts—heart vs. head, impetuosity vs. cautiousness, optimism vs. pessimism, ego vs. deeper, spiritual self. If you are the kind of person who is always thinking twenty different things at once and do not really know what you want, do not despair. Natural magic can help you find out by putting you in closer touch with your true will.

Will in magic is associated with the element of fire and the energy of the planet Mars. When we make decisions to act and overcome inertia, a failing of earth, we are calling on earth's opposite element—fire. Fire is associated with energy and courage. It endures the rigors of existence and triumphs. By developing our fire energy, we gain the courage to overcome obstacles that challenge us. Fire acts like the Sun on a plant. It helps us develop and grow. Will is the energy that gives us "get up and go." Fire is never static. It seeks and welcomes changes. It forces us to act, even when decisions are difficult.

@

Will Meditation

This is an exercise to help you develop and harness your inner fire. Find a comfortable chair where you can sit with your spine straight, kneel on your haunches or sit cross-legged if you prefer. Relax and open your chakras. Once they are open, visualize a column of white light pouring down over your crown chakra. The white light enters the crown of your head and flows through you. It flows down through your skull, cleansing your psyche, clearing your mind. It flows through your third eye, washing it in white light, giving you clear vision. It flows through your throat chakra, freeing up your voice, giving you the power to speak and to listen and understand. It flows through your heart chakra, removing barriers that prevent you from interacting with others. It flows through your solar plexus chakra, filling you with healing energy. It flows through your sacral chakra, putting you in touch with your instinctual self. It flows through your base of spine chakra, freeing up your physical energy and giving you strength. Allow the white light to flow down through you, taking away negative energy and any blockages or barriers to the flow of your energy, will, power, and love. Bathe all your chakras in the cleansing light. With the flow of the white light, all negative energy is removed. You feel the clear, light energy of spiritual presence filling you and uniting you with the spiritual realm. The light continues to flow down through you and over you. It is a continuous white stream without beginning, without end. The streaming light clears out all negative thoughts. It clears out jealousy and anger, frustration and irritability. It clears out all barriers that prevent you from realizing your inner potential. It leaves you focused in the present, with a strong desire to order your life in the way you wish. Allow the light to cease to flow. The clear sense of purpose that contact with the Divine Light has given you remains. You find that you are in your own space, with a focused energy and purpose that you can use in the days to come. Repeat this exercise whenever you have need of focused energy.

Mars

Mars is an energy we can bring into our lives to wake up the psyche. In early Roman mythology, Mars is a popular god of fertility and agriculture. Interestingly, Gunter Sachs's astrological research* shows that farming is one of the top two Arien occupations. Later, Mars becomes a patron of young men and their activities, including athlet-

*Sachs (1998): 190.

ics and war. The Gauquelins' astrological research shows that successful athletes are more likely to have Mars predominant in their
birth charts—either directly above them in the heavens or on the
eastern horizon. Mars gives his name to March. The Norse equivalent of Mars is Tyr, who gives his name to Tuesday. The ram symbol
for Aries reflects the fertility aspect of Mars. Mars's primary festival
in ancient Rome was the Quinquartus, five days of celebration
around the Spring Equinox, the beginning of Aries. The planet Mars
is a red ball of rock with carbon dioxide, "dry" ice at its pole, and
two Moons—Phobos and Deimos. The red appearance of Mars in
the sky compared to the other planets led to an association between
the planet and blood, and led to the association with war. Red is a
color associated in the human psyche with anger, fire, energy, and
physical strength.

Saying Yes to the Universe

The "will" meditation is about clearing your psyche and removing
blockages. When you feel inwardly free, you are more able to take
notice of and say "yes" to the opportunities that the universe presents to you. You can tread boldly and go forward with courage. Saying "yes" means developing a positive and outward-looking attitude
to the universe. This means that you become active rather than passive, a shaper rather than a watcher, proactive rather than reactive. If
you would like to become more proactive, how can you begin? First,
decide that you will. Second, the next time a new opportunity presents itself, try it. You are likely to find that once you have decided to
say "yes," an opportunity will present itself quickly. The universe is
checking you out, seeing if you mean what you say. To develop your
"yes" qualities, take the initiative. Don't wait for others to do something, do it yourself. If you want to contact someone, make the first
move. Reach out to people. If there is an activity you would like to
happen but no one is organizing it, organize it; take the lead. If there

is a far-off place you have always wanted to visit, visit it. Travel broadens your horizons. The more we take the initiative, the better we can open ourselves to possibility and spontaneity. We allow ourselves to let go of previously arranged plans and ideas and respond to the moment. Some people are naturally like this. They are extroverts. They like novelty, going to new places, meeting new people. Psychologists will often tell you that you cannot change your basic personality. This is true to a certain extent, but only to a certain extent. Some of us are suppressed extroverts; others are introverts only up until the second drink. We all have competing impulses to engage or to retreat, to take risks or to play safe. Magical self is intrepid and spontaneous self. It is prepared to take risks. The more you practice, the easier it gets.

Waking up Your Brain

Why is spontaneity important? Spontaneity means responses to ideas from yourself or others that are not responses you would otherwise have. If you are a natural risk taker—the sort of person who makes a natural entrepreneur—you will be used to doing this. If you have been brought up to be cautious and thoughtful, to look before you leap, then you will have to learn new habits of thought. We can encourage spontaneity by breaking habits. All esoteric teaching tells us that one of the problems with human progression is that half the time we sleepwalk our way through life. You will notice that you cease to "see" your route to work. Whether driving, walking, or taking public transport, the journey becomes an automatic program that you run. You wake up at various points along it and notice where you are and then go back to your daydreaming or whatever. You don't really "see" it anymore. Similarly, after a while you cease to see pictures on your wall. Your vision becomes habituated to them, so you no longer notice them. While I was at school, my psychic Gemini mother often rearranged the furniture. I would come home and find we had completely different room arrangements. I would "see" things again, notice them; there would be a different energy in the room. Moving things around is also a brilliant way of keeping things clean. All that accumulated dust hidden away in corners and under sofas is exposed, so you can get rid of it. Getting rid of accumulated waste is psychologically energizing as well as healthy. Changing your environment is one way of waking up the brain. Here are some other ways to make your psyche more active.

@

Waking up Your Psyche

Change the angle of your desk. Change your hair color. Take a different route to work. Visit somewhere you have always meant to go but never got round to. People habitually sit in the same place when they eat, go to meetings, or go to lectures. Sit somewhere different. You will make eye contact with different people and see the room or situation from a new perspective. You may be one of the many people who were subtly encouraged as an infant to change from left-handedness to right-handedness by your mother moving the spoon into your right hand if you picked it up with the "wrong" one. If so, try doing some activities with your left hand and see if it works better for you. Wear your watch on your right wrist. Use your left hand to eat, for your computer mouse, to brush your teeth, for phone calls. Try out new sensory experiences. No, I don't mean just new sexual positions. Listen to a different type of music. If you are not a theater-goer or an art gallery visitor, go as an experiment and see if you enjoy it. Try out a new cuisine. Read a different newspaper. When your brain is more awake and active, you will find it easier to concentrate and have focused purpose. When our brains are tired and lazy, they drift, daydream, and can easily float into negative thinking. Awake brains are positive, focused brains. Be awake.

Mars Ritual

Mars rituals are useful if you have a lot to do and need energy, if you've been going through a period of depression and need to shake it off, if you have to be confrontational, or if you have been too timid and accommodating in the past. Magical altars usually have symbols of all four elements on them, but there may be times when you want to emphasize and encourage the energy of a particular element. The red planet Mars is closely associated with fire. Instead of the usual quarter invocations and visualizations, invoke the fiery aspect of each element. I'll explain what I mean.

Elements can manifest in different forms—hot or cold, liquid or solid. Air relates to the elements in their most insubstantial form, fire relates to heated versions of the elements, water to the elements mixed with water, and earth to the elements in their most solid form. Think about this in relation to fire. What is the airiest and least substantial way in which fire can manifest itself? Light, spark, or reflected light of the Sun—a rose, orange, and red-tinted dawn sky? What about the hottest version—fire of fire? What might you visualize? Think of an immense amount of intensely hot fire—the heart of the Sun? What about fire of water? We need an image of a watery fire—tricky; what about burning steam or boiling water? What about fire of earth? Volcanic lava, which is molten earth, burning coal? Choose four visualizations for fire of air, fire of fire, fire of water, and fire of earth. Below are some suggestions to help you, but remember there are no absolute rights and wrongs. Choose what seems right for you. Remember that decision-making is one of the Martian qualities you want to cultivate.

ELEMENTS OF ELEMENTS

Element	Air Of	Fire Of	Water Of	Earth Of
Air	Sky	Lightning, hot wind	Cloud	Dust
Fire	Glow	Heart of the Sun	Steam	Phosphorus
Water	Mist or rain	Hot springs	Sea	Ice
Earth	Quicksand	Molten lava	Mud	Rock

The Rite

As preparation for the ritual, create a Mars altar. Cover a table or other flat surface with a red cloth. Decorate it with red candles and red flowers. Find a piece of red rock, such as red sandstone or red granite. You could add bloodstone and hematite, or something made of iron, the metal of Mars. Find a red vase for your flowers. Fill a red bowl with water. Use red candles and a Mars incense. For a wand, use holly, the warrior tree. If you have a fiery picture, place it on or near your altar. You could decorate your altar with fiery tarot cards. The Ace of Wands, Queen of Wands, and King of Wands are all good, as are the major arcana cards of Strength, ruled by Leo; Temperance, ruled by Sagittarius; and the Emperor, ruled by Aries. There is a major arcana card ruled by Mars, but this is the Tower, the card of unexpected disasters, which is not what you want. Make sure the room is warm—remember you are invoking a fiery planet. Once everything is ready, relax and take a bath. You can prepare your psyche further by lighting the bathroom with red candles and, before your rite, by drinking a spicy tea.

To begin your rite, cast a circle and invoke fire of air, fire of fire, fire of water, and fire of earth at the four directions.

Stand in the east and visualize fire of air—maybe you visualize a red, orange, rose, and gold dawn sky and a warm wind. The warm wind fills you with the power of illumination, the ability to see what must be done and do it. Meditate on this for a few moments, then say:

> Powers of the East, by fire of air,
> I summon, stir, and call you up,
> to guard my circle and witness my rite.

At the south, visualize fire of fire, feel its warmth seeping into your muscles, relaxing and yet energizing you, giving you the gift of inner strength. Meditate on this for a few moments, and then invoke the south by fire of fire. At the west, visualize bubbling hot springs. Feel the warmth of the steam rising from them, cleansing your skin and bringing purification, another of the gifts of fire, and the warmth of love and passion. Meditate on this for a few moments, then invoke fire of water. At the north, the place of fire of earth, visualize a volcano spewing out molten lava. This is the destructive power of fire, anger, and righteous wrath. Sense the power and energy of anger, but do not draw it into you. Meditate on its fiery power and sense that it is a power buried deep within you, part of you, but one to be used only cautiously, wisely, and well. Call upon the north as fire of earth. Your circle is now complete.

Now turn to the center, the realm of spirit and say an invocation to the god Mars, or if you prefer a goddess, say an invocation to Sekhmet, lioness-headed goddess of the Egyptians, or to another deity with fire associations. Remember that Mars is a warrior but also a god of athletics—using the body in harmony and strength. He is associated too with sexual passion and is a patron of agriculture and fertility. His season is Spring, which brings new growth, new beginnings, the waking of earth energy, March hares, the birth of young animals, flowers, the power to overcome winter's dark, the end of the cold times of depression, joy, birds singing. Some of these images, together with images of your own, can be woven into an invocation to Mars. If you prefer to invoke a goddess, Sekhmet is a goddess of war who defends what is hers, but she is also a goddess of healing.

Hers is the strength to drive out disease. Her image is that of a woman in a straight shift, sitting on a throne. Behind her lioness head is a golden solar disc to show that she is the beloved daughter of the sun god Ra. In her right hand, she holds a staff with a lotus flower at the top. In her left hand, she holds an ankh, a looped cross. This is a sign of life, but also a symbolic key that opens the door to the temple of the mysteries. As you say your invocation to god or goddess, visualize an image of the deity manifesting behind your altar to bless and energize your rite.

ANKH

Once you have invoked the divine energy, sit, stand, or kneel in front of your altar with your spine straight and allow your breathing to become slow and steady. Once you are relaxed, visualize a column of white light pouring down over the crown of your head. The white light enters your crown and flows through you. It flows down through your skull, cleansing your psyche. It flows right through your body and down into the floor beneath. With the flow of white light, all negative energy is removed from you. You feel a clear, light energy filling you, uniting you with the spiritual realm. The light continues to flow down through you and over you. It is a continuous white stream without beginning and without end. The streaming light clears out all negative thought. It clears out jealousy and anger. It clears out the barriers that prevent you from realizing your potential. It leaves you focused in the present, with a strong desire to order your life in the way that you wish. Now say an affirmation.

Mars Affirmation

I have the power to change what seems changeless;
I am an Energizer in the world;
I have the will to change the pattern of my existence,
with love and passion, I can harness that will;
deep within me are reserves of strength, energy, and power.

Allow the light that you are visualizing to cease to flow. The clear sense of purpose that contact with the light has given you remains. You find that you are in your own space, with a focused energy and purpose that you can use when you wish. You can repeat the affirmation whenever you need to have focused energy. To close your rite, bless cakes and wine, and eat and drink. Cake or biscuit with ginger in it would be appropriate. Thank the god or goddess, then bid farewell to your fiery quarters.

To back up your ritual, take the red imagery into your everyday life. Say the affirmation every day for a week. Add a touch of red to your clothing. You don't have to dress head to foot in the color, but one of these—a red tie, earrings, shoes, socks, a necklace, a buttonhole—can add a little fire to a business suit. Put a Mars-related substance into your work environment—a piece of hematite as a paperweight or red flowers, for instance. Buy a red folder for meetings. Take notes with a red pen. All these are simple things, but they work on the simple age-old magical principle of sympathetic magic.

✦

POINTERS FOR PRACTICE

Magic is a way of reprogramming our unconscious mind so we have a different set of expectations about how the world will treat us. When we have different unconscious expectations, people treat us differently. When we empower ourselves, others see us as empowered. We are instinctively drawn to empowered people. The world treats us differently when we have a positive evaluation of ourselves. Make a Mars talisman when you need to feel empowered, and to strengthen your decisiveness and will.

CHAPTER TWENTY

Magic and Depression

. . . if we should wish to uplift a while and otherwise console a person who is too occupied by Saturnine contemplation or oppressed with cares . . . the best discipline is to recall to the mean those declining to either side through certain pursuits and remedies of Phoebus [the Sun] and Jupiter . . .

MARSILIO FICINO (1489) *LIBRI DE VITA*

Saturn, the planet traditionally associated with melancholia, is associated with the element of earth. When we describe depression, our images are often earthy. We feel buried, drowned, as though we are wading through treacle or pushing a boulder uphill. We feel heavy, lethargic, slow. Earth and water make mud. We talk of sinking into depression or becoming "stuck in the mud." To get out, we need energy, but we have no energy. What can we do? If you are beginning to think magically, you will sense the answer. You need to create energy that can act as an antidote to excess water and earth. Marsilio Ficino was a Renaissance doctor and magician, president of the Florentine Platonic Academy, commentator and translator of Plato, Plotinus, and the *Corpus Hermeticum,* who invented a system of planetary magic that was a precursor to modern psychology. He recommends Sun and Jupiter as antidotes to Saturn because they are planets associated with the element of fire, and fire warms.

When we are depressed, "stuck in the mud," we know what we

should be doing. The problem is letting go of our present state and allowing ourselves to do it. Sometimes we need a "down" phase. When things go wrong, it is good to let go a little; to acknowledge our grief; to have a period of mourning, of suspended animation. This is a recovery period, a time to deal with shock and lick our wounds so they can heal. And then, at the right time, when we have had our time of convalescence and recuperation, it is time to move forward. Magic is helpful here. It can provide the extra energy we need, a trigger to boost the psyche that says, "Believe in yourself. You have courage and power."

I will describe a magical working that some friends and I did to help someone move forward from a broken relationship. It would work equally well for someone recovering from a different kind of personal distress, such as losing a job. You will notice that we did not do all the work. When someone is in a negative situation, he or she needs the help of others, but that help involves showing the person how to help him- or herself. Magic is about empowerment, and if we are doing magic for someone else, it is he or she who needs to feel empowered, not us.

☽

HELPING SOMEONE MOVE FORWARD

One Saturday afternoon, some friends and I make an incense for Emma. We include myrrh, used in ancient embalming; cypress from inconsolable Cyparissus, who mourned eternally after accidentally killing his favorite stag; and cassia oil and aloes gum, used in ancient medicine to fight disease but also as an erotic incense. We are making an incense of Saturn. We are working to rid her of a disease, the disease of being locked in the past. Emma has been mourning for six months the end of a long-term relationship. It's like a death. The relationship has died; sometimes she wishes she was dead; sometimes she wishes death for her former partner; but it's early spring and it's time to let go and move forward.

We give her hugs, so she knows she is loved. We ask her to start pounding the ingredients: pounding is therapeutic. We all take a turn. We ask her to burn the incense every evening for seven days, and each evening to say good-bye to the relationship. We ask her to imagine it as a ship setting off to sea. We show her the Waite tarot card of the two of wands. A man stands on a terrace looking out to sea. He holds a miniature world in his hands. He is in charge of his fate. We know from the next card in the suit, the three of wands, that he is watching a ship. We ask her to visualize each evening that she is the watcher, holding her destiny in her hands. She is watching a ship sailing further and further away from the shore. It is taking away with it the cargo of the past, good and bad, joy and grief, leaving her in charge of her future. On the seventh evening, we tell her that she should let the image of the ship disappear over the horizon and then mentally walk away, keeping the miniaturized world.

Emma comes back the next week, noticeably happier. In a toy shop, she has found a child's rubber ball with the world painted on it, and she is using this in her meditation. She takes it to work with her and puts it on her desk to remind her that her destiny is in her own hands. We have another session of incense pounding. This time we make an incense of the Sun and we bring her small gifts, gifts with Jupiterian symbolism—an amethyst necklace, some blue candles, a bowl of purple and yellow crocuses, some purple anemones, a tiny oak tree in a pot, some cedar oil, a piece of lapis lazuli. We ask her to keep her gifts near her and on each of the next seven evenings to burn the incense of the Sun to bring new energy into her life. We suggest that she visualize herself as the Queen of Wands in the tarot—a woman filled with energy and in charge of her own destiny. Each evening she is to open her chakras and visualize herself strong and empowered with the energy of the Sun. Emma moves forward to embrace the rest of her life.

☽

When We Get Stuck

Part of Emma's problem was depression. Some types of depression have physiological causes associated with changes in brain chemistry and hormonal fluctuations. The way you think can be a contributing factor, but if you are physiologically depressed, you need pharmacological help. Most people, however, are not physiologically depressed. They are just plain depressed. Many of us go through phases when we become stuck. The future seems hopeless, the present disastrous, and we are full of regrets about the past. We are like rabbits paralyzed in headlights. Instead of a will like fire, our will is frozen like ice. We are stuck in a deep black hole. Thinking can lead us into that hole, especially if we focus on the past. We can be caught up in the trap of "if only." If only I hadn't done this, gotten involved with this person, taken this job, bought this house, said "no" to that opportunity—life would have been better. Of course life might have been better; it might also have been a lot worse. We do not know what other directions our lives would have taken if we had done things differently. We only know where we are now. We have a say in the future, but the past is unchangeable history.

It is important to treat every day of our lives as Day One—a new beginning. If we start each day afresh, we can focus on the here and now and on what we want to achieve in the future, rather than on what we have left behind. When we are depressed, we make errors of thinking: I feel awful, there must be something wrong with me, it must be my fault, things will always be like this, they can never get any better, I'm useless . . . And on it goes. If you are trapped in this kind of negative groove, you need to take a deep breath and take charge. In the future, you will be in control, not your illogical thinking. Tackling depression can be a mixture of magic and what fantasy novelist Terry Pratchett calls "headology," one of the main skills of his witches. First, if you are unhappy about something that has happened in the past, forget about fault. Blame never solves anything. It focuses on past causes, not future changes. What you want are future changes. A good place to start your life-change is the "What if" game.

@
What If?

Playing the "What if" game is easy. Sit down in a quiet room and light two candles, one red for fire and one golden yellow for the Sun. Dim the lighting and play some relaxing music. Relax, open your chakras, then do the will meditation described in Chapter 19. With your mind clear, imagine how your life might be if you were not depressed. What would people notice about you that was different? Choose three things about yourself or your environment that you would change if you were not depressed. Would you change your hairstyle, clean your home, cook a meal, wash the windows, change your car, paint a room, change a light bulb, buy some different clothes, phone a friend, apply for a new job, sign up for a yoga class, buy a mountain bike, end a relationship, try to make new friends?

The next stage is action. Do one of the things you would do if you were not depressed. Doing the first thing will be the hardest, so choose whichever is easiest or most pressing. Depression creates inertia, and you need to act rather than being inert. Don't spend a long time deciding, just do one thing. If you are so depressed that you can't make decisions, write the alternatives on separate pieces of paper. Shut your eyes, jumble them up, grab one, open your eyes, and whatever it is, do it. Do it even though you are depressed; even if every step you take feels as though you are wading through thigh-high mud; even if everything inside you is screaming, "No! I can't do this. I want to opt out. It's too difficult, too painful!" If you are depressed enough, even getting to the supermarket and back is a major triumph. Doing things when you are depressed is like pushing water uphill. It is hard. Once you have done one thing, do a second, then a third. As your psyche gets used to the idea that you can do things, even if part of you is depressed and doesn't want to, the rigid control mechanisms, the programming that tells you that you can't do anything because you are depressed, lets go just a bit. And you prove yourself wrong. You can do things—you've just done one. And then you do another one, then another.

Sun and Jupiter energies are good for depression, but sometimes you need something more. You need a little Mars. Mars is associated with the qualities of passion, energy, will, courage, and anger. The anger is important. It is difficult to believe when you are severely depressed and so tired and dispirited that you can hardly get out of bed, but depression can be closely related to repressed anger that is not allowed to escape and so turns in on itself. Beneath all that earth and water, there may be a fiery volcano just waiting to erupt. Anger is not a constructive emotion. What you need is a positive way of tapping that latent fiery energy. Once you have achieved the easiest item on your "What if" list—you've finally turned up that drooping hem, sewn on the missing button, painted over that ghastly orange wall, had that strange noise in your engine checked out—once you have taken the first step to help yourself, you could do a Mars ritual to help you do more. Remember, you have already made a small beginning, even without the aid of a ritual. The ritual will help you harness more energy for the next onslaught in sorting out your life.

@

Mars for Energy

If you feel stuck and need to move forward, a Mars ritual can give you the energy and impetus you need to do something about your life.

Self-Acceptance

I used to be Snow White, but I drifted.

—MAE WEST

Magic is about self-exploration. Through ritual and meditation, we discover more about ourselves. It is a knowledge that seeps in via the unconscious. We are unaware that we have acquired it and then suddenly it emerges into consciousness. When we do not know the answer to one of life's questions, we find that we can allow our unconscious minds to work on it in dream, through divination, and in meditation, and the answer emerges fully formed into our minds. We are learning to use our psyches in a new way, a way that trusts the deeper self within. With enlargement of consciousness come deeper wisdom and deeper insights into right and wrong. This can be painful. As we evolve, we become more acutely aware of our failings, dishonesties, hypocrisies, cruelties, and self-deceptions; of the side of ourselves that is manipulative, egotistical, selfish, aggressive, and is not always well-disposed toward others. Looking glasses and reflections in water play an important role in myth and magical tales. The hero of the story (male or female) sees his or her reflection and discovers something that he or she did not know before. Reflections take us out of our everyday consciousness, where we are wrapped up in our own little dream world of fact and fantasy, dreams and aspirations, hopes, anxieties, and fears. They allow us to see. When we see, we are given new data to integrate into our psyches. New data changes us. Things can never be the same as they were. New data takes us forward.

The more we understand ourselves, the more we start to see through others and ourselves. You may notice as your conscience grows more acute that you dislike some of the ways you act. That's okay, because magic can help you change so that you act better, but where you *do* look back on past actions with regret, it's important to remember Grandma's old adage: "There's no use crying over spilled milk." You have to put the past behind you. Do not waste time telling yourself what a nasty, rotten, useless person you are. Instead, let this energy out of your head, where it makes you miserable, and get rid of it. The past is only useful when it teaches us about how to act in the present and future. It is there for us to draw lessons from, not to wallow in. Maybe you foul up an important presentation at work, your job interview goes horribly wrong, you say something awful to your best friend after your fifth Bacardi Breezer, you end a relationship in a cruel and heartless way. If something doesn't go as well as it should, this is a challenge, an opportunity to learn something. Think, "Okay, I'm not perfect and I fouled up, but I don't have to make the same mistake again."

In magical thinking, there is no perfection this side of manifestation. Perfection is not part of reality, but part of the otherworld—the world beyond matter, the world of dreams and ideals. Here on planet Earth, we must translate ideas into actions. Inevitably, there is a discrepancy between what we dream and what we achieve. The first discrepancy we have to deal with is between what we are and what we would like to be. We will get more out of life if we learn to enjoy who we are, aspire to be the best we can be, and accept that we often fall short of what we wish. Accepting our shortcomings does not mean complacency and a lack of desire to change. It does mean living with reality. However good we are at life and magic, we are not going to be able to make things exactly as we want. What we can do is to give it our best shot. Natural magicians teach "magical realism," which means steering a course between the boring drab dullness of cynicism and the naivete of romanticism, where we are so out of touch with reality that we think we can do the impossible.

Putting the Past Behind You

Sometimes we become stuck because we find ourselves involved in emotional situations where we find it difficult to let go. A lot of these involve anger or grief, often both. It might be a death, a breakup of a relationship, loss of a job, an injury, loss of wealth. These are all the hazards that are part of the exciting and sometimes frightening business of living. If you are having problems letting go, some simple ritual actions can help you let go of many different types of past experiences—things you wished you had or hadn't done, things people did to you, random life events that just happen—by allowing you to release pent-up energy and transform it into something else. When you want to let go, to "cut the ties that bind," it is good to consign your thoughts to the past through a quicker route than burying something in the earth. You need the releasing and cleansing power of fire.

@

Rite to Let Go

If you want to let go of the past, you need to play a few psychological tricks on yourself. We hang on to the past because letting go is difficult. It's especially difficult to let go of deep emotions, so we need to practice. A few days before your ritual, spring clean your home and get rid of anything that you do not use—old clothes, CDs, old towels that you've kept for spares "just in case," discarded flower pots, broken items that you will never fix. Whatever time of year, have a spring cleaning and clearing. Now you've started to create the right energy in your psyche, an energy that is letting go of what you do not need.

For your ritual, set up an altar with a yellow, orange, or gold altar cloth, flowers and candles, a Sun or Mercury incense, a bowl of earth, a pen, and some yellow or orange paper. The Sun is associated with healing and strength, Mercury with movement. Yellow is a color associated with the Sun, and orange with Mercury. Here, a mixture of the two can bring you positive rationality and creative energy. For cakes and wine, choose white wine and a cake or biscuit with orange flavor.

Open your chakras, cast a circle, and call upon the powers of the four directions to witness your rite and to lend you their energy and power to help you move forward. Then sit in your ritual space, take up pen and paper, and write down in one sentence the past event you want to leave behind. Leave a space and write in one sentence any feelings that you have about it that you want to consign to the past. Leave a space and write a third sentence—what you want for the future. Cut the paper into three strips, one for each sentence. Take the first sentence—what happened—and read it aloud. Now burn the strip in a candle flame. Say as you burn it, "I let go of this event in my life. Let it be consumed in the past." Put the ashes in your bowl of earth. Take the second strip. Read it aloud, then burn it, saying, "This is the present, I am moving forward into the future." Again, put the ashes in your bowl. Third, take the final strip. Read it aloud and say, "This is what I want for the future." Then fold it up in your hands. Draw energy into your chakras, energize your hands, and visualize the energy like golden light being absorbed into the third strip of paper. When you cannot energize the piece of paper any more, put it on your altar and end your rite by blessing cakes and wine, libating, and thanking and bidding farewell to the four directions. Dispose of your earth and ashes somewhere outside. Keep your third piece of paper somewhere safe, but near you, such as in your bedroom, under your pillow, or in a small pouch you can wear around your neck. By reading aloud what you have written you are bringing it out of the hidden world of your head and into reality. Reality is much more straightforward than what goes on in our heads. By burning two of the strips, you are performing a symbolic action— you are consigning to the past that which you cannot change and keeping the strip that represents the future and making it your own.

✦

POINTERS FOR PRACTICE

The past no longer exists. It cannot be changed—not even by magic. The present and the future are full of potential and new possibilities. If you are depressed, play the "What if" game and start to make small changes in your life. Bringing Sun, Jupiter, or Mars energy into your life can help you move forward. You are not perfect, and as your insight deepens, you will see much about yourself that you do not like. Remember to forgive yourself for not being perfect. A "letting go" ritual can help you put negative past experiences and regrets behind you.

CHAPTER TWENTY-ONE

Sacred Time

M̲agic is not just a set of exercises for getting your own way.
Natural magic has its own spiritual current, which is nature religion.
For many people, their most profound spiritual experiences are not
in organized religious settings. They are outside in nature, in sex
with a person they love, in relationships with their children, or in a
gathering of people who have come together to venerate that which
is closest to their hearts and draw closer not only to the Divine outside but to the Divine within one another. Nature spirituality venerates the natural world and sees the Divine as dwelling within nature
rather than being set apart from it. Divine energy inhabits every part
of creation, so that land, sea, star, tree, and leaf are all ways that we
can see the Divine in everyday life and turn our thoughts to that
which lies beyond the boundaries of everyday existence. Magic practiced purely as spellcraft can become selfish and egocentric. As part
of our magic, we need in our lives reminders that we are part of a
greater human family that in turn is part of a biosphere, in turn part
of the cosmos. We are cells in the cosmic body, constantly inter-
changing energies with the greater whole. This gives us responsibilities as well as the gift of individuality. Our lives work better and we
are happier if we have a clear vision of how our lives connect with
the whole. The seasonal festivals celebrated by many natural magicians are ways of renewing our links with the cosmos and of reminding ourselves that we have much to give to the world and that

it is important that we give it. The festivals are also ways of linking us with nature's tides.

Celebrating the festivals is a way of attuning to the magical tides, to the forces of nature that create tides of life, death, and life again. When we celebrate the seasonal cycle, these tides become realities in our lives. They bring renewal, healing, rest after troubled times. When we know the tides, we can work our magic in conjunction with them. We work then with the flow of nature and not against it. Nature spirituality is not about seeking to impose our will on the universe but about harmonizing ourselves with the outer world, a harmony that brings harmony within. It is less flashy than spellcraft, less easy to explain, and deep—a deep rooting in earth, time, nature, past, and future. We are recognizing that we are part of the cosmos, children of Earth, and sea, and stars.

There are eight festivals in the magical year. The equinoxes, when day and night are equal, and the solstices, the shortest and longest days, are four of the magical festivals. The other four derive from the Celtic year cycle, which reflects human activity rather than astrological configurations. Contemporary natural magicians often use the Irish Celtic names for the festivals—Imbolc, Beltane, Lughnasadh and Samhain—but they are also known by traditional English names: Candlemas, May Eve, Lammas, and Halloween. The festival dates span two days because the festivals start at sunset and last for twenty-four hours to the next sunset. The dates given are the usual dates, but there can be slight variations with leap years, and astronomical phenomena such as the longest day can shift slightly in different years.

Celebrating the Seasons

To create a ritual for the seasonal festivals, create an altar using appropriate symbolism. Try to hold your ritual on a day when you do not have to go to work and can take a walk in the countryside or a city park to see what is happening in nature and to gather leaves, flowers, pine cones, acorns, feathers, stones, and other items from the natural world to decorate your altar. For the ritual itself, you can use the same way of casting a circle as you use in a magical ritual. Create an invocation to the gods, perhaps invoking the Divine as Goddess and God with imagery appropriate to the season. If you are celebrating the festival with friends, you could choose someone to represent a deity in the ritual. If you want to do magic in the ritual, choose a purpose appropriate to the seasonal tide. You can perform your rite on the exact date, but a few days before or after is also fine.

*Imbolc**

Imbolc, or Candlemas, is on January 31–February 1. Nature is awakening from its winter rest. Nature is beginning to produce signs of life. In the plant world, the first bulbs shoot. In the animal world, it is lambing time. In North America, the groundhog may wake. The days grow noticeably longer, so in traditional celebrations at this time of the year, there is a theme of the return of the light. The Christian calendar celebrates the feast of Candlemas at Imbolc. It is still winter, but spring is close at hand. In temperate regions, bulbs thrust their fresh green shoots through the earth—small signs of new life appearing. Imbolc is a time of optimism and planning new beginnings. In the traditional agricultural cycle, it was plowing time, when the days had grown long enough for the sun to warm the earth and unfreeze it. Fields would be made ready for spring sowing by turning over and aerating the soil and adding manure to fertilize it. Psychologically, we start to wake up after winter, and if we link the

---

*If you live in a temperate climate, the seasonal festival imagery described here will be similar to your local area. If you live in a hotter or colder climate, you will need to adapt the ideas to your region.

symbolism of the seasonal cycle to our own lives, this is a good time to do magic to plan and prepare new projects, which we can launch in the spring months to come. It is also a good time to renew New Year's resolutions. Healing magic is traditional at this time, so think of ways of improving your health. This is also the time of the festival of Brigid, once an Irish goddess, then a saint, and now honored as a goddess once more. She is known as Bride (pronounced Breed) in Scotland and is the origin of the English word Bride. She is a virgin goddess and represents nature reawakening and bringing new life to the land. Think of the colors outside in nature—the white of snow and snowflakes and the fresh green of new shoots. These would be good colors to choose to decorate your altar and for candle magic. To help you think about how you might celebrate Imbolc, here is how I celebrated Imbolc 1989.

◡

AN IMBOLC CELEBRATION

A white-veiled woman representing Bride stands at the edge of the magic circle, a silver crown of lighted candles upon her head. She is led down a pathway of flickering candles through the darkness and into the circle. Standing before the altar, she gives the blessing of Brigid. She is in a trance, and those who wish to ask her for prophecies or for blessings for the coming year. Her presence gives energy to the circle, the energy of creativity and the energy of healing, for Brigid's gifts include the power to heal. There is power here, and love. We prepare to bless candles to be given to the sick, energized with the healing power of the circle. We focus our minds to put some of that energy into candles for those who cannot take part. We consecrate white candles by passing them through the symbols of the four elements—incense for air, a candle flame for fire, consecrated water for water, and finally we sprinkle the candles with a little salt, symbolic of earth. We select one candle and light it. This we will use to light the rest. We pass white candles around the circle to-

SEASONAL FESTIVAL CORRESPONDENCE

Season	Natural and Agricultural Cycle	Altar Decorations	Color	Things to Do
Imbolc January 31– February 1	First bulb shoot, lambing, ewes lactate; first plowing, oats are sown	Snowdrops and other late winter bulbs, candles	White, pale green	Candle magic, healing magic, magic to initiate new project; renew New Year's resolutions
Spring Equinox March 20–21	Barley is sown; birds build nests and lay eggs; first leaves on the trees, spring flowers	Spring flowers, painted green eggs, catkins, seed cake	Green	Seed planting, fertility magic, magic to begin new enterprises and worldly activities
Beltane April 30– May 1	Trees blossom	Hawthorn and other blossom, ribbons, flowery crowns, decorated poles	Green, white, and pink	Sex magic, fertility magic, magic for worldly success; spend time with your lover, renew your passion, tend your garden, pamper your body, buy yourself new clothes, take up a sport, take children into nature and teach them the names of trees, plants, and birds
Midsummer June 21–22	Grass is cut for silage	Roses, oak leaves, symbols of the Sun	Yellow, red, green	Magic for men and for worldly affairs
Lughnasadh, Lammas July 31– August 1	Wheat harvest	Newly cut wheat, corn dollies, fresh-baked bread, sickles	Gold, orange	Magic for letting go, divorce, holiday

Season	Natural and Agricultural Cycle	Altar Decorations	Color	Things to Do
Autumn Equinox September 21–22	Winter wheat is sown, maize harvest, fruit harvest	Apples, fallen leaves, pine cones, antlers	Orange, brown, gold red	Magic to increase intellectual, psychic, or spiritual powers, study
Samhain October 31–November 1	Trees planting from Samhain to Beltane, rye planting	Apples, spirals, branches of dead leaves, black mirrors, crystal balls, cauldrons	Brown, black	Divination, remember dead relatives and friends, tend graves, honor war dead, make wills, do accounts, sign contracts, pay debts, watch spooky movies, tell ghost stories, have a party, feast, plant a tree, eat apples
Yule December 21–22	Rest and feasting	An evergreen tree (preferably one can be replanted); anything reminiscent of the Sun—golden apples, holly and mistletoe, sparkling crystals, candles, a hearth fire	Black, gold, white, red, green	Celebration, magic for children's health or to conceive, give presents, give to charity, visit relatives and friends, feed birds, sit by a log fire, tell stories

gether with a small bowl of eucalyptus oil. We take a little of the oil on our fingers, oiling each candle from the center. We visualize the person we are consecrating the candle for, saying his or her name softly, until it flows into a chant that becomes a hypnotic, wordless singing. There is energy in the circle, an energy that tingles, flows, surrounds us. There comes a point when the chanting ceases; simultaneously by unconscious agreement we stop. From the lighting candle, each of us lights a candle for a person we are healing. We place the candles on the altar, focusing on the flame as healing light. Together we say:

> Strong as the wind is our will,
> strong as fire is our desire,
> strong as the sea, our spells shall be,
> strong as earth that gives them birth.
> so mote it be!

We let go of the visualization and send a last thought to those we are healing. At the end of the circle, we extinguish the candles and wrap the individual candles so they can be given to those who have asked for healing. We tell them to burn a little of the candle every evening for a month. Each evening at the same time, we focus on those we are healing, a linking of thought and intention, in love.

☽

Spring Equinox

Spring Equinox takes place on March 20–21 and is a major turning point of the year. The hours of dark and light are equal and now the light is winning. We move into a major phase of growth. Sap rises in the trees. The sexual urge awakens in the animal world and in our own. Trees resonate with birdsong. Birds signal their territories with sound, make nests with frantic purpose, and lay eggs to fill them.

Spring flowers bloom. There are blues not seen at other times of the year, and bright yellows. The first leaves appear on the trees. Fields are sown with crops for the summer. For a Spring Equinox rite, decorate an altar with true spring flowers, those appropriate to the season rather than forced flowers from greenhouses. Choose green or yellow for your candles. Spring is a good time for fertility magic and magic to start new enterprises and activities. It is an energetic time of the year and a good time for any magic that involves putting energy into something. One traditional way of doing magic at this time of year is to energize seeds. Here is how I marked one particularly meaningful equinox.

☽

SPRING EQUINOX SEED SOWING

March 21, 1980, is our first Spring Equinox after starting our mediumship classes. Days are growing warmer and longer. The garden is full of daffodils. My husband, Chris, and I cover an altar with a green altar cloth embroidered with flowers and birds. We decorate it with a vase of daffodils and add green candles and a bowl of earth and seeds. We create a ritual. We invoke the Divine Feminine as Goddess, as the Spring Maiden, and her male counterpart as the youthful horned hunter of the woods. We sow seeds in earth to symbolize their mating, the coming together of the two creative forces of the universe to bring new energy and life. Each person takes a small pot and a handful of seeds. We energize the seeds by drawing etheric energy into our hands. We flood our hands with golden light. We visualize an intention, something we would like to see grow and manifest in our lives over the next three months. We hold the image in our minds and we project energy, through our bodies, into our arms and hands, and into the seeds. We are impregnating the seeds with a personal magical wish. We plant our seeds. I give each person a name label so we do not mix up the pots. We cover the small pots with cling film and the gardening-challenged ask me to care for theirs as well as our own. We put the pots of seeds on the kitchen windowsill. The seeds are all the same kind and receive the same amount of heat, light, and water, but some do not grow, and others are stunted. Chris gets Aries competitive about it and keeps willing his seeds to grow. They shoot up, much taller than everyone else's—too tall. They become weak and flop. Ego involvement is not a good idea in magic. Other shoots grow perfectly. Some of us have energized our seeds correctly and others have not. Some wishes are stronger and want to grow; others wither. Where the seeds do not flourish, the wishes do not manifest.

How can we explain why a seed, a wish, a ritual act of visualization and energizing should relate to whether something happens in the world? Are the seeds synchronized with the intention so they are predicting what will happen, or does the correct magical energy make both seed and intention grow? I do not know, but the differences between the pots are startling.

ⓔ

Try Seed Magic for Yourself

Beltane

Beltane, May Eve and May Day, is on April 30–May 1. Beltane is a word derived from Gaelic. It means "bright fire." It is a time when trees are covered in blossoms and flowers are blooming. Days grow longer and the increased hours of sunlight give us a psychological boost. The life force is strong, and it is a good time to remember the sensual. Beltane takes place in the astrological sign of Taurus, which is ruled by the planet Venus. This is the time for all things Venusian. It is a good time for love magic and to devote time and attention to any lover you have. Renew your passion, pamper your body, go away for a weekend into the countryside and see the beauty of nature. If you have children, teach them the names of trees, plants, and birds. For a Beltane rite, find blossoms and flowers to decorate your altar. There is an old superstition that it is unlucky to bring hawthorn blossom into the home—except for witches. So if you are a natural magician, you can count yourself included. Tend to your garden and indoor plants, as well as to yourself. Remember that Venus to the Romans was Lady of the Gardens. Check how your spring seeds are doing. By now, they may need transplanting to a larger container or outside. Green leaves and white and pink blossoms are colors we find in nature during this season; so use these colors for your altar and candles. This is an ideal time for love magic.

Midsummer

Midsummer, June 21–22, is also known as the Summer Solstice and the Longest Day. Trees are thick with green leaves. On the Longest Day, it is traditional to celebrate the power of the Sun. This is a good time to bring Sun energy into your life. Solar energy is associated with health, wealth, and material well-being. The Sun is associated in mythology with royalty and kingship. In the modern world, this translates into worldly success and fame. Now is a good time for success magic. You could do some candle magic or make a Sun talisman. Midsummer is a time of bright colors in nature—roses and other summer flowers. Decorate your altar in reds, golds, and greens and with golden or yellow candles.

Lughnasadh

Lughnasadh, July 31–August 1, is also known as Lammas, which means Loaf Mass. It is the time of the wheat harvest and is a thanksgiving for the safe harvest of the wheat. A special loaf would be baked from the newly gathered grain. This is a time to decorate the altar with golds and oranges, the colors of ripened grain. What about magic? At Lughnasadh, summer Sun is still strong, maybe too strong, but the days are shortening. Although it is summer, a time of positive energy, the signs of decay are already present. Wheat is golden because the fresh greenness that it had when it first grew has been burned out of it by the Sun. It suffers the same vagaries of aging as our human bodies. We too grow, mature, peak, and then decline. Decline is not necessarily negative. There are some energies that we want to decline. Lughnasadh is a good time of the year for magic to let go of negative energies. If we have been through a painful divorce or relationship breakup, this is a good time to do magic to let go of the past and move forward. Like Imbolc, Lughnasadh can be a healing time, a time to let go of the negative energy of illness. Sometimes this comes about through conscious magic, but celebrating the seasonal festivals has a deep effect on the unconscious mind. What we enact symbolically becomes a reality. Magic works in many ways, not just through specific rites or spells. We have to remember the power of synchronicity. The best example of this in my own life was an incident that involved a good friend of mine, Stephen, who had been struggling with AIDS.

☾

LUGHNASADH, '95

Stephen comes out of the hospital. He is coming to stay with us in France to celebrate Lughnasadh. The thought of him traveling worries me: he's uninsurable. I don't know what will happen if he relapses. We choose by lot a man to represent the god in the Lammas rite. The Lammas god represents the spirit of the wheat that is chopped down so that people might be fed. The message is of death, sacrifice, and rebirth. A woman offers the men straws. Stephen draws the shortest straw. The sun is low and golden, near to sinking. The women who are to dance the reaping emerge in black robes, crowns of ripened wheat and poppies on their heads. Each holds a silver sickle whose blade turns to gold in the evening light. The circle is cast within our circle of standing stones. We salute the four directions, by blade and sign, and call to the guardians of our land. Wind comes up from the east and dies away. In the south, a planet hangs over the horizon, a bright beacon. To the west, the sunset; to the north, a silver birch and a white quartz altar gleam in the fading light. A dance begins; the glittering blades of the sickles curve inward and meet and outward again, in hypnosis-inducing crescents. The women circle, swaying in and out from the central fire. The Sun at last is beginning to sink low. Pink streaks in the west turn blood red. A song begins, one woman, an ancient lament, the song of the reaper. Sadness, death, yearning, darkness, and sacrifice are in her voice and words. The old order passes, the summer Sun is squeezing the life force from the land. She shows signs of aging. The black-robed women surround the men, drawing them into an inner circle surrounded by sickle-bearing women. They say:

> He shall be cut down in the wheat for me,
> he shall lie upon the warm earth for me,
> he shall give his life to the land for me,
> he shall renew the world.

A clashing of sickle blades, Stephen falls. A black cloth is drawn over him. The Sun sets—twilight. Women strew wheat ears and poppies over the black cloth. Red, gold, and black, the colors of harvest. The women chant, joining the singers:

> He shall be cut down in the wheat for me,
> sustenance shall he be to all.
> Take these, the gifts of land and heart,
> and bear our secret wishes to the gods.
> Dark Mother, Earth Mother, take him to your embrace.

Stars appear like lights being switched on. Another chant calls the dead god to rise, like new shoots of wheat. The power that lies in the earth brings renewal; the dead husk of wheat is also the seed that brings new life.

> Die not but live,
> fall not, but renew.

A stirring beneath the black cloth. Stephen stands before us, tall, straight, strong, powerful. He speaks of death, life, and renewal. The rite ends, a thing of power. Shortly after, the doctors try a new treatment. Stephen's blood count goes up and up again. He lives.

☽

Autumn Equinox

Autumn Equinox takes place on September 21–22. The hours of day and night are equal. We stand poised on the threshold of autumn. Soon the nights will grow longer. It is the time of the fruit harvests and maize harvest, when the last crops of the summer season are gathered and used or stored. As we enter the darker time of the year, outdoor activities become less attractive. There is a natural turning inward to our inner worlds and the life of the mind. It is a good time to sign up for new courses or to undertake a spiritual retreat. A time of meditation and contemplation can give us insights into how we can best make use of our time in the winter months to come. This is a good season for magic to assist with intellectual matters or our personal development. If we have spending problems, then autumn is a good time to work with the sober energy of Saturn. Decorate your altar with the colors of autumn leaves—orange, brown, gold, red—and with autumn leaves themselves, and with apples, a gift of autumn.

☽

Samhain

Samhain, October 31–November 1, is also called Halloween, or All Hallows Eve. It is a turning point, poised between one cycle of rest, renewal, and growth and another. It is food storage time. In the woods and parks, bright red hips attract birds and squirrels. Squirrels store away chestnuts—shining, round, brown, full of starch and goodness. Ponds grow colorful with the incoming northern migration. Brightly painted arctic ducks take over when less hardy birds fly south. In ancient Ireland, at Samhain, warriors sheathed their swords while bards sang in the halls and exaggerated their exploits, as is the task of bards. As for blades, it was the butcher's shining ax that made its sharp journey—and met with flesh, bringing death to pigs and cattle that could not be kept through winter. Salted meat was winter's fare. And in the halls of the chieftains and the hovels of peasants, extra places were laid, to feed not the living but the dead. It was time for the ancestors to return to their descendants, to feast and make merry with them. Samhain stands outside ordinary time. It is between the worlds, poised on the threshold between past and future. Those who have transcended earthly life and live in the eternal present can come to meet with us who know and love them.

In Europe, Samhain was an important date in the legal year. It was a time to make wills, do accounts, sign contracts, and pay debts. Samhain is a good time to do magic for any legal or contractual process you are involved with. You could do some candle magic or make a talisman. This is also a traditional time for divination for the year to come. Decorate your altar with black and orange—black for the dark time of the year and for death, and orange for the fallen leaves. All is not somber gloom at Samhain. Halloween is of course a time of celebration and fun. To celebrate Halloween, watch spooky movies, tell ghost stories, or have a party. This is also, in temperate climates, the beginning of the tree-planting season. Plant a tree to honor the memory of a friend or relative or to give thanks for blessings received during the year. Samhain is also a good time to re-member the dead. We can honor our ancestors by making an altar with photographs and mementos and lighting candles to honor their memories and to send them good wishes in the life beyond. Each Samhain, I honor the memory of my mother. Here I will de-scribe the first Samhain after her death.

SAMHAIN, '95

Leaves fall, trees are stripped bare. Shortening days—the clocks go backwards. The pace of life slows. With the ebbing tide of life, the old grow weaker. I take my mother out in a wheelchair to view the last bright red autumn leaves, her urgent wish. The days are unsea-sonably warm. She does not go out again. She died on October 29—two days before Samhain. Her body not yet cold, bells are rung and masses for her soul are said in monasteries and in parish churches. Soon after Samhain, on All Soul's Day, we bury her—a Catholic rite with Pagan overtones. We throw rosemary in the grave for remem-brance. In the trees around the graveyard, I see her spirit, my father waiting. Hand in hand, they walk away. On the gravestone, beneath their names, I have carved, "United in Love and Light." In the evening with our Wiccan friends, we dance the Spiral Dance in re-membrance; my mother was a dancer.

Yule

Yule is on December 21–22, the Longest Night. It is also called Win-ter Solstice, or Midwinter. The seasonal cycle changes. Days are still shortening, temperatures growing colder, but on the shortest day of the year, we undergo a psychological shift. It is almost as though the psyche says, "That's it. Enough! Time for a celebration." Winter Solstice celebrations are an important part of many cultures. In the darkest time of the year, it is important to reaffirm life and, in the mythology of Europe, it was the time of the rebirth of the Sun. Christianity took this time for its own feast of celebration, not for the Sun, but the Son. Yule is connected with birth and the celebration of a child, so it is a good time for magic for children's health or to conceive. Link to the seasonal tide of celebration by giving presents, donating to charity, visiting relatives and friends, and feeding birds. Cover your altar with a red or gold cloth and decorate it with evergreens and the traditional holly and mistletoe. Add sparkling crystals and warm red and gold candles, anything that reminds you of warmth and love in this cold time of the year.

★

POINTERS FOR PRACTICE

Natural magic has its own spiritual current, which is nature religion. Nature religion is natural religion, a way to venerate the cosmos that is our home. Celebrating the seasons is a way of harmonizing ourselves with the outer world of nature. We are part of nature, and we feel rooted and whole when we remember to honor the planet that gives us life. Celebrating the seasons also reminds us that we are planetary citizens with global responsibilities. We need to work to keep our planet a safe, healthy, and abundant home for generations to come.

CHAPTER TWENTY-TWO

Sacred Place

Natural magic makes sacred that which is natural. It sanctifies time by honoring the changing seasonal tides that reflect changes in Nature but that also parallel the changing tides within our lives and psyches. Natural magic also sanctifies place. In Chapter 6, I discussed that magic begins at home, by creating centers of energy and peace within our homes. If we have a garden, or even a balcony or roof terrace, we can create positive energies in these spaces around us too. You can bring a deity statue into your home to create a sacred shrine and energy center. You could also place a statue in your garden to create a center of peace and meditation. Many garden suppliers now have statues of Greek deities, Egyptian Basts, and Buddhas. The cats that visit our garden in France like to sit in front of our large Bast statue, imitating its pose and looking for all the world as though they are praying. The birds prefer our outdoor Buddha, whose cupped hands collected rain and create a natural birdbath. We have surrounded our Buddha with flowers, and Bast sits on a plinth beneath an arch of flowers and climbing plants. On our London balcony, a bronze Buddha smiles benignly into the living room, creating an atmosphere of harmony and peace. You can treat your whole garden as your personal space and apply the feng shui grid in Chapter 6 to determine which parts of the garden would be good for different features, depending on what in your life you want to emphasize. The central space is your energy center, so whatever you put there represents your central being. Think about what you might like that to be—a tree, a statue of a favorite deity or other being, a fountain, a sundial, a beautiful boulder, a seating area for friends and family to gather. What might best represent what you want to make central in your life?

Placing objects in your garden that remind you of the sacred and timeless will make it a haven of peace and a place where you can rest and re-energize yourself.

Tree planting has its own special magic. Plant trees in the appropriate season for your locality. This is the late autumn and milder winter months when the ground is not frozen but Nature is dormant, so the tree can rest a while and get used to its new environment before having to grow. There is an ancient European tradition that any major event should be marked by planting a tree. We still maintain this tradition in a secular way when political leaders plant trees to mark special occasions. Many folk traditions talk beautifully about planting "trees of thanks," so when something special has happened to us—a magical ritual to get a job, for instance, has worked, or we or someone close to us has given birth—then we give something to Nature. Planting a tree can also be a special way of remembering someone who has died. As the tree grows, so we can remember him or her and wish them well in the life beyond and any new life to come. The principles of natural magic are derived from Nature. Nature produces new growth but this matures, withers, falls, and replenishes the nutrients in the soil so that in its turn it can create more new growth. Giving a gift to Nature or to a charitable or spiritual body when something we have sought with the aid of magic manifests for us is a good principle in magic. It is our personal way of contributing to the cycle of growth.

When your magic is successful, give something back to the world in return. In this way, your gain is also the world's gain.

Natural magic is earthy magic in the sense that magic creates a strong connection with Nature in the form of the species that share our planet with us and the elements, including the land on which we live. Connecting with the land around us is important. When we move homes, we uproot ourselves. We will feel psychologically more secure if we root ourselves to our new neighborhood. We can do this by creating sacred shrines that act as energy centers in our homes. We can also find a deep sense of connectedness by visiting sacred sites in our locality. They are places where generations of human beings have worshipped for hundreds or thousands of years. They may not be your direct ancestors, but it is important to link with the memories inherent in places. They give us roots and connectedness, important human needs; especially now that our societies are so fragmented and migratory.

Meditating in Your Own Sacred Space

Wherever you live, there will be sacred sites, ancient earth mounds, standing stones, tombs, temples, churches. Whether it is a sacred place outside in Nature or a human-made building, the atmosphere is likely to be charged and powerful. Regardless of the religious tradition, if you go into places where people have prayed, meditated, and performed rituals for centuries, you will find that the atmosphere "zings." The silence rings with sound. If you meditate there, you will come away renewed and refreshed. If there is no sacred place in your area, make your own. Choose a tree that seems to you to be especially beautiful, strong, or evocative and make this a place that you visit regularly to meditate for a while and to step outside your everyday life and your hopes and fears.

CIRCLES AND SPIRALS

Brittany is a land of spirals. The traditional dances move in spirals. The neolithic tombs built over a period between four and nine thousand years ago are carved with spirals. Some artistic friends come to stay and decide to create a more elaborate form of spiral—a labyrinth—on our land. They search for the right place—the lawn? I gently dissuade them. It will look great now, but you try mowing a labyrinth. We find a clearing in the pine plantation that looks just right, a circular space with a tree in the center. They collect small rocks. Hours of trips with the wheelbarrow later, the jumbled rocks reveal a shape—around a central pine tree, a meditative labyrinth.

THE LABYRINTH

At night, we fill empty yogurt jars with night-lights and hang them in the trees. One by one in silence, we walk the labyrinth. The labyrinth walk is mysterious. It takes much longer to go in than to come out. Walking it makes some people so dizzy they fall over. Others find it difficult to maintain the silence. It embarrasses them to be still, to contemplate, to watch someone else perform an action that they will soon copy. Eventually, people "get it." They find that if they concentrate on the walking, if they maintain the silence, if they forget that others are watching, they reach a point of transcendence. The journey around the labyrinth becomes all journeys—a metaphor for life, for the seasons' change, for the evolution of the planet, for the slowly ever-changing cosmos. The way out of the labyrinth retraces the way in, but it appears different, never the same. The traveler is changed by the journey. This is the secret of the labyrinth.

Sometimes we bless the sacred cup. One person carries the cup to the center to libate the Earth and tree. Another follows and takes the cup from the first, drinks, and becomes the cupbearer, holder of the sacred office, guardian of the Grail at the *axis mundi*, the turning point of time and space. Sometimes the labyrinth becomes a place of initiation, where initiates are tested and riddles answered. A bridegroom seeks to be worthy of his bride, a priestess of her high priestesshood. Some learn the labyrinth's magic. They whisper their wishes to the tree at the center and their wishes come true. I walk the labyrinth for healing, weaving someone's pain into the spiral walking. The labyrinth grows stronger.

If you have a garden or yard, you could create your own stone circle, or maybe a labyrinth.

Elemental Experiences

Gardening or creating sacred space on the land connects us to earth. We can connect with the other elements by seeking them out in Nature. When we invoke the four elements to surround a magic circle we are creating a microcosm, a miniature representation of the world around us. It is a miniature world in which we are in control and we act as the creative force, the Divine mind. You can think of this symbolically or more literally, depending on what seems to resonate with your personal beliefs. To invoke the elements, we need to understand them, think about them, attune ourselves to them, and experience them by going out of our centrally heated houses and apartments into the natural world. Sometimes our local environment becomes so familiar to us that we no longer notice what is there.

@

An Exercise to Experience the Elementals

Try this exercise yourself. Sit quietly, open your chakras, and recall some places where you have had intense experience of the elements in Nature. See, feel, touch, taste the element.

You can also experience the elements in the everyday world around you, urban or rural. Wind is the most obvious manifestation of the element of air. Go out in a strong wind or to a high place, a mountain, a skyscraper, and feel the wind against you. Wind can create giant waves, destroy homes; yet when gentle it is the breath of life. Meditate on fire by walking in the Sun or by lighting an outdoor fire. Feel the heat of the Sun or fire on your skin. Feel your skin soaking up the Sun's rays—health-giving but, with our thinning ozone layer, dangerous in excess. Let the heat of the Sun warm your muscles, bringing relaxation. Water is seas and rivers, pools and rain. Go for a walk by water. Paddle in a stream, walk in the rain, swim in a lake or the sea. Cup some water in your hand and feel its coolness. It is liquid rather than solid but it seeks form. The molecules adhere to one another when they can. Drink the water if you know it is safe. Many natural springs have healing properties, but today the water table is often polluted by agrochemicals. To experience the element of earth, go to a rocky or stony place. Take a piece of rock in your hand—cold to the touch or warmed by the Sun. Feel its longevity, endurance, resistance. Feel earth in the form of soil. Take soft earth in your hands. Feel its moisture or dryness—lumps to shape into satisfying mud pies, crumbling grains, sticky clay. Think of the different colors of earth that you have seen—red, brown, black, yellow, gray. Place your hand on the ground and feel the pulse of the Earth. Beneath the surface, soil teems with life—worms, insects, moles, mice, rabbits, growing roots, and upward-thrusting shoots. Although seemingly static, there is a constant movement within earth. The earth element is rich and abundant. Walking, hiking, and gardening are good ways of making contact with earth.

Elemental Quest

To intensify your experience of the elements around you, you could go on an elemental quest—a day spent looking for symbols of air, fire, water, and earth. Recently, we took our summer retreatants on an elemental quest in the Forest of Brocéliande in Brittany. Only eight thousand acres remain of the vast forest that gave the interior its Breton name of *Ar goat,* the Wooded Land. Brocéliande was once mysterious and impenetrable. The Romans stuck to their roads and defending their trade routes, leaving the wild Celts and their druids to keep to their woods. This is Merlin and Arthur territory. England's Glastonbury and Wales's Cardiff have their Arthur claims, but the minstrels that wove the Arthurian myth for public consumption in the Medieval era were French. Many of the events in the lives of Merlin, Morganne le Fay, Viviane, and Lancelot take place in Brittany. A château still stands by the lake at Comper, gazing forever at its reflection in a mirrored lake below, like Merlin's crystal castle. This was where Lancelot's mother Viviane, the Lady of the Lake, raised him. Merlin was a magician, of wilder blood than Viviane's, a forest dweller. He preferred the company of birds and animals to humans. Another culture would have called him shaman. In the forest, at the sacred spring of Barenton, he fell in love with Viviane. Some say she was a fairy, others a magician and enchantress, but her goal was knowledge, the secrets of Merlin's magic. Once she had tricked him into giving her what she sought, she imprisoned him within nine magic circles, magical rings. He was lost to the world, nevermore to return, so the legend says, but others say that one day he will come again.

☽

AN ELEMENTAL QUEST IN BRITTANY

We go first to the Fontaigne de Barenton to collect water. The French minstrel Chrétien de Troyes sang of its wonders.

> The spring that bubbles, you will see,
> though its water is colder than marble.
> Shaded by the most beautiful tree
> that was ever made by Nature.

It is said that if you drink the water and then splash water three times on the steps to the spring, you will raise a storm, roaring lions, and a horseman in black armor. Until the twentieth century, the parish priest performed this duty when drought struck. We need no thundery weather, so we drink but leave the charms of the horseman and his lion for another day. Instead, we wait and watch for the bubbles of pure nitrogen that are said to grant people's wishes. Before the coming of Christianity, druids set up a psychiatric hospital here. Legends say that the spring has healing properties, but chemical analysis reveals nothing special about the water. Maybe it was the peace of the vast forest that healed sick minds. Today, people still make pilgrimages to the spring, leaving as offerings posies and crystals. There are people quietly sitting in meditation—a beautiful sight in the forest of dappled sunshine.

Out from underneath the tree canopy, into the hot Sun, we go in search of fire. We head for the Church of the Holy Grail at Tréhorenteuc. Christian imagery mixes happily with Pagan and Arthurian myth, a stained glass window of the Holy Grail and a painting of the Knights of the Round Table. We intend to buy votive candles, but the church is shut. We improvise and gather red berberis and red flowers from the garden instead and make spiky posies to decorate our rite. Unintended pricked fingers add to the red. Back in the forest, we search the ground for fallen feathers to symbolize air. A red sandstone rock becomes our symbol of earth.

Equipped with our elemental symbols, we go in search of a neolithic burial chamber that legend calls the Tomb of Viviane. Guidebooks say it is difficult to find, but the guidebooks are out of date. The French are beginning to acquire the enthusiasm of the British for neolithic monuments. Tombs and sacred places are not yet swamped with tourist buses, but we find a family already at the tomb. We wait and they leave. There is a small window of opportunity in the afternoon's tourist circuit. We cast a circle and stand at the quarters holding our elemental symbols. We invoke the energies of the elements. In the north, from the Tomb of Viviane, I call above the void of the Valley of No Return, where Arthur's half-sister Morganne imprisoned faithless lovers—a strange experience. We ask for the blessing of the Breton deities, the guardians of this land, and then bless Breton cake and wine. We pour libations. One of us plays a pipe and music echoes over the valley—the pipes of the dancing god whom some call Shiva, others Pan. We have entered a timeless zone in the long summer afternoon and evening. We are at peace.

When we remember and honor the elements in Nature, the natural environment assumes a new importance. Intellectually, we know that our environment is threatened, but when we experience this for ourselves, the meaning is driven home. If we go on an elemental quest in a national park or an unspoiled area like Brocéliande, we can experience the elements as they are meant to be, but their elemental beauty is threatened. We find a beautiful river covered in unsightly foam from a factory's discharge. We must cover our bodies in sunscreen to garden because the protective ozone layer that filters out harmful UV rays is so thin. When petrol-laden air makes us cough as we walk by the roadside, our deeper selves realize something is very wrong. It makes practicing recycling and campaigning to protect those places of natural beauty and tree resources that remain that much more important. Natural magic becomes a spirituality and environmental ethic that venerates our planet in all its richness and values what it has to offer.

◡

★

POINTERS FOR PRACTICE

When you move homes, make an effort to explore the natural locality and connect with your new land. Visit sacred sites in your locality or adopt a favorite tree that you can visit regularly to meditate there. If you have a garden, make sacred energy spots by creating a circle or a spiral or installing a deity statue. Connect with the elements by going on an elemental quest. Think about what you can do to protect our environment and venerate our planet. It is our home and gives us life.

CHAPTER TWENTY-THREE

Magic 201

To attain the Sanctum Regnum, in other words, the knowledge and power of the Magi, there are four indispensable conditions—an intelligence illuminated by study, an intrepidity which nothing can check, a will which cannot be broken and a discretion which nothing can corrupt and nothing intoxicate. To KNOW, *to* DARE, *to* WILL, *to keep* SILENCE—*such are the four words of the magus.*

ELIPHAS LEVI, *TRANSCENDENTAL MAGIC*

Lost in the Otherworld

One of the commandments of the traditional magical lodges was to "keep silent." Silence and magic go well together. Strange things happen if you start to do magic, mysterious things; but is it wise to bore your friends with your wonderful psychic and magical experiences? To anyone not involved, they are meaningless. Becoming a natural magician is a bit like being a voyager to another planet where the rules of time, space, and gravity are different. This new world is full of mirages and hallucinations, and navigating your way around it takes discernment. You have to judge right from wrong, false from true.

If you want to practice magic, you need to be able to distinguish fantasy from reality. This is difficult because many people interested in magic are highly imaginative and creative. Whether imagination is good or bad depends on how we use it. Creative arts, new inventions, and new ideas spring from those blessed with imagination, and magic stimulates the creative imagination. It is no coincidence that many artists, writers, and dancers are interested in magic. Fantasy can also be a trap. In the world of imagination, we can be heroes or great lovers. We can be whoever we want to be. In our own inner worlds, we get to call the shots. Some people are attracted to magic because they want to be special or different, and by "different" I mean better, superior, more powerful. The vision of magical power can be a compensation for personal inadequacies.

If you network on the magical circuit, you are unlikely to meet Hollywood-style Satanists. Well, only if you try very, very hard, and are desperately keen on that kind of thing. You will find self-proclaimed masters, channelers of extraterrestrials, reincarnated Inca princesses, and people who are convinced they are witches burned at the stake in seventeenth-century Glastonbury (people weren't burned at the stake for witchcraft in England). There are very white people claiming to be pipe carriers of Indian peoples, and specially mandated by the elders to sell you their secrets for large fees, and there are Celtic priestesses who have never seen Ireland or any other part of the Celtic world. If fantasy becomes a replacement for reality, it saps our ability to make reality what we want. This is described symbolically in myth and fairy tale. In many cultures, there are stories of people who enter the magical realm, the world of fairy. The fairy realm is delightful—time flies, years pass like days. Eventually they want to return to the world but the world has moved on. They have been left behind; all they knew and loved has passed away. To enter the magical world can be to enter the world of the ever young, Never-Never Land, the world of Peter Pan, where no one ever grows up, but this is a misuse of magic. Magic is to enhance reality, not to become a substitute for it.

Magical Crutches

Magic can help us live more productive and useful lives in the world. Magic can also be an escapist crutch for the weak. We are too scared to confront someone who is abusing us, so we do a spell against them, or if we are more ethically minded, we do a spell to curb their activities rather than actively harm them. Traditional magic is full of the curses of the disempowered. "Curse the woman who stole my dress," writes the Roman lady on her petition left at the sanctuary of a Romanized Celtic goddess. If you feel disempowered, it is easy to imagine that magic can solve all your problems, give you the word of power that will make the strong tremble and those who think they are greater than you sink to their knees. Are you someone who others put down, whose life doesn't work well, who is scared of every-day existence, who finds it difficult to cope with the vagaries of life? If so, magic can help you deal with those problems, but it is important to remember that the impetus has to come from you. You are the engine, the driving force in your life. Magic is about taking responsibility for yourself and what happens to you. It is about no longer being a victim. It is not about becoming someone who dominates or controls others.

Magic is not about infantile wish fulfillment. "I speak and it is so," reflects our childhood desires for omnipotence; for the world to be made in our image and to conform to our desires. Magic is a way of helping us smooth our path in the world, but no magic can make the world exactly what we want it to be. Our thoughts and desires are but currents and eddies that encounter competing currents and eddies. Nor should we want the world to conform exactly to our desires, for our desires are bound by the horizon of our conscious mind's imagination at the time. How often have you heard someone say, "I could never have imagined that I could do this. I would never have imagined that things could turn out this way." Sometimes, things have not turned out well at all, but more often than not, people are saying that they have achieved more than their wildest dreams. We want magic to help us on our journey, but we do not want it to limit us. We need to be open to the endless possibilities that the world has to offer. We want to steer the boat, but we don't need to control the sea. The sea of life takes us to amazing places.

Fear

To voyage into the unknown, we must face our fears. Demons, vampires, the "things that go bump in the night" are our projections of those things within ourselves that we fear to see. They are aspects of what the psychologist Carl Jung called the "shadow." Indian spiritual leader Mahatma Gandhi once said that the only devils in the world are those running around in the human heart, and it is there that the battle must be fought. People are often afraid of magic because they imagine that if they had magical power they would use magic as a weapon. Suppose all your negative thoughts were charged with the power to harm: when you wished your boss would drop dead, she did? You wish that the traffic cop who has just given you a ticket could be consigned to eternal flames, and he is? Fortunately, magical power is not that strong, and the universe's impetus is toward creativity and evolution. If you try to work negative magic, the universe will opppose it. Also you can protect yourself from doing unethical magic by having a good level of self-knowledge, knowing your own weaknesses, being ruthlessly honest with yourself, and having high ethical standards. Within us are selfishness and altruism, egotism and heroic self-sacrifice. And we know which is right. Within us is a deep ethical sense. We know the actions and behaviors that build good and just societies, and those that lead to tyranny, selfishness, and oppression. In magic, as in life, we know to choose correctly if we are not to cause ourselves harm.

Often, traditional village witches and shamans were amoral.

They were as ready to cause disease, if paid the right fee, as to effect cures, but the damage done by negative magic is to the perpetrator. The truth about magic is that it is an energy, one that changes its creator. In order to project negative energy, you have to create negative energy within yourself. Negative energy attracts negative energy. You become accident prone, people react aggressively toward you—even perfect strangers. It is as though you are giving off the wrong pheromones—and you have only yourself to blame. Contemporary magic is an ethical practice. It is about attuning to the creative forces of the universe and working in harmony with them. If you are constantly working with and manifesting positive energies, you begin to change. The petty desires of the ego fade and seem trivial. You develop a new center of consciousness, the self, and the self gives you a new perspective on life, one in which you are not the center of the universe. You see the needs of those immediately close to you, those of your wider kinship and social group, those of all of humankind, and finally of all creation. You come to respect them and want to incorporate them into your worldview. "May all beings be happy" is a famous Buddhist phrase, and one that goes well with natural magic.

Linus's Blanket

Magic can be a way of alleviating our anxieties. We end up doing spells and rituals of protection to make everything in our lives go right, so nothing bad will ever happen to us. Magic used in this way is a double-edged sword. Founding father of psychoanalysis Sigmund Freud used the term "obsessional" to refer to people who have an obsessive need to control the world around them. Obsessional behavior can be some of the most psychiatrically difficult to eradicate. Obsessives may wash their hands repeatedly until they are raw and bleeding in an attempt to rid themselves of germs. They take hours to go out because they must check that every door and window is locked, and by the time they have been all the way around, they can't remember whether they checked the first window properly—and around they go again. All of us can suffer from obsessional behavior in periods of our lives when we feel insecure. You may have been through a phase where you had to keep going back to your car to check that you had locked the doors. This is due to anxiety—not about your car, but about life in general. Our minds are full of worries, so we do activities automatically, without focusing on them, then cannot remember whether we did them or not, and go back to the beginning again.

What has this to do with magic? Superficially, magic can seem a brilliant panacea for anxiety, a way of being in control, but it can make things worse. You cannot go out without going through small rituals of protection such as touching your lucky statue. You become paranoid if you've forgotten to wear your protective talisman. Magic is a wonderful playground for the obsessive. If you read some traditional books about magic, you will find that they are full of instructions about how to protect yourself from psychic attack by other magicians. Thinking you are being psychically attacked is symptomatic of your personal problems. Medieval people often made witchcraft accusations against people they had wronged. They had refused to give them alms, felt guilty about it, and started feeling ill at ease with themselves. When we feel ill at ease, we tend to do things badly, and things go wrong. Why are things going wrong, we ask ourselves? Maybe it's got something to do with something that's happened to me. What about that time I refused to give that woman alms? Maybe she's cursed me? Maybe she's a witch who's cast a spell on me. You get the picture. We do something to someone that we shouldn't. We feel guilty and anxious and afraid that they might be out to get us. The next thing is that we imagine they are psychically attacking us or cursing us.

An important part of becoming a natural magician is to learn to manage your thought processes. Remember the philosopher Descartes: "Cogito ergo sum," "I think therefore I am." We can turn this around and say, "I am what I think." There are limits to this, of course. If you are a 5' 3" brunet, no amount of thinking and visualization will turn you into a 5' 9" blond. However, you can become a 5' 4" blond with the aid of heels and hair dye, and some confidence-boosting magic will make you more radiant so people will see you as more attractive. Life is a compromise.

Magic and Superstition

Let me give an example. The *British Medical Journal* of December 8, 2001 reported a study by David Phillips and colleagues at the University of California, San Diego on "The *Hound of the Baskervilles* effect," about deaths among Chinese and Japanese Americans. The study covered nearly fifty million people who died in the United States between 1973 and 1998. In Chinese and Japanese cultures, the number four is considered very unlucky. Apartment blocks are often built without the number four because number four units won't sell. Chinese and Japanese hospitals have no fourth floors or rooms with the number four. Even in the military, Chinese military aircraft designations omit the number four. The reason? In Mandarin, Cantonese, and Japanese, the word "shi," four, sounds almost the same as the word for death.

We could laugh this off as meaningless superstition, but it has very real effects. Professor Phillips's intriguing Californian study showed that Chinese and Japanese Americans were much more likely to have fatal heart attacks on the fourth of the month than on any other day. Such is the superstition about "four" that if people are already physically ill, the additional psychological stress of the inauspicious date causes increased adrenaline secretion and irregular heartbeat, and this is enough to tip some people over the edge. The Chinese phobia about the number four cuts no ice, though, with the British legal system. In January 2002, gift shop owner Tak Ping Yeung of London's Chinatown was left with a six-figure legal bill after Judge Anthony Hallerton dismissed his claim that his landlord was violating his human rights by asking him to move his shop to similar premises two doors down, at number four.

Superstition about numbers is not confined to Far Eastern culture. In Britain, car license plates with 666 on them had to be withdrawn, but this isn't an example of fear and phobias; other drivers were so mesmerized by the number that they kept crashing into them. The fear of number thirteen is so widespread in Western culture that it has its own name: "triskaidekaphobia." Canary Wharf, London's nearest equivalent to the Twin Towers, has no thirteenth floor. Many people believe that Friday the 13th is particularly unlucky. There is even a special word for people with phobias about Friday the 13th—"paraskevidekatriaphobics." A study by the Mid-Downs Health Authority in England showed that car drivers were 50 percent more likely to have an accident on Friday the 13th than on any other day.

Of course, there is nothing in the least bit magical about a date. It is simply an arbitrary way of numbering the days in a year, but when we are anxious we have more accidents. Superstition, particularly negative superstition, can kill. Many research studies show that a high percentage of people given a placebo, a harmless substance sometimes given as a substitute for medicine, will respond positively and get better faster. Negative superstitions, fears, and phobias, act like their opposite—nocebos. We think something bad will happen to us, so it does. Such is the power of the human mind.

Self-Determination

When I was initiated into a kabbalistic magical lodge, I was told, "We in this Temple do not live under the Law of Accident." This was intoned by a baritone voice from between a black and a white pillar in a room with a black-and-white tiled floor, lit by flickering candlelight, through drifting incense smoke, and the voice was unexpected. These things have a habit of sticking in one's memory. My youthful, inexperienced self had no idea what this meant, but it sounded impressive. "We do not live under the Law of Accident." It was the grit in the oyster shell syndrome. The phrase resonated away in the backrooms of my memory until it became obvious what it meant. It had been obvious all along: magic is about carving out your own destiny. When we first take up magic, we are avid enthusiasts. We read tarot or runes at the drop of a witch's hat—usually, despite all warnings against it, for ourselves. As we mature in our magical practice, our intuition grows more acute and we need formal divination systems less. We cease to be passive receptors on the stage of the world, waiting for fate to control our lives. Instead, we become proactive doers.

Our first attempts at magic are usually to sort out our own life problems. After a while, you find that you do not need to do so many spells because many problems sort themselves out without your direct intervention. I say "direct intervention" because your magical mindset is influencing what is going on by applying the right principles and energies to it, but you do not actively have to do a spell. Instead of doing magic, we become magic. We are in the driving seat of our incarnatory vehicles and heading up the highways of our choosing. We learn to forge our own destinies and to cut our own paths. Obstacles arise, but we deal with them and overcome them. We learn to move forward. Within us is the true self, a seed struggling to grow, a babe waiting to emerge from the womb. It has purposes, purposes that are outside anything we can conceive of with our limited conscious minds. It wants things for us, it has places to go, things to achieve. As the voice of the self becomes stronger within us, we find our lives changing and growing in ways that we never expected. This is the aim of natural magic.

★

POINTERS FOR PRACTICE

Magic is not a prop or a crutch. Contemporary magic is an ethical practice that teaches us to attune ourselves to the creative forces of the universe and work in harmony with them. As you manifest positive energies, you begin to change and develop a new perspective on life. The voice of the self grows stronger, and we find our lives changing in ways we could never have expected. We cease to do magic. We become magic.

CHAPTER TWENTY-FOUR

Magical Self

A human being is part of the whole, called by us "universe," a part limited in time and space. He experiences himself, his thoughts and feelings, as something separate from the rest—a kind of optical delusion of his consciousness. This delusion is a kind of prison for us, restricting us to our personal decisions and to affection for a few persons near to us. Our task must be to free ourselves from this prison by widening our circle of compassion to embrace all living creatures and the whole of nature in its beauty.

ALBERT EINSTEIN, *THE NEW YORK TIMES*, MARCH 19, 1972

What do we want out of life? Our bodies have fundamental needs—food to keep them healthy. Once fed, we need shelter and protection. Once we have satisfied our bodily and security needs, we need sex, relationships, and companionship. Once we have a community of support, we need to exercise talents and skills that give us self-esteem and ways of exercising the mind. Beyond that, we have a need for self-actualization—to become the whole person we were always meant to be. This requires a deep connection with our spiritual center. Natural magic has evolved to fulfill human needs, but it is not a quick fix. Like anything else, it needs inputs to get outputs. It needs practice and some dedication. If we are willing to give a little of ourselves, the returns are enormous, but they may not be what we originally expected. Magic changes our vision and outlook. Many things that seem major preoccupations when we start become relatively trivial as we develop a less egocentric view of the world. As we realize who and what we really are, we realize that many desires and goals that once seemed compelling are not really "ours" at all. They are based on the expectations of our upbringing, peer group, the media, and popular culture. Magic is not really part of popular culture, despite the newspaper astrology columns, instant one-weekend-course feng shui experts, and coffee-table spell books. It is deeper, older, ancient in fact. It comes from the deepest, innermost recesses of human memory. If we are true natural magicians, it is part of the core of our being, and we learn to love and respect this strange, mystical, otherworldly but always practical art.

Magical Self

Magic in all its manifestations requires a leap of the imagination. It is about having the courage to see the world differently. As a child of the twentieth century, adults told me many things that seemed to me obviously untrue. People had souls and animals did not, the Divine was male and never female, trees did not have consciousness. I thought adults were mad. I learned not to tell people what I really thought, but it didn't prevent me from thinking. Now, in the twenty-first century, we come closer to being able to tell people what we really think. The leap of the imagination that we take when we dare to see the world in a new way is revisioning. We reimagine how things might be, allowing ourselves to have a sense of wonder about the cosmos around us. It is a reenchanting of the world, a creative act, and in the human psyche, the worlds of myth, imagination, creativity, and magic are closely related. In Irish tradition, creativity is one of the gifts of the goddess Brigid, who became St. Bridget when Ireland became Christian. Creativity is also a gift of the many-talented god Lugh, a harper, poet, silversmith, and much else besides. Lugh is associated in Celtic myth with sunlight, and Bride with fire. Light and fire give illumination in the darkness, so they are natural symbolic images that often appear in connection with creativity. Creative inspiration comes from a deeper source of your being than your everyday conscious mind. It comes from a deeper level that is present within all of us. We have only to access it.

Bringing It All Together

To discover more about your vision—your life journey, where you want to go and what you want to do next, you can go on an inner journey into the dark cave. What do caves symbolize? Dark earth, an unknown place, for our ancestors a place of safety and of fear. If we defend the cave, it can protect us from storms and wild animals. It can provide a place to make fire to keep us warm. If the cave is already occupied by another species—lion, poisonous spider, snake, bear—then the dark cave entrance is a place of danger. If we want possession, we will have to fight. Caves are passageways into the Earth. They are mysterious roads to the underworld. They go into the heart of our mother the Earth. They take us to the Earth's hearth fire, her heart fire, over which hangs a sacred vessel, the Cauldron of Transformation. In Welsh myth, the cauldron belongs to the goddess Cerridwen. Cerridwen is a magician, a witch, a brewer of magic potions that can provide unlimited wisdom, eternal youth. Cerridwen is a black-haired goddess, a Dark Mother of dreams.

@

Cauldron Journey

The cauldron journey is a ritual to help you find inspiration for your life's journey. It will take some time, and you should allow at least two hours. It brings together many of the techniques I have described—visualization and energizing, seeking inspiration, circle casting—to create a ritual to help you into the future. It is not a ritual to do casually, but something to help you in the year ahead. It is a good ritual to perform on a major seasonal festival, a point of transition and change, or on a full Moon. Take a day off work to prepare for your ritual. Give yourself thinking space. Have a quiet day, switch off your phones, and don't log on to email. Take some time to meditate and to go for a walk.

Prepare what you will need for the circle—the usual altar implements, candles for the four directions, flowers, cake or bread, and wine. For the quarter candles, you might like to choose four colors representing the elements in a pure form—say sky-blue for air, red for fire, blue-green for water, brown for earth. Although it is a symbolic journey into the Earth's heart, into the center of your own being, the power of the Moon can stimulate your psyche and guide you. You might like to choose lunar colors for your altar candles—white, silver, or pale violet. As a preparation for the rite, you could make a Moon incense.

For the visualization, write down the key stages of the visualization and then learn them so that you can make the inner journey without referring to notes. Reading the instructions midway through your visualization will interfere with your ability to enter a deeper state of consciousness. To record what you see in the visualization, you will need drawing paper, some writing paper and a pen, some colored pens, and a small piece of white card on which to draw a talisman. A piece about the size of a tarot card would be fine, or you could have something larger if you prefer. The talisman will act as a personal symbol for the next year or so of your life, so you might want to have it on view in your bedroom.

For the rite, set up your ritual space with your wand, the elemental symbols, an altar to the north of the circle, and candles for the four directions. At the center of the circle, place a light to symbolize the inspiration that you are seeking. Open your chakras, create your circle, and call upon the four directions to assist you with your inner journey. You could ask air to send you new knowledge, fire to send new energy, water to send new vision, and earth to give you the strength to undertake this next stage of your life's journey. Finally, invoke spirit at the center of the circle and ask for inspiration from the spiritual realm to show you the direction in which you should go and grow.

Sit, kneel or lie down in your sacred space, whichever you prefer. Relax and go within yourself. Let your breathing become regular, your mind become still. Allow all the busy thoughts of daily life to drift away. Sink gently into stillness.

Begin the visualization. It is night. Above you stars shine and the Moon is bright and clear. Note the surroundings. Wherever you are, you feel peaceful and at home in this place.

After a while, you see in the moonlight a figure coming toward you. This is a guide who will take you on your journey. The guide may be male, female, animal, a being of light, or in some other form. Greet your guide and follow him or her until you come to the mouth of a cave. At the entrance to the cave, your guide pauses and indicates that you are to enter alone, while he or she waits for you and keeps watch at the entrance. You go into the cave but you can see, for there are flickering flames in the darkness. Flaming torches light the way. Walk into the cave until it opens out into an underground chamber.

In the center of the underground chamber is a fire pit with a burning fire over which hangs a cauldron. This is the cauldron of the goddess Cerridwen, a goddess of transformation. Steam rises from the cauldron straight upward. Looking upward you can see a natural chimney in the rock that leads upward toward the stars.

Sit down by the fire pit and look into the flames. The rising steam from the cauldron will clear, so you can look into the cauldron of Cerridwen. The dark surface of the liquid in the cauldron becomes a black mirror.

Gaze into the dark mirror—the mirror of the future—and ask yourself, what is the one thing that you would most like to achieve in your life during the coming year? Shapes will appear, perhaps figures, or sudden thoughts will arise from your unconscious. Take a little time to do this and let one idea or concept take over. This is what you are going to bring into your life at this time. Let a phrase form in your mind to represent what you want to achieve.

When you have done this, the cauldron begins to bubble again, steam rising upward. Focus on the rising steam and ask yourself if anything within you makes what you want to accomplish more difficult. Are there any internal barriers that might prevent you from accomplishing your new aim? Allow images to form in your mind of any barriers, things you need to let go of and want out of your life. Once an idea has formed, focus on this for a moment, forming an image of it in the steam. Then let it go. Let it dissolve in the steam, rising up on the steam, out of the chimney in the cave. It dissolves and moves away.

Remembering your phrase about what you want to achieve and the barriers that you have dissolved that hold you back, return to the entrance of the cave, where your guide awaits. Allow your guide to lead you back to the place in Nature where you started the visualization. Thank your guide for assisting you on your journey and in your own time return to the world of the circle.

When you are ready, record your experiences. Write down the phrase that expresses what you want to achieve. On a separate small strip of paper, write down any internal barriers that stand in your way. Then draw your journey. Don't worry if your drawing skills are no better than the average five year old's. The drawing is not an artwork, but a way of anchoring the experience. It will help you notice symbolism and significances that you missed at the time. Draw the surroundings where you began your journey, your guide, the tunnel, and the cavern.

Now that you have made your record, it is time to turn what you want to achieve into a personal talisman, using the same technique. Turn your phrase into a symbol by eliminating the vowels and any repeated letters, until you are left with the core of what you are seeking to manifest. Take these final letters and turn them into a shape. You may want to experiment a few times before you achieve something you like. If you wish, fill in some of the spaces with colors that emphasize your intent; blue, for instance, if you want calm and peace, red for energy and health, gold for material success, orange for careers. When your design is complete, transfer it to your piece of white card.

The final stage is to empower the talisman by consecrating it. Relax after the hard work you've done so far; then draw energy through your chakras into your hands. Consecrate your talisman by passing it quickly through incense smoke for air, taking it back through the heat of a candle flame for fire, flicking a few specks of water on the back for water and pressing on the soil of your earth bowl. Now allow energy to flow from your hands into the symbol, empowering it. Visualize the symbol, then close your eyes and visualize it without looking at it. Keep looking at it until you really can visualize it with your eyes shut. Then say, "As I do will, so mote it be." Prop up the talisman on your altar. Bless cakes and wine, offer libation, eat and drink.

When you are ready, bid farewell to the quarters. Your rite is ended, but the work has not. Your talisman will empower you, but now you have to seek opportunities to bring what you want to achieve into being. The magic gives you a current of energy that will help take you to your goal. Your empowered self can do the rest.

Landscape of the Unconscious

Inner journeys like the Cauldron Journey are designed to help us communicate with our unconscious minds, which "think" in symbols. The unconscious consists of our personal experiences that have not yet come into conscious awareness, or which we have suppressed. Also, there is a deeper level of the psyche known as the collective unconscious. This is the repository of a mythological, magical, and symbolic level of thinking that is common to all humankind. In the dreams and myths of all peoples, certain symbols tend to have universal meaning. Mountains are associated with aspirations, spirituality, communicating with the gods. Caves and tunnels take us into the unconscious. They are like a return to the womb, to the place of the Goddess. Guides are helpful parts of our psyches, not our normal everyday personalities, but aspects of ourselves that are in touch with our unconscious, instinctual, and spiritual natures. They are way-showers. Sometimes they appear as helpful animals. This is frequently the case in fairy tale and myth. Night is the time when we feel closest to the unconscious, to dreamtime.

◡

MY CAULDRON JOURNEY

Samhain 2001, Chris and I run a workshop for St. James's Church in London's Piccadilly. The church is a beautiful seventeenth-century building and it offers hospitality and openness for all faiths—a model for religious institutions everywhere, but one not often found. It has been a strange Samhain. The workshop attendees are English, American, and from many European countries. The events of September 11 have made this festival of death and rebirth more significant and poignant than ever before. We talk of the frightening powers of hate and fanaticism, of the negative side of the psyche, and of how it can overwhelm us. Then we bring to mind the positive, how such events can show us what is important in the world and what is not.

I make the Cauldron Journey at the workshop and what comes is not exactly what I asked for—as is often the way in magic—but it is what I need. I am given a message. Four small women, almost dwarflike, come out of the passageways and stand around me, propping up my waist. I feel a cord being wrapped around my waist, a girdle. They are giving me strength. They are saying, "You are supported, remember." I am not alone. I ask what I should let go of, what eternal barriers prevent me from finding the support I need. A leaf floats upward on the cauldron steam, out of the chimney and away into the starry night. "I am a leaf on the wind," is the phrase in my mind. This is what I must let go of, the feeling I am a leaf in the wind, to be blown about by the vagaries of fate. I am a magician. I have the power to decide my own destiny. I see a chain—a chain of interlocking events, causality as a scientist might say. Everything that happens has purpose; everything is linked to and causes everything else. Nothing is lost. Everything has meaning. I take a piece of paper and write:

supported

I strike out the vowels because the system is based on Hebrew magical tradition, and Hebrew uses no vowels. Then I remove any duplicated letters, leaving:

sprtd

I weave this into an image of letters.

PERSONAL SYMBOL

I feel drawn to color some of the sections of the symbol. I use gold for solar energy, green for new beginnings, and violet for the opening of the third eye. I don't know why I want these particular colors, but they seem right. As we work together to create our talismans, there is an extraordinary feeling of peace, a flowering of creativity and beauty as people create symbols of their hopes and aspirations.

☾

Alchemical Journey

Life in magical tradition is seen as a journey, usually a reincarnatory journey with many lifetimes that ends in the Divine. Two distinct spiritual currents cut across traditional religious divisions. One sees the Divine as external to us, a force to be worshiped, adored, feared, placated. The other sees the Divine as a state of consciousness within us and within the universe. The orientation you have will depend on your upbringing and experience. Even if your beliefs seem fixed, they are unlikely to remain unchanged. Magic is about change, and it evolves our thinking. If you walk the magical path, you will have new and surprising experiences that will change your worldview. In magic, it is a good idea to travel with light baggage. You do not need a complex set of beliefs that you have to discard when you find evidence that refutes them. We do not need to believe in too many things—in fact, the fewer the better. Complex belief systems are intellectual games; fun in their way, but they are not to be taken too seriously. They are games for the mind, not pathways for the spirit. Magic requires truth, love, realism and observation, energy and power, wisdom and impartiality, and vision. It also requires us to follow the magical commands: to know (air), to dare (water), to will (fire), and to keep silent (earth). There is also a fifth command, that of spirit—to reveal.

When we invoke the elements at the quarters, we invoke air, fire, water, and earth. We journey from the least substantial element, that of air, to the most substantial, earth. What are we doing? We are bringing energy into manifestation—out of the realm of the immaterial, we bring spirit into the world and reveal it. We imbue matter with spirit and make immanent the Divine. The final element of the

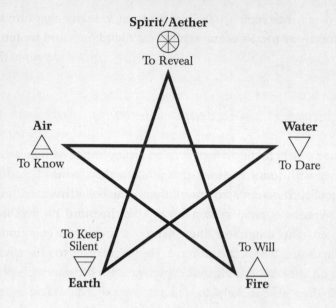

Spirit/Aether

To Reveal

Air

To Know

Water

To Dare

To Keep
Silent

To Will

Earth

Fire

THE PENTAGRAM OF NATURAL MAGIC

sequence is spirit, the mysterious fifth element that is both within and beyond the other four. We come to the center of the circle, the place of the altar, the place of transcendence and initiation, the place of the cauldron. Magic is a journey to uncover the creative spirit within. It is a beginning, a first step on the long path, a never-ending process that continues all around us and manifests itself within us. It lies at the deepest core of our being and at the universe's deepest heart. Magic is not for the faint-hearted, but it is for those who are prepared to take responsibility for themselves and for the Divine spirit within them. This can be daunting. Those who follow any magical path take risks by committing themselves to the "way less traveled." They take risks by voicing, expressing, and creating new forms and modes of personal expression; by exploring their being and finding ways for this to be expressed.

In our spiritual journey, we must have both force and form. We need energy and ideas, as well as the technical skills that turn them into form—image, word, movement, or sound. To grow, we must be willing to listen to the voice of the universe. For some people this is God, for others Goddess, for some the force of life itself. Whatever our spiritual belief, as natural magicians we can see that our universe is purposeful and seeks to manifest itself in all the myriad and wondrous forms that it can. As magicians, we become instruments for the creative forces of the universe. We become at one with the gods and we seek to do the greater will of the universe. As instruments of the universe, we draw close to the collective unconscious, the collective psyche of humankind. We dive into its depths and draw on commonalities, those symbols, archetypes, inspirations, and ideas that take us beyond our own experience, to become manifesters of ideas and images that speak to the societies of which we are members. We transcend the boundaries of our individual selves and access the group mind of us all. We become the eyes, ears, hands, and brains of creative deity.

In magical tradition, the aim of human beings is to transform ourselves to become like the gods. To do this we must balance our personalities and rectify imbalances. As we become more balanced and we explore the different qualities that comprise our personalities, we come to a deeper realization—that we are not our personalities. Within us is a center, a deeper place, which is the self. The self is a spark of the Divine, hidden beneath the complexity, confusion, emotions, desires, worries, and conflicting impulses that make up our everyday selves. As we progress on our magical path, we find ourselves in moments of stillness and balance at the center of our magical circles, symbolic images of the balanced cosmos, touching something deeper within our core being. We come to realize that something within us is undying and eternal. It does not belong to the material world of time, space, and events, but to the eternal world that precedes material creation and to which it shall return when this phase of cosmic evolution draws to its end. We come to understand the age-old saying, "I am that I am."

Life Task

Becoming what we truly are is often described in the magical tradition as finding one's true will. It is also described in the magical tradition as the Great Work. Why should something so personal be given such an exalted title? As each one of us evolves to take our rightful place in the world, so the human psyche as a whole evolves. Each of us is a cell in the collective brain—the better each cell functions, the better the whole. When a cell is dysfunctional, unhealthy, or simply not performing at its optimum, the functioning of the whole is affected. Think about it. If each of us sorted ourselves out and found the way we could best contribute to society, how much more energy, wealth, abundance, and beauty there would be. It is important that we realize the moment to improve our lives is now, not tomorrow, or the next day, or next week. States of consciousness are contagious. As each person advances, the collective psyche of humankind advances just a fraction. The change is minute, but cumulatively over the millennia, the change is great. To evolve spiritually, we need to establish a dialogue with the deeper self, the inner guide. "Follow me," says the voice of the self, and we follow the best and highest part of ourselves, thinking that we are following Goddess or God. When the link with the self grows strong, the self comes and overshadows us, folding us in its wings, and guiding us on our life's journey. We seek to do its will and not the will of the ego. Then, finally, we become the self and realize that what we saw as Divine was but a way station on the journey to the true mystery, which is far beyond our everyday minds. The psychologist Carl Jung once said, in *Modern Man in Search of a Soul:*

> But we must not forget that only a few people are artists in life; that the art of life is the most distinguished and rarest of all the arts.

To become a magician is to become a magical artist in life. Let us make of our lives a creative magical act, of joy, beauty, pain, sorrow, and above all of aspiration—the courage to take the great leap forward and to reach for the stars.

POINTERS FOR PRACTICE

Magic changes our vision and outlook. Many things that seem like major preoccupations when we start become relatively trivial as we develop a less egocentric view of the world. To discover more about your personal vision, do the Cauldron Journey exercise to find inspiration for the next stage of your life. Remember that by finding the way we can best contribute to society, we are helping society evolve and grow. This is the way of the true natural magician.

BIBLIOGRAPHY

Aarons, M. *The Tapestry of Life: Through the Mediumship of Lilian Bailey.* London: Psychic Press, 1979.

Agrippa, H. C., JF trans. *De Occulta Philosophia.* London: Gregory Moule, 1651.

Anon. *The Key of Solomon the King (Clavicula Salomonis).* S Liddell, 1972 ed. MacGregor, Mathers trans. London: Routledge & Kegan Paul. Original manuscript sixteenth century.

Assagioli, R. *The Act of Will.* Wellingborough: Turnstone Press, 1974 ed.

Austin, J. *Zen and the Brain: Towards an Understanding of Meditation and Consciousness.* Cambridge, Mass: MIT Press, 2001 ed.

Barrett, F. *The Magus or Celestial Intelligencer: A Complete System of Occult Philosophy.* Seacaucus, NJ: Citadel. First published 1801, 1967 ed.

Cardeña, E., Lynn, S. J. and Krippner, S. *Varieties of Anomalous Experience: Examining the Scientific Evidence.* Washington, DC: American Psychological Association, 2000.

Christ, C. P. *Rebirth of the Goddess: Finding Meaning in Feminist Spirituality.* New York: Routledge, 1997.

Crowley, V. *A Woman's Guide to the Earth Traditions.* London: Thorsons, 2001.

———*Wicca: The Old Religion in the New Millennium.* London: Thorsons, 1996.

———*A Woman's Guide to the Earth Traditions.* London: Thorsons, 2000.

———*A Woman's Kabbalah.* London: Thorsons, 2000.

Crowley, V. and Crowley, C. *Your Dark Side: How to Turn Your Inner Negativity into Positive Energy.* London: Thorsons, 2001.

Fortune, D. *Moon Magic*. York Beach, Maine: Samuel Weiser, 1978 ed.

———*The Mystical Qabalah*. London: Ernest Benn Ltd.,1935.

Gauquelin, M. *Birthtimes: A Scientific Investigation of the Secrets of Astrology*. New York: Hill and Wang, 1983.

———*The Cosmic Clocks: From Astrology to Modern Science*. St Albans: Granada, 1973 ed.

Griffin, W. ed. *Daughters of the Goddess: Studies in Healing, Identity, and Empowerment*. Lanham, Md: Altamira Press, 1999.

Hale, G. *How to Feng Shui your Home*. London: Lorenz Books, 2000.

Howell, F. C. *Making Magic with Gaia: Practices that Heal Ourselves and Our Planet*. Boston: Red Wheel/Weiser, 2002.

Jeffers, S. *Feel the Fear and Do It Anyway*. London: Arrow, 1996.

Jung, C. G. *Memories, Dreams and Reflections*. London: Fontana, 1995 ed.

———*Modern Man in Search of a Soul*. London: Routledge & Kegan Paul, 1973 ed.

Leland, C. G. *Aradia: The Gospel of the Witches*. London: CW Daniel Company, 1974 ed.

Levi, E. *Transcendental Magic: Its Doctrine and Ritual*. London: Rider, 1968 ed. (First published 1896.)

Markham, G. *The English Hous-wife*. London: Hannah Sawbridge, 1683 ed.

Paterson, J. M. *Tree Wisdom: The Definitive Guidebook to the Myth, Folklore and Healing Power of Trees*. London: Thorsons, 1996.

Ring, K. *Predicting the Weather by the Moon*. Christchurch, NZ: Hazard, 2000.

Roberts, Royston M. *Serendipity, Accidental Discoveries in Science*. New York: John Wiley and Sons, 1989.

Sachs, G. *The Astrology File: Scientific Proof of the Link Between Star Signs and Human Behavior*. London: Orion, 1998.

Shah, S. I. *The Secret Lore of Magic: Books of the Sorcerers*. London: Abacus/Sphere, 1972 ed.

Starý, F. and Jirásek, V. *Herbs: A Concise Guide in Colour*. London: Hamlyn, 1973.

Wallis Budge, Sir E. A. *Amulets and Talismans*. New York: Collier/Macmillan, 1970 ed. (First published 1930.)

Zohar, D. and Marshall, I. *Spiritual Intelligence: The Ultimate Intelligence*. London: Bloomsbury, 2000.

ABOUT THE AUTHOR

Vivianne Crowley, Ph.D, is a psychologist, university lecturer, and management consultant. For twenty-five years, she has been a teacher of magic, inspiring thousands on their spiritual path. Her books include *Wicca* and *Way of Wicca*.